Irigaray and Deleuze

Irigaray & Deleuze

Experiments in Visceral Philosophy

Tamsin Lorraine

Cornell University Press

Ithaca and London

For information, address
Cornell University Press,
Sage House,
512 East State Street,
Ithaca, New York 14850.
First published 1999 by
Cornell University Press
First printing, Cornell Paperbacks, 1999
Printed in the United States of America
Cornell University Press strives to
use environmentally responsible
suppliers and materials to the fullest
extent possible in the publishing of its
books. Such materials include vegetable-
based, low-VOC inks and acid-free papers
that are recycled, totally chlorine-free,
or partly composed of nonwood
fibers.

Library of Congress
Cataloging-in-Publication Data
Lorraine, Tamsin E.
    Irigaray and Deleuze : experiments in
visceral philosophy / Tamsin Lorraine.
        p.   cm.
    Includes bibliographical references
(p.   ) and index.
    ISBN 0-8014-3623-0 (cl. : alk. paper)
ISBN 0-8014-8586-X (pa. : alk. paper).
    1. Irigaray, Luce. 2. Deleuze,
Gilles. 3. Body, Human (Philosophy).
4. Feminist theory.   I. Title.
    B2430.I74L67   1999   99-18218
    194—dc21

CLOTH PRINTING

10 9 8 7 6 5 4 3 2 1

PAPERBACK PRINTING

10 9 8 7 6 5 4 3 2 1

Contents

Preface

In his book *Chaosmosis: An Ethico-Aesthetic Paradigm* Félix Guattari claims that different societies offer different possibilities in the formation and maintenance of interdependent human selves, that these possibilities change over time, and that we need models for the processes of self-making that will facilitate the reappropriation of these processes by social subjects. Guattari is careful to distinguish his own characterizations of psychic processes from scientific theories. Rather than reflect what must be the case about human existence, his cartographies and psychological models are meant to coexist with the day-to-day processes of individuals and collectives that are actively engaged in the project of living lives as human beings. What he claims matters in his own modeling of subjectivity is whether or not his characterizations effectively make possible an "autopoiesis" of the means of production of subjectivity. That is, Guattari creates cartographies of the social processes involved in the making of selves in order to foster subjectivities that break free from hegemonic forms and enable individuals and collectives to own creatively their own identities along with the processes that support them. It is to this kind of project that I hope to contribute. In the pages to come I explore the work of Luce Irigaray and of Gilles Deleuze, often in tandem with his collaborative work with Guattari, in order to suggest a model of subjectivity that could help to provide practical answers to the problem of how we could and should live in the world and with others.

In keeping with the poststructuralist tradition in French philosophy from which this work is largely drawn, I assume that human selves are neither substances with determinate properties nor egoic structures that accrue personal histories in a predictably orderly way. Instead, I assume that the selves we experience as our own are the product of a historically conditioned process involving both corporeal and psychic aspects of existence, that this process needs to be instituted and continually reiterated in a social context in order to give birth to and maintain the subject at the corporeal level of embodiment as well as the psychic level of self, and that language and social positioning within a larger social field play a crucial role in this process. In taking up a position in the social field as a speaker of language, a human being takes up a perspective from which to develop a narrative of the self. This perspective is constituted through a combination of the embodied subject who materializes a specific social positioning and whatever social positions are available given the social structures of significance through which the subject materializes herself.

In this work I attempt to simplify two complex thinkers into relatively digestible readings with the practical purpose of proposing a new way of thinking about ourselves, our relationship to the world, and our ways of thinking, speaking, and being as part of that world. This attempt is inevitably reductionistic and is thus bound to close down some of the more radical implications of their thought. Irigaray in particular has openly expressed her objection to such readings, saying that rendering her work through straightforward commentary can do no more than distort her thought. Given that she is attempting to open up a new way of thinking, one must go to her work, read it for oneself, and let it work its effects without trying to master it with reductionistic prose. I appreciate Irigaray's concern and urge my readers to seek out the writers I discuss here in order to see just how inadequate this work is in doing full justice to the richness of theirs, and to discover their own ways of reading. But as a writer and a reader I am more inclined to Deleuze's invitation to experiment. My experiment in the pages to come draws from their work a model of subjectivity designed to overcome traditional mind/body dualisms in a way that I believe to be both personally revitalizing and ethically responsible. It is my hope that at least some of my readers will be inspired to engage in creating models of subjectivity of their own and to implement those models in their own experiments in living, thinking, and writing.

I want to extend my heartfelt gratitude to all the people who stimulated and provoked my thinking during the time I was writing this book. My thanks to everyone involved in the NEH Summer Institute on the body held in Santa Cruz in the summer of 1994. This Institute was not only beautifully organized and intellectually rewarding, but it was also a lot of fun! It was here that I conceived the project of this book in its initial form. The anonymous reviewers who read earlier versions of this manuscript gave me helpful encouragement and suggestions. My editor, Alison Shonkwiler, offered astute advice and eased my periods of discouragement by demonstrating consistent patience and enthusiasm. My colleagues at Swarthmore College, especially Richard Eldridge and George Moskos, have given me supportive and attentive feedback and advice. The Wisdom crowd sparked my initial interest in Deleuze and was a wonderful source of inspiration and support. I particularly thank Thomas Thorp, Brian Schroeder, and Brian Seitz for making the retreats at Wisdom happen and for their lively approach to philosophical questions. I also thank all the other participants at Wisdom, especially Charlie Shepherdson and Mark Tanzer. I treasure the time I spent with such wonderful company in such a special setting; the open-minded respect and creative sharing in which we were able to engage provided a heartwarming paradigm of what philosophical discussion can be. I extend special thanks to Tina Chanter and Kelly Oliver for being inspirational role models as well as provocative interlocutors; their work and support always challenge me to do better. And, as always, I express my profound appreciation for the presence of Alison Brown and my sister, Shawn, in my life. Alison always excites me to new ways of thinking and incites me to take risks I would not otherwise take; Shawn is a true friend in every sense of the word whose belief in me has never failed.

I dedicate this book to my students at Swarthmore College whose alert attention and insatiable appetite for new ideas challenges me to think more deeply and to communicate as fully and directly as I can. Their enthusiasm and creativity help to sustain my own line of flight.

TAMSIN LORRAINE

Swarthmore, Pennsylvania

Abbreviations

BOOKS BY LUCE IRIGARAY

ESD *An Ethics of Sexual Difference.* Translated by Carolyn Burke and Gillian C. Gill. Ithaca: Cornell University Press, 1993.

ILTY *I Love to You: Sketch for a Felicity within History.* Translated by Alison Martin. New York: Routledge, 1996.

JTN *Je, Tu, Nous: Toward a Culture of Difference.* Translated by Alison Martin. New York: Routledge, 1993.

ML *Marine Lover of Friedrich Nietzsche.* Translated by Gillian C. Gill. New York: Columbia University Press, 1991.

S *Speculum of the Other Woman.* Translated by Gillian C. Gill. Ithaca: Cornell University Press, 1985.

S&G *Sexes and Genealogies.* Translated by Gillian C. Gill. New York: Columbia University Press, 1993.

TD *Thinking the Difference: For a Peaceful Revolution.* Translated by Karin Montin. New York: Routledge, 1994.

TS *This Sex Which Is Not One.* Translated by Catherine Porter and Carolyn Burke. Ithaca: Cornell University Press, 1985.

BOOKS BY GILLES DELEUZE

B *Bergsonism.* Translated by Hugh Tomlinson and Barbara Habberjam. New York: Zone Books, 1991.

D *Dialogues.* With Claire Parnet. Translated by Hugh Tomlinson and Barabara Habberjam. New York: Columbia University Press, 1987.

D&R *Difference and Repetition.* Translated by Paul Patton. New York: Columbia University Press, 1994.

F *Foucault.* Translated by Seán Hand. Minneapolis: University of Minnesota Press, 1988.

FB *Francis Bacon: Logique de la sensation.* Paris: Éditions de la Différence, 1981.

KCP *Kant's Critical Philosophy: The Doctrine of the Faculties.* Translated by Hugh Tomlinson and Barbara Habberjam. Minneapolis: University of Minnesota Press, 1984.

LS   *The Logic of Sense.* Translated by Mark Lester. Edited by Constan-
      tin V. Boundas. New York: Columbia University Press, 1990.
N   *Negotiations: 1972–1990.* Translated by Martin Joughin. Euro-
      pean Perspectives: A Series in Social Thought and Cultural Crit-
      icism, ed. Lawrence D. Kriztman. New York: Columbia Univer-
      sity Press, 1995.
NP   *Nietzsche and Philosophy.* Translated by Hugh Tomlinson. Euro-
      pean Perspectives, New York: Columbia University Press, 1983.

BOOKS BY GILLES DELEUZE AND FÉLIX GUATTARI

A-O   *Anti-Oedipus: Capitalism and Schizophrenia.* Translated by Robert
      Hurley, Mark Seem, and Helen R. Lane. Minneapolis: University
      of Minnesota Press, 1983.
ATP   *A Thousand Plateaus: Capitalism and Schizophrenia.* Translated by
      Brian Massumi. Minneapolis: University of Minnesota Press,
      1987.
K   *Kafka: Toward a Minor Literature.* Translated by Dana Polan. Min-
      neapolis: University of Minnesota Press, 1986.
WP   *What Is Philosophy?* Translated by Hugh Tomlinson and Graham
      Burchell. New York: Columbia University Press, 1994.

Irigaray and Deleuze

Introduction

Body Talk

We live in a world in which the specific form our bodies take very much matters; sex, race, physical anomalies, and any physically marked differences from or convergence with the dominant "norm" have ramifications that extend into every part of our lives. Not all corporeal differences are equally significant. Whether I have brown or black eyes does not matter as much as whether my skin is black or white. In addition, corporeal differences that are perhaps less tangible since they are not genetically determined — the way one carries oneself, the way one speaks, behaviors that betray one's class — can also have a deeply pervasive impact which is difficult to escape and which forms an inevitable part of the fabric of one's life. Whatever one's politics or beliefs about what it means to be human, the specific body one inhabits inevitably affects the path one's life takes. Our bodies have social significance with which we are forced to come to terms. They enter into our senses of identity, the ways we behave, and the ways we interact with others. To theorize the body, then, means in part to refuse to ignore this aspect of social existence on the misguided assumption that we interact as if we were all equally human and that what this means is not inextricably linked with the specific forms our bodies take.

That said, however, it is tricky to know how to take this body into account. Do we assume that anyone who is female has one kind of body and that anyone who is male has another? Do we assume that race is clearly demarcated in specific ways? How do we theorize this body, how do we account for its role in subjectivity, how do we account for its effects? How do we account for how and when it enters into our own senses of identity as well as the way it enters into how others perceive and treat us? Lately there has been some very interesting work done on the body by feminists as well as many others.[1] Western culture tends to associate women with the body in a reductionistic way that makes women seem somehow less than human; feminists have explored this assumption by exploring the connection between human "nature" and embodiment. If women are more identified with their bodies than men with theirs, why is this the case, and is it really because women are less able to reason beyond the contingencies of the flesh and the impermanence of sensuous existence?

Despite the association of women with the body, it is by no means an area of life that philosophers have entirely neglected. Hegel and Marx emphasize the role of human labor in the development of consciousness, Husserl and Heidegger return to the lived experience of perception to ground philosophy, and Nietzsche and Freud claim that the body and the physiological aspects of living are crucial to human consciousness in ways of which we may not be aware. More recently, theorists of various disciplines have attempted to theorize the body itself. Psychoanalysis has continued to develop accounts of conscious experience as it emerges from the initial corporeal organization of the subject in relation to her or his parents. Literary theorists, historians, sociologists, anthropologists, and philosophers have also tried to account for the variety of ways in which the human body has been represented over the centuries and to theorize its significance for human life.

In her groundbreaking book *Volatile Bodies*, Elizabeth Grosz presents a compelling agenda for an approach to the body that would provide new insight into the puzzles of various kinds of dualisms in the philosophical tradition as well as into alternative conceptions of subjectivity, gender relations, and the relationship of self to other. According to Grosz, traditional approaches to the body include investigating the body as an object of the natural sciences, construing it as a kind of tool of consciousness (or a vessel occupied by an "animating, willful subjectivity"), or conceiving of it as a passive medium of expression that renders communicable what is essentially private (Grosz 1994c, 8). All these approaches imply a mind/body dualism. Theories that reduce human consciousness to physiological processes, as well as those that depict consciousness as either a disembodied process or the effect of a mental thing, fail to capture the ambiguity of human existence. Human beings come to experience the world as conscious, sentient, embodied subjects through a process in which no clear distinctions can be made between mind and body, thought and matter, reason and emotion, interiority and exteriority, or self and other.

Philosophy has tended to replicate the mind/body dualism by elevating a disembodied mind and disavowing the body. In addition, it has excluded the feminine by implicitly coding it as aligned with the unreason associated with the body. Grosz suggests that to overcome the blind spot created by the refusal of the body and the feminine, philosophers should regard the body "as the threshold or borderline concept that hovers perilously and undecidably at the pivotal point of binary pairs" (Grosz 1994c, 23). That is, rather than revalorizing the body as the unprivileged term of the various dichotomies with which it is associated, she suggests theorizing the body as a unique kind of object which problematizes binary oppositions. She evokes the metaphor of a Möbius strip to model "the inflection of mind into body and body into mind" and the "ways in which, through a kind of twisting or inversion, one side becomes another." It is the body viewed as this kind of peculiar object that is neither simply a psychical interior nor a corporeal exterior but something with a kind of "uncontrollable drift of the inside into the outside and the outside into the inside" (xii) that would provide a perspective from which to rethink the opposition between inside and outside, private and public, self and other, as well as other binary pairs associated with the mind/body opposition (21).

Confronting the ambiguity of the body entails questioning the "natural" coherence and solidity of bodies and complicates our understanding of the social identities "attached" to those bodies. If bodies are not corporeal containers for consciousness but are instead fully implicated in the dynamic process of social living, then our tendency to consider our bodies the preserve of the "natural" part of our identities is false. Our embodied selves are as implicated in our specific historical situation as the social selves of our conscious experience. This means that there can be no easy distinction between body and mind; the notion of a body with determinate boundaries, just like the notion of a psychic self, is the constituted effect of dynamic forces which are always in movement.

With the "linguistic turn" toward philosophical questions about the nature of language and the discursive subjectivity of language users, theorists of various kinds have elaborated how human subjects are implicated in systems of signification. At times this work has tended toward, or been read as tending toward, a conception of the human subject that is socially situated only with respect to the abstract signifers of a system of social significance.[2] Such accounts tend to drop out the embodied subject in order to concentrate on the speaking subject who is able to situate herself within the matrix of linguistic systems of meaning. An important aspect of human subjectivity is one's situatedness within symbolic systems and one's ability to produce words that will be recognized by others as the words of a subject who "makes sense." Julia Kristeva, Michel Foucault, Luce Irigaray, Gilles Deleuze, and Félix Guattari have created theories of subjectivity that emphasize the implication of such discursive situatedness in corporeal practices that are equally situated and yet entail an extralinguistic dimension of meaning. Their work provides some of the exciting approaches toward conceptions of humanity that are able to account for "the inflection of mind into body and body into mind" which Grosz has in mind. The conception of the human subject which emerges from their work is that of a problematic intertwining of contingent and often conflicting social identities assumed at the level of imaginary identifications involving a morphology of the body (that is, an ongoing materialization of the body in the specific forms that it takes), as well as at the level of conscious thought. The body of such a subject is not a stable entity with unambiguous boundaries, but a temporal becoming which is always culturally mediated and integrally linked to the equally dynamic process of psychic selfhood.

In this book I focus in particular on the work of Irigaray and of Deleuze, sometimes in collaboration with Guattari, in order to engage in a project of overcoming mind/body dualisms which have been detrimental to women as well as other "marginalized" groups, and in order to elaborate a vocabulary for talking about ourselves in relation to the world and human others in terms of the dynamic flow of a process of being that is corporeal as well as discursive. I approach this project from a perspective informed by feminist writers who, like Grosz, call for an account of how the body comes into play in the production of the knowledges that inform our self-understanding and our conceptions of what is desirable as well as what is possible for human relationships and ethical community; but it is from Irigaray's work that I derive the main inspiration for the form my project takes.[3]

Irigaray argues that contemporary culture is bifurcated by a sexual division of labor in which the body and the "natural" are relegated to the feminine and the more "cultural" products of symbolic significance are relegated to the masculine. She further argues that this bifurcation has serious ethical implications which have led to an impoverished life for us all and have encouraged us to create symbolic support for feminine subjectivity. Such support would make possible a genuine dialogue between two kinds of subjects. Genuine communication between two genders could lead to undermining the body/mind bifurcation of contemporary culture, foster practices of perception in which all subjects took responsibility for integrating body and mind, and open up important ethical and political opportunities for a new way of life. In this book I develop Irigaray's account of a (masculinist) specular economy of subjectivity which fosters divisive mind/body dualisms, and I explore Irigaray's work, along with the work of Deleuze, to develop a theory of embodied subjectivity that could provide an alternative to contemporary forms of specular subjectivity. Deleuze argues that we need to encourage experimentation with nomadic subjectivity. Human life is organized into strata which are implicated with nonhuman strata of life. Nomadic subjects can destratify from rigid forms of organization by creating "planes of consistency" that put heterogeneous elements of existence into continuous variation. I appeal to Deleuze's reading of Foucault to highlight how nomadic subjects can integrate discursive and nondiscursive aspects of social life. Deleuze's work provides an important resource for characterizing how subjects can foster creative engagement with the world of dynamic becoming of which they are an integral part. I elaborate Irigaray's theory of specular subjectivity as a useful description of some aspects of contemporary social life. Understanding ourselves through such a description could suggest alternative ways of being. Thorizing those alternatives, on my view, constitutes a positive step in making them a reality.

Because terms such as 'human nature', 'self', 'woman', and 'man' imply static substances (with or without changing attributes), they fail to capture the dynamic quality of the process of being-subject these theorists emphasize. Although the terminology used to describe this process is by no means uniform, various writers have contributed new terms for that process as well as new ways of understanding more traditional designations for human selfhood. I use the term 'subject' to refer to a grammatical position the 'I' can take up with respect to conventional meaning and 'self' to refer to the reference point or image by which a human being can orient the developing narrative of her life. Since the self of a narrative seems to take on a specific form by accruing qualities and characteristics in the living of a life, 'subject' seems to be the more appropriate term for indicating a social self in the context of positioning itself vis-à-vis a larger social field that is importantly oriented through language as well as other systems of social significance. 'Subjectivity' refers to the notion of the subject as a process that must continually repeat itself in order to maintain a specific form and an 'economy' or 'structuring' of subjectivity to the various means by which a subject can regulate and stabilize this process of being a subject.

Grosz has described the project of Luce Irigaray as that of "rethinking knowledges as the products of sexually specific bodies" (Grosz 1995, 41). Irigaray demonstrates through readings of key philosophical texts that the supposedly sexually indifferent status of knowledges (i.e., their claims to be universal rather than the product of masculine interests) is linked with a "culturally inscribed correlation of men with the category of mind and of women with the category of body." It is due to the association of women with the body, the irrational, and the natural that men can take on the position of subjects of "pure" knowledge: "By positioning women as *the* body, they can project themselves and their products as *disembodied*, pure, and uncontaminated" (42). It is the project of this book to investigate ways of overcoming the detrimental impact of mind/body dualisms that privilege the former at the expense of the latter. In keeping with this project, I introduce the terms 'conceptual logics' and 'corporeal logics' to mark the pervasive impact of such dualisms in contemporary culture. Both Irigaray and Deleuze challenge any conception of the human subject as a unified, rational agent and instead theorize subjectivity as the effect of a dynamic process involving heterogeneity and difference which includes corporeal as well as psychic elements. They challenge conventional notions of perception which assume that objects of perception are similar to other objects perceived in the past, as well as notions of conception which assume that objects of thought must conform to already established norms. Both challenge the traditional model of thinking and instead theorize thinking as always encountering what is singular and unprecedented. I follow Irigaray and Deleuze in conceiving of philosophizing as a practice — one that does not necessarily give clear-cut results, but one that sets us on a path of experimentation and receptivity to the unknown. Questions concerning the body, its relationship to mind, and the nature of embodied subjectivity lead each of them to a critique of traditional notions of identity and representational thought. For both, the body and the self are not the contained objects they may appear to be, but are rather the effects of processes of which we are more or less unaware. Investigating these processes enables us to rethink our engagement with them and instigate new experiences in embodied living.

In keeping with the challenge of their theories to traditional notions of the body as well as of the mind, I use the term 'corporeal logics' to refer to the background processes informing the perceptual awareness of sensation and what are traditionally known as the "irrational" processes of mood, intuitive "gut" feelings, and emotions, and I use the term 'conceptual logics' to refer to the background processes informing the conceptual awareness of what are traditionally known as the "rational" processes of logical and articulate thought. Referring to both sides of the mind/body dualism in terms of a logic underlines the socially situated nature of such logics and the insight that "natural" bodies are as informed by social processes as are minds. Maintaining a distinction between the two through the use of the two terms underlines the pervasive cultural bifurcation Irigaray insists upon, which relegates products of the "mind" to one group in society and products of the "body" to the other. Although I am not as convinced as Irigaray that gender is the only or even the most important way to mark the groups associated with these dualisms, I believe she is right to insist that theorizing the mechanisms of this dualism is crucial to our struggles to create a more ethical future.

Distinguishing corporeal and conceptual logics speaks to the way in which contemporary meaning systems are arranged in keeping with mind/body dualisms; we actually do tend to separate our understanding of life according to this split.[4] What we know on a rational, cerebral level is not what we know on an emotional, corporeal level. The gap between a subject's conceptual and corporeal logics can be profound since the realms of conceptual and corporeal "sense" not only are oriented in different directions but are also likely to diverge ever more widely, especially in a culture that emphasizes mind/body dualisms. Both Irigaray and Deleuze are engaged in a project of transforming how we think, speak, and live. In the reading I give here of their work, I emphasize how this transformation involves reconnecting our bodies and minds at the corporeal level as well as at the level of discursive systems of meaning and note the beneficial effects the integration of what we might call somatic knowledge with conceptual knowledge could have for a culture intent on valorizing the latter at the expense of the former.

My exploration of the body is in part a response to the sense of alienation that seems to pervade contemporary cultural life and that was so compellingly diagnosed by Nietzsche. Nietzsche taunts the person who thinks that his self is just his consciousness or rational capacity. For Nietzsche, this part of the self is just the "little self" — a small effect of a much larger self that is "the body." In denying this larger self, we not only deny the greater part of who we are but also close off possibilities of living. This larger self turns out to be the effect of natural and social forces extending beyond us that only contingently converge to manifest a given individual. This Nietzschean theme is picked up by Heidegger, Irigaray, and Deleuze. The work of Irigaray and Deleuze emerges from a French philosophical tradition marked by the Cartesian influence which led to a specifically French reaction to Hegel, Husserl, and Heidegger as well as Nietzsche, Marx, and Freud.[5] Heidegger's interest in Nietzsche prompted a French resurgence of interest in Nietzsche.[6] Whatever their disagreements with this tradition — Irigaray's break with the Lacanian community or Deleuze's insistence on doing his commentaries on "maverick" philosophers such as Nietzsche, Spinoza, and Bergson rather than Descartes, Hegel, and Heidegger — the questions and issues that emerge in their work bear the marks of that tradition.

To set the scene for my reading of Irigaray and Deleuze, I briefly present the role of the body in Heidegger's work in the next section of this introduction. I am interested in why he seems to draw back from what we might call "body" talk despite his insistence on our Being-in-the-world. I also explore his notion of following the path of genuine thinking. I claim that this path entails integrating corporeal logics with conceptual logics and so engages one in what we might call a corporeal practice of thinking. Irigaray's and Deleuze's projects, different as they are, both involve a shift in thinking that must take place on a corporeal as well as a conceptual level. Reading Irigaray and Deleuze in light of the notion of thinking as an integrative practice meant to bring about a transformation in corporeal morphology as well as cognitive understanding provides an approach to their work that has provocative implications for reconceiving ethical self-other relations.

In the final section I motivate a project that would foster a way of thinking, speaking, and being that integrates conceptual thought with corporeal logic, and I briefly sketch out the resonances between Irigaray and Deleuze in light of such a project.

Heidegger and the Body

Heidegger's notions of curiosity, idle talk, and ambiguity in *Being and Time* are interesting when examined in light of the discursive notion of subjectivity that emerges in poststructuralist accounts of human selfhood. Saussurean linguistics, Lévi-Straussian anthropology, Lacanian psychoanalysis, and Foucauldian notions of the subject could be read as indicating that human subjects are the effects of social systems of significance that require human beings to take up a position as a speaking subject with respect to other social subjects. The specific form that one's subjectivity takes would then be contingent on how one's position in the larger structural whole of human significance relates to other possible positions. The notions of curiosity, idle talk, and ambiguity which Heidegger delineates in *Being and Time* refer to the ease with which a speaker of language can take up perspectives with respect to what it is possible to say. His interpretation of these notions suggests that one can take up such a perspective without seriously considering the choices involved in thus positioning oneself. When one is curious in a superficial way, engaged in idle talk, or deliberately ambiguous rather than taking a stand, one is adopting a free-floating attitude that can easily shift. There is no resistance or friction in such shifts; one moves easily from one attitude to the next. Even those obstacles set up by cultural mores and taboos do not have to be respected in idle talk. One's actual social position or locatedness can be waived without loss of "meaning" at the level of public discourse. That is, one can engage in many forms of conversation with others without having to confront one's own situation as an embodied human being (Heidegger 1962, ¶35–38).

On Heidegger's account, relating to one's own death brings one back to one's own embodiment and the physical limitations of being in time and space — and in particular a specific culturally encoded time and space. Confronting one's mortality means, in part, confronting the disintegration of one's bodily boundaries. When one dies, one will not only no longer have possibilities in the sense of having a position in a cultural matrix; one will also no longer have sentient experience. On the one hand, Heidegger's *Dasein* (his term for human existence) has possibilities that "make sense" in relation to the meaning systems of a specific society. On the other, insofar as *Dasein* is living "authentically," possibilities are manifested within the constraints presented by a uniquely embodied situation. Authenticity, then, insists on a kind of situatedness that involves both the discursive meanings of a cultural field of significance and the corporeal experiences of an embodied subject.

Dasein as Being-in-the-world is always projecting itself toward a future about which it cares. The 'they' — Heidegger's term for public discourse which dictates what "one" should do in a given situation — provides *Dasein* with a range of meaningful cultural projects from which to choose.

Projects that do not fully engage the *Dasein* living them out are inauthentic. Heidegger's uncanny "call" of conscience which prompts "authentic" commitment to one's choices (as opposed to the evasive irresponsibility of someone who views her choices from the perspective of, for example, idle talk) could be read as a call to attend to the corporeal logic of the body.[7]

> Conscience summons Dasein's Self from its lostness in the "they." The Self to which the appeal is made remains indefinite and empty in its "what." When Dasein interprets itself in terms of that with which it concerns itself, the call passes over *what* Dasein, proximally and for the most part, understands itself *as*. And yet the Self has been reached, unequivocally and unmistakably. . . . The caller is unfamiliar to the everyday they-self; it is something like an *alien* voice. What could be more alien to the "they," lost in the manifold 'world' of its concern, than the Self which has been individualized down to itself in uncanniness and been thrown into the "nothing"? (Heidegger 1962, 317–22, ¶56)

The call away from the 'they' could be conceived as a call toward a heterogeneous logic that speaks of the dynamic formations of a body in process. To turn away from this call is to turn away from what moves us at the level of bodily fluxes and flows — the fleeting sensations, emotions, and half-thoughts of the more decidely corporeal aspects of human selves. This call is reticent and silent in the sense that it does not and cannot utilize the same logics as those of language. The call summons *Dasein* away from the public discourse of the 'they,' because the same things that are meaningful to the subject at the symbolic level of conventional social significance are not necessarily meaningful at the level of that subject's corporeal logic. Different words evoke emotional resonance in keeping with an experiential fund of encoded experience which relates to the biography of the individual. This biography has both corporeal and conceptual components. Authenticity involves an integrative act of bringing together the two levels of corporeal and conceptual meaning in a vitalizing way. It thus adds an emotional richness to authentic living that the dispersed living of inauthentic life cannot have.

Heidegger's notion of mood indicates the corporeal rootedness of the prereflective understanding more primordial than our theoretical understanding of life. The 'they' cannot dictate *Dasein's* mood. Anxiety is explicitly analyzed by Heidegger as a mood that speaks to the ultimate lack of discursive foundation for any specific project *Dasein* may choose (Heidegger 1962, ¶40). Heidegger's notion of the call could thus be read as a call to rethink our engagements with the projects that are meaningful to us because of the 'they' in a way that incorporates direction from the corporeal logics of an embodied subject who has had to develop a determinate physical form as well as a psychic self. Heidegger's mystification of the gap between the 'they' and the uncanny call pulling one away from the 'they' could be the first step toward the reactionary suggestion to uphold the "destiny" of one's traditional culture, for example, as manifested by the Nazi Party of Heidegger's cultural situation; such mystification tends to leave only the already articulated possibilities of the tradition as opportunities for authentic action. Developing a richer vocabulary for corporeal processes might provide symbolic support for creative integration of corporeal and conceptual logics that could generate new choices in authentic living.

We will find that Irigaray and Deleuze also appeal to silence for creative rejuvenation. Irigaray advocates listening to silence (see Chapter 4). Deleuze advocates approaching the gap between mute word and blind thing that intimates something beyond both corporeal and conceptual logics (see Chapter 8). Irigaray's feminine subject is receptive to the sensible transcendental. This transcendental is immanent in all sensous experience and yet is transcendent in the sense of eluding any determinate form experience takes. Deleuze's nomadic subject is receptive to the imperceptible. The imperceptible is also immanent in conscious experience; molecular becomings occur at thresholds below the level of the perceivable and conceivable and yet can set into motion new formations of both. Irigaray's sensible transcendental opens subjectivity to a feminine divine which is a horizon of dynamic becoming. Deleuze's becoming-imperceptible opens subjectivity to a virtual chaos of incompossible becoming. A practice of thinking that entails integrating corporeal and conceptual logics entails, for Irigaray and Deleuze as well as Heidegger, receptivity to an immanent "beyond" in which binary oppositions no longer hold.

One of the theses of this book is that we can and should attempt to theorize more of the corporeal aspect of being human into conscious awareness. An elaboration of corporeal logics could provide a vocabulary of the body that would allow us to symbolize and integrate more of the extralinguistic realm of embodied living into our consciousness. Since symbolizing corporeal logics must always pursue a dynamic process, such a project would entail the transformation of Western representational thought into another, perhaps more life-affirming, form of thought. Heidegger, like Irigaray and Deleuze, suggests that thinking, speaking, and writing can and should involve something like a transformative practice. None of these thinkers are interested in thinking and writing practices that merely pass along information. They are all looking for some kind of qualitative change in the lived experience of their readers as well as in themselves. One way that this is expressed is through an emphasis on the path of thinking, or the process of reading, speaking, and writing, as opposed to the results produced in the content of the thinker's thought. They direct our attention to thinking and writing as practices with transformative possibilities rooted in material processes not all of which are accessible to conscious awareness. Focusing attention on these processes through the notion of the body, rather than the notions of the unconscious or of Being, has the advantage of calling our attention to the fringes of our own awareness. It emphasizes the potential accessibility of these processes without at the same time minimizing their strangeness or the bizarre effects they could have on what it is that we think we already know.[8]

Conceptual Thought and Corporeal Logics

The Freudian notion of drives suggests that they are neither completely biological nor completely cultural. Thus, for psychoanalytic theory, and particularly Lacanian psychoanalytic theory, the body can provide a kind of link between soma and psyche, the place where body and mind meet. That theorizing this link turns out to problematize the distinction between body and mind does not diminish its importance for understanding how the body/mind distinction emerges. One could argue that Heidegger attempts to overcome mind/body dualisms but reintroduces one by privileging a radically other "call" stripped of its corporeal roots in material process. Irigaray stresses the importance of acknowledging and representing sexual difference in a cultural economy that aligns matter-nature-body with the feminine and divinity-culture-mind with the masculine. Deleuze elaborates perceptual and conceptual forms of organization and advocates pushing each to its limits in order to encounter the outside that can transform both. All three assume a form of the mind/body split that can and should be continually bridged in an integrative practice.[9] I have, somewhat crudely, referred to two levels of human subjectivity as the corporeal and conceptual levels in order to characterize the dualism with which we live. Although I will discuss these two levels at times as if they were nonproblematically distinct, they not only are theorized quite differently by different theorists but also are inextricably linked. My characterizations of Irigaray's and Deleuze's work should make clear just how problematic and ultimately arbitrary any distinction between the two must be. Although Irigaray's and Deleuze's approaches may suggest different ways of understanding the distinction and relationship between body and mind, both nevertheless advocate a way of thinking and being that would explore the connections between the two in the context of encountering what lies beyond both.

The French poststructuralism that emerged in the wake of and in response to phenomenology and existentialism looked for the affective roots of language and held out hope that cultural politics, and in particular avantgarde literature, could achieve what Marxism could not: a shift in consciousness that would lead to significant social change. This French line of thought suggests that language does not simply describe human reality but is an important constitutive factor in conscious experience.[10] Stylistic innovations can be crucial to introducing new ways of thinking and being that can transform our awareness. In the work of Irigaray and Deleuze, the concern with style becomes accountable to a reality that lies beyond the perceivable, conceivable reality of conventional conscious experience. Innovations in style respond to what lies beyond the familiar. It is only insofar as such innovations emerge from "authentic" encounters that they speak to something of genuine significance rather than simply engage in empty play. Philosophy for both becomes not simply a form of communication but a practice that asks basic questions about life and reality and breaks down dualisms in order to intensify the experience of living and bring us back in touch with what most strongly moves us.

For Irigaray and Deleuze, writing theory is a practice that brings — or should bring — the writer into more intense immediate contact with herself and the affective materiality of her existence, which feeds and motivates her words. Writing and reading is effective insofar as it is able to intensify the sense that one's experience is meaningful in a fully somatic sense of the word. Repeating what has already been said is not likely to instigate the kind of thinking that enlivens one's sense of meaningful connection with the world. It is stylistically evocative language that emerges from encounter with the world that can have this effect. And it is because of the way the unconscious fills in the gap provoked by the failure to stick to the letter of conventional meaning that this effect comes about. The response to aporetic suspensions of conventional meaning can evoke somatic responses that adhere to corporeal rather than conceptual patterns of response. Such responses can destabilize our physical forms as well as our psychic selves. This destabilization in turn can initiate fresh integration of corporeal and conceptual levels of subjectivity. Irigaray and Deleuze suggest that confrontation with the limits of what is perceivable (through corporeal logics) and what is conceivable (through the conceptual logics of discursive systems of meaning) leads us to an infinite beyond both that is our most important resource in the rejuvenation of human life.

Neither Irigaray nor Deleuze believes that there is something like a pure experience that can be unearthed and experienced once we have removed the blind spots and distortions of contemporary culture. There is no touchstone, no ultimate base on which we can build a more veridical or authentic experience. There is no body that has access to a pure realm of sensation, and there is no transcendent realm of forms to which we can refer our thinking. To avoid reference to a foundational transcendent, Irigaray and Deleuze attempt to invent a new way of thinking and writing. Irigaray characterizes and critiques a masculine form of subjectivity in order to gesture toward an alternative form of subjectivity. This alternative form of subjectivity would produce an individual with a heightened state of consciousness who would be more in the present, more attuned to the body with its "natural" rhythms, less rigid, and more ethical by virtue of a heightened awareness of and flexibility toward others with all their differences. Her notion of a sensible transcendental indicates an immanent form of transcendence that could foster receptivity to difference without dictating the specific forms that difference should take. Deleuze too is trying to promote an alternative image of thinking that would result not just in a different way of thinking but in a heightened state of consciousness. Like Irigaray, he is interested in promoting a way of living that does not erase or deny the multiplicity of life but instead receptively and creatively affirms it. The notion of the nomadic subject that he creates in tandem with Guattari evokes an individual who continually reinvents herself through ongoing attunement of the fluxes and flows of material life to the specific contingencies of social existence. The notion of becoming-imperceptible implies continual confrontation with the limits of conventional perceptions and conceptions of life and the invention of new modes of being through the pursuit of the immanent unfolding of desire.

Irigaray and Deleuze diagnose and attempt to provide a cure for the cultural problems that they perceive. They offer images of subjectivity and thinking that incorporate aspects of the "unconscious" and assume a much richer kind of connectedness to our world and others than do traditional conceptions of the self. Their attempts to elaborate what I have called corporeal logics into their account of human existence, as well as their attempts to conceive of practices that could integrate corporeal and conceptual levels of subjectivity, make their work an ideal resource for creating a model of subjectivity that could overcome the mind/body dualisms that impoverish contemporary culture.

Developing an embodied theory of subjectivity will turn out to require developing a theoretical method that encourages a self-transformative process on the part of the theorist. Theorizing embodiment involves re-thinking not only who we are but also how we think about who we are. And since this integrates into the thinking process aspects of being human that have often been pushed to one side, at least in the Western tradition of philosophical thought, it stands to reason that the *how* of this thinking should be as radically affected as the *what* of that thinking in the process.

My perspective here is ultimately a feminist one, with all the benefits and limitations that such a perspective implies. Although I have tried to be sensitive to other kinds of embodied differences, and although I believe that an image of thinking premised on a logic of difference rather than a logic of identity would be beneficial for other kinds of differences, for the purposes of this project I have been especially interested in considering the gender inflections that emerge as one explores and experiments with the dissonances and resonances between Irigaray and Deleuze. I believe that the specular economy elaborated by Irigaray with respect to mascu-line subjects and feminine others, however, could also be elaborated with respect to active subjects and supportive others who are divided across axes of difference other than that of gender.

The impetus for this project is the desire to work toward a social reality in which the participation of all human beings would be fully supported and recognized. The way we think about how human beings come to be and maintain social selves has important repercussions for questions about what constitutes an ethical social order. Shifts in consciousness and social practices on the part of specific groups of people cannot help but affect the social field as a whole. Such shifts can cause disruption, dislocation, and disorienting rifts in social meaning. A theory of embodied subjectivity can help us map corporeal connections among people and thus indicate how different forms of subjectivity are interdependent and mutually informing. Challenging traditional boundaries among bodies and among minds as well as between bodies and minds allows us to rethink the interdependent nature of subjectivity. Insight into how cultural practices and discursive systems of meaning inform subjectivity could suggest strategies for facili-tating constructive change. For Deleuze and Irigaray, thinking, speaking, and writing, if done creatively, can transform us not only at the conceptual level but at the level of corporeal morphology as well. Insofar as we are able to engage in a practice of thinking, speaking, and writing that over-comes the mind/body split, we will be able to break out of forms of life that have already been lived and thought and to invent new forms of life more suitable to our present circumstances.

Irigaray not only lays out a theory of masculine subjectivity with its specular, feminine other, she also seeds her entire corpus with hints of an alternative feminine subjectivity — one that eludes the masculine perspective as well as one that has not yet, perhaps, been achieved. In fact, the category of the "feminine" is neither straightforward nor unitary for Irigaray. In addition to depicting the feminine other as seen by the masculine subject, Irigaray depicts the feminine other co-opted by masculine subjectivity (that is, the feminine other who buys into the way the masculine subject views her), the feminine other of the masculine subject as she is apart from the masculine subject's perspective, and the feminine other in the process of articulating herself as a subject and thus providing an alternative paradigm for subjectivity that may not yet be actualized. In Chapter 1, I lay out Irigaray's project and give an overview of these various conceptions of the feminine.

In Chapter 2 I explore Irigaray's attempted dialogue with Nietzsche in *Marine Lover*. At the same time that Irigaray is clearly drawn to Nietzsche's "deconstruction" of sense experience which inevitably also challenges the subject of that experience, she also chides him for not going far enough. If anyone should have succeeded in evoking the body, one might think that it would be Nietzsche. After all, he advocates being true to the earth and speaking honestly of the body, and he paved the way for just the kind of challenge to traditional conceptions of the subject that Irigaray herself would seem to want. Yet in much of *Marine Lover* she derides him for his blind spot when it comes to the feminine other. Irigaray "argues" that despite his acknowledgment of how the category of the feminine works vis-à-vis the masculine subject, he is no closer than other masculine subjects to being able to conceive of the feminine subject apart from the masculine economy. For Irigaray, this blind spot ultimately leads him to a somatophobia similar to that which haunts masculine subjects less inclined toward taking the first approach to articulating the feminine. By enacting the role of the feminine other emerging from Nietzsche's texts in an attempted dialogue with Nietzsche, Irigaray gives a voice to his feminine other. With an examination of *Marine Lover*, I investigate the possibility of shattering mirrors by enabling the mirror to speak, and I explore Irigaray's elaboration of Nietzsche's feminine other at the threshold of claiming her subjectivity.

In Chapter 3 I examine Irigaray's notion of the "sensible transcendental" — a realm that can never be captured in language and yet with which we are always in direct contact — through a reading of "La Mystérique" (a section on medieval mystics in *Speculum*), her evocation of intrauterine experience in *An Ethics of Sexual Difference*, and her depiction of angels of passage and a feminine divine in *Sexes and Genealogies*. In living toward the horizon of the sensible transcendental, one dissolves one's perceptions and self-same-identity. For Irigaray, however, such dissolution is contained through attentive response to that which is always contiguous to conscious awareness; by attending to the gap between corporeal and conceptual logics, especially in relation to an embodied other, one can find the point of contact that can lead to rejuvenating transformations of both.

In Chapter 4 I address Irigaray's proposal for shattering mirrors as it emerges in *Sexes and Genealogies* and *I Love to You*. Irigaray insists on getting the masculine subject to acknowledge the feminine other in her push toward a new kind of subject in part because implicit forms of feminine subjectivity are, according to Irigaray, our best bet for rejuvenating culture. Since the masculine economy of subjectivity requires feminine others, empowering women by fostering their active subjectivity (according to the masculine model) not only is impractical but also would obliterate an alternative economy of subjectivity that already exists in nascent form. It is dialogue between two different subjects that could usher in a new, more ethical way of life.

I then turn to Deleuze. Although Heidegger was not operating out of a psychoanalytic framework, his influence on the Lacanian reading of Freud which influences Irigaray's work is clear. Deleuze, like Irigaray, albeit from a different perspective, challenges this tradition and investigates certain philosophers who are "deviant" in one way or another in order to create a conception of thinking, speaking, and writing that evokes the body in a way that moves beyond a psychoanalytic framework. He contrasts the traditional image of philosophical thought (which he argues is so limiting as to kill genuine thinking entirely) and creates his own conceptions of nomadic thinking, speaking, and writing that do not just provide an alternative to the traditional ones but create an alternative conception of subjectivity in the process. In *Anti-Oedipus*, Deleuze and Guattari contest the Lacanian account of (masculine) subjectivity and develop a model in which molecular flows stabilize into the molar aggregates of human subjects with recognizable bodies and selves. They advocate a project of schizoanalysis that would thwart social hegemony and foster experiments in nomadic living. In other works by Deleuze, and Deleuze and Guattari, these experiments go by the names of "becoming-imperceptible" and even "doing philosophy" (among others). In Chapter 5 I discuss the model of subjectivity Deleuze and Guattari present in *Anti-Oedipus*, give a preliminary sketch of their conceptions of becoming-imperceptible and philosophy, and explore these experiments as projects in symbolizing viable alternative models of subjectivity.

In Chapter 6 I present Deleuze's version of Nietzsche. The main difference in Irigaray's and Deleuze's readings of Nietzsche has to do with Nietzsche's notion of the eternal return. Irigaray insists that Nietzsche's eternal return involves a notion of the repetition of the same. Because of his failure to acknowledge the creative contribution to becoming made by the feminine, he can never enter into a real relationship with the feminine other upon whom his identity depends. Deleuze, by contrast, insists that Nietzsche's notion of the eternal return is not about the repetition of the same, but rather involves a repetition of difference which is ultimately based on a logic of difference rather than a logic of identity. The Dionysian subject of the eternal return has no need of affirming a self-identical self and is instead engaged in an ongoing process of metamorphosis. This audacious experiment in subjectivity, however, entails the dissolution of personal identity. Comparing the two conceptions of the eternal return brings out the dilemma of stabilizing a self out of dynamic processes of becoming.

In Chapter 7 I elaborate on the model of subjectivity Deleuze and Guattari develop in *Anti-Oedipus* by extending this model to include the model presented in their book *A Thousand Plateaus*. In the latter work, desiring-machines become assemblages and schizoanalysis becomes destratification. Their conceptual innovations enrich their initial model and provide a vocabulary for nomadic experiments which resonates in interesting ways with Irigaray's very different presentation of feminine experiments in subjectivity. I further draw out these resonances by exploring the trajectory of becoming-minority (as it emerges in Deleuze and Guattari's book *Kafka*), becoming-woman, and becoming-imperceptible, and the notions of a line of flight and the body without organs.

In Chapter 8 I appeal to Deleuze's reading of Foucault to highlight how destratification can be a practice that integrates corporeal and conceptual logics, and I suggest that the notion of a Foucauldian 'diagram' (or the construction of an 'abstract machine' as described by Deleuze and Guattari in *A Thousand Plateaus*) can provide a useful tool for putting individual projects of destratification into the context of a larger social field in which we may want to select certain lines of flight rather than others. In addition, I suggest that Irigaray's work could be read as a diagram of sexual difference, and I advocate multiple mappings of the social field. I then give a reading of Deleuze and Guattari's notions of philosophy and art as it emerges in *What Is Philosophy?* in order to develop further their notion of the virtual as the counterpart to Irigaray's notion of a feminine divine. Irigaray insists on the receptivity to the divine of a living subject in continual contact with embodied others in a sensual world; Deleuze and Guattari lay out approaches to the virtual that may provide new perspectives on such living.

In Chapter 9 I attempt a synthesis of Irigaray and Deleuze. Irigaray's conception of the sensible transcendental and Deleuze's conception of becoming-imperceptible entail a critique of traditional notions of perception and representation as well as of the subject. These critiques are developed in tandem with new theories of subjectivity that symbolize the process of challenging conventional norms of perception and conception which subjects must continually undergo in order to integrate the dynamic becoming of life. Both theorists suggest that there is a realm of the infinite that is immanent in our sense perception — an inexhaustible realm that is "outside" our ordinary experience and yet always there at the edges of our feeling, thought, and perception. I consider the dilemmas raised for personal identity by the receptivity to dynamic becoming advocated by Irigaray and Deleuze, and I suggest ways to combine Irigaray's concern for personal identity with Deleuze's detailed account of the pre-personal singularities of life processes. At the same time that Deleuze acknowledges that others are always implicated in our flights, he does not insist on recognition of the feminine other in the way that Irigaray does. And at the same time that Irigaray insists on the feminine other, she does not allow, perhaps, the same range of lines of flight as Deleuze. Reading the two together opens up new ways of thinking about subjectivity, self-other relations, and mind/body dualisms.

1
Irigaray's Project

In an interview conducted in 1994, Luce Irigaray described the evolution of her work through three phases.[1] The first phase was a critique "of the auto-mono-centrism of the western subject" in which she showed "how a single subject, traditionally the masculine subject, had constructed the world and interpreted the world according to a single perspective." The second phase investigated "those mediations that could permit the existence of a feminine subjectivity" (JLI 97). And the third phase explored ways to define "a new model of possible relations between man and woman, without the submission of either one to the other" (96). Irigaray insists on the philosophical nature of her work, commenting that "the thing most refused to a woman is to do philosophy." She says that, like Nietzsche and Heidegger, she attempts to open up new ways of thinking. She believes that in order to carry out the project of her current phase — to define "a philosophy, an ethic, a relationship between two different subjects" (97) — she needs to break out of the constraints posed by a single discourse and indicate how this discourse is limited to a single subject. Inventing two equal subjects is, according to Irigaray, the same as inventing a new sociocultural order.

In this chapter and the next three, I present Irigaray's project of describing and giving voice to the feminine other she believes to have been silenced by a masculinist economy of subjectivity, and I elaborate the alternative (feminine) economy of subjectivity that, if given proper symbolic support, would destabilize masculine subjectivity and so initiate the emergence of a new sociocultural order.[2] Acknowledgment and symbolization of femininity will inevitably involve some recognition of how specific human others are constitutive of our own identities on a psychic and corporeal level. Taking into account the unconscious as well as conscious aspects of ourselves involves taking into account corporeal morphology — a way of moving in space, a way of defining our body boundaries, and a range of other factors that enter into how we think and speak which involve the sensual and affective materials out of which personally meaningful language emerges. It is crucial, on Irigaray's account, to acknowledge how human others participate in our own subjectivity if we are to be able to invent new ways of symbolizing our corporeality. It is only symbolization that actively acknowledges the constitutive role of the other that will allow us to reconceive and institute more ethical forms of subjectivity.

The implicit assumption of Irigaray's project is that it is more ethical to work toward a cultural imaginary that would support the subjectivity of all through active recognition of our interdependence and mutually constitutive activity than to allow the silencing of an other (or group of others) in order to maintain one's own subjectivity. Irigaray values reciprocity based on the recognition and affirmation of difference rather than on a reductive notion of equality. Such a notion of reciprocity entails our continually bringing to light and symbolizing the multiple ways in which we premise our identities on blindness to the other. Irigaray privileges sexual difference, and in some places even suggests that the "irreducible" difference between woman and man is an "ontological" difference. Her work as a whole, however, suggests that this claim must be read in the context of a culturally specific situation. Language, on Irigaray's view, is not a transparent medium through which we refer to a separate reality, but is a constitutive factor of human existence. Categories of language, including gender categories, have decisive histories inflected by changing cultural conditions; Irigaray deliberately engages in a kind of deconstructive play with the positive content of sexual terms in order to demonstrate their historical layers and to exhibit a supplementary dimension to their meaning that could lead to their reversal (see Weed 1994, 101).[3] Irigaray must always be read as working against the content of what can be represented in language through a strategic use of style. Although she privileges sexual difference in her reworking of cultural symbolism in the attempt to overcome the blind spots of a "masculinist" logic of the same, acknowledgment of sexual difference would ultimately have to lead to an open-ended subjectivity premised on an ongoing recognition of multiple differences and continual, mutually constitutive self, other, and world transformation.

In this chapter I present Irigaray's critique of masculine subjectivity. In the first section I discuss Irigaray's critique of Freud's blind spot with respect to femininity. As we will see, Irigaray believes this blind spot to be an inevitable symptom of a masculine economy that has repercussions for the Western tradition of philosophy as well as Western culture as a whole. In the next section I characterize Irigaray's project of fostering the recognition of sexual difference. And in the final section I discuss the strategies Irigaray has developed for reading philosophical texts in order to liberate what they have to offer the project of articulating alternative economies of being and thinking. In the next three chapters I explore her dialogue with and critique of Nietzsche's project (Chapter 2), her notion of the sensible transcendental (Chapter 3), and further strategies for achieving what she calls double subjectivity (Chapter 4).

Throughout this chapter as well as the next three, I characterize Irigaray's work in terms of sexual difference. Although the feminine other turns out to conform to no one determinate form, its relation to the masculine subject in the specular economy of a masculinist culture is seen to be that of a supportive other to an "active" subject. It is my belief that active subject–supportive other relationships also play out along axes of difference other than that of sexual difference. These include, but are not limited to, those of race, class, sexual preference, and ethnicity. Irigaray's characterization of a specular economy which privileges one subject at the expense of the other is crucial for alerting us to the inevitably interdependent nature of subjectivity and the ethical implications of the alternative conceptions of subjectivity we create. I do not believe, however, that sexual difference is foundational in the sense of being the one difference to which all members of our specular economy are subjected in the same way. Although Irigaray sometimes uses the adjectives 'female' and 'male', I have tried consistently to use the adjectives 'feminine' and 'masculine' to indicate that these adjectives refer to social positioning rather than essential (biological) attributes of an individual. I use the terms 'masculine subject' and 'feminine other' throughout my discussions of specular subjectivity in order to indicate that in a masculinist specular economy it is the masculine subject who functions as the "active" subject at the expense of the subjectivity of his feminine counterpart. I characterize these two positions with respect to a masculinist specular economy in perfect working order. Fortunately no actual economy ever works so perfectly; it is unlikely that an embodied human being will fully manifest either position without complication or "excess." To consider other forms of a specular economy — still operating on the division of labor Irigaray describes between "producers" of cultural capital and "reproducers" of embodied subjects — I use the terms 'active subject' and 'supportive other'. It is my belief that aspects of what Irigaray describes in terms of a masculinist specular economy should be applied to these other forms of specularity; moving beyond the theoretical confines of a psychoanalytic framework allows us to see how this could be the case. I appeal both to Irigaray's notion of the feminine as a category of excess and, in later chapters, to Deleuze and Guattari's critique of psychoanalysis to indicate how to move beyond such a psychoanalytic framework.

Irigaray and the Constitution of the Subject

In *An Ethics of Sexual Difference* (1993a), Luce Irigaray performs a reading of various philosophical texts in order to ferret out the limits of a discourse that operates according to what she has called the logic of the same — a logic practiced by an inevitably masculine speaking subject — and to hint at a conception of mutuality beyond the limits of the texts she examines. The subject of philosophical discourse is inevitably masculine not because of a lack of female philosophers but because of the failure of the symbolic meaning systems of our society to enable female speakers to speak as women or to support them in doing so.[4] Irigaray suggests that our current norm for subjectivity operates according to a specular logic: the contemporary masculine subject reflects himself onto a feminine other in order to affirm himself repeatedly as a self-identical and self-sufficient subject. Corporeal identity is maintained despite fluctuating bodily processes owing to the displacement of "in-between" sensation and affection to an other. The masculine subject denies the feminine other's role in providing the ongoing and literally material support required to maintain the illusion of a self-contained and repeatable identity and reduces her to the other of a self-same subject. This entails denying the feminine other subjectivity in her own right.

According to Irigaray's Lacanian-informed version of masculine subjectivity, taking up a position as a speaking subject requires clear-cut distinctions between oneself as subject and one's objects. Human subjects emerge from corporeal entanglement with the mother and develop selves with definite corporeal and conceptual boundaries. According to Lacan, this begins when the infant layers up a "fictional" ego through a series of imaginary identifications with images that ensure pleasurable maternal contact. The subject further emerges out of this state of confused boundaries by taking up a position as a speaking subject from which he can represent his desire for maternal contact with words. Representations of the pleasurable maternal contact that would satisfy the subject's desire undergo transformation as the subject substitutes socially appropriate objects of desire for the originary one. The masculine subject reaffirms the boundaries thus created through a process of reification that pushes confusion and lack of clarity onto the feminine other, despite his unceasing engagement with the world as an embodied being. Living always and inevitably involves continual and all-encompassing corporeal contact with the world. Irigaray's work hints at an alternative subjectivity that is more fluid than the masculine subject, a subject that is always immersed in the world and others and whose boundaries are always shifting. She associates this subjectivity with the feminine because it is women who are more often associated with madness, the unconscious, and the body, and because she believes that women have less symbolic support for differentiating from others and maintaining a separate self-identical identity as women.

Irigaray's notion of the 'feminine' turns out to be multifaceted. The feminine as specular other is the masculinist perspective on the feminine — the feminine other the masculine subject must see in order for his economy of subjectivity to continue. The feminine as co-opted by masculine subjectivity is the feminine other who takes herself to be this specular other. Because the co-opted feminine other has limited cultural resources for symbolizing and stabilizing an alternative feminine economy of subjectivity, she is abandoned to the role of specular other. In actively living this role, however, she is already moving beyond the masculinist fantasy of who she is. This movement is captured and elaborated by Irigaray in her symbolization of the feminine as she is apart from masculine subjectivity. Positive characterizations of this feminine movement provide the initial symbolic support required for the emergence of the truly alternative economy of a feminine subject. While Irigaray does not believe that any one person could achieve such an economy in isolation, her dream of the feminine subject is a dream that two distinct subjects — masculine and feminine — could meet as equals without obliterating their differences.

The Feminine as Specular Other

In a critique of Freud's blind spot in his description of femininity, Irigaray claims that Freud strikes not one but two critical blows at the scene of representation.[5] The first blow occurs in his destruction of "a certain conception of the present, or of presence, when he stresses secondary revision, overdetermination, repetition compulsion, the death drive, etc., or when he indicates, in his practice, the impact of so-called unconscious mechanisms on the discourse of the 'subject' " (S 28); Freud's theorization of "unconscious" processes challenges the notion that what appears on the stage of consciousness is self-evidently "true" or "real." The second blow occurs in his definition of sexual difference as a function of the a priori of the same. By exhibiting what Irigaray calls a symptom of a "prisoner of a certain economy of the logos" — that is, by insisting that masculine sexual pleasure is the paradigm for all sexual pleasure — he exposes the sexual indifference that has ensured metaphysical coherence and closure for contemporary forms of masculine subjectivity. Just as his theory articulates how conscious awareness is informed by the processes that make it possible, his descriptions of feminine and masculine sexuality reveal what needs to be the case for masculine sexuality to function. Freud thus not only inadvertently reveals the unconscious processes that condition consciousness, but also compellingly manifests himself the symptoms of a subject relegating certain aspects of femininity to the unconscious in order to preserve a specific awareness of masculinity. According to Freud, feminine sexual pleasure "does not exist" (29). All desire is understood according to a masculine paradigm for representing the relationship to one's origins in the maternal body; the phallus becomes "an appropriation of the relation to origin and of the desire for and as origin" (33). Since no desire specific to woman's own sex organs is possible on this model, it is little wonder that she is said to suffer from penis envy and the need to obtain vicarious sexual pleasure through association with men.

Like Freud, Irigaray believes that a third term is needed to break into the mother-infant dyad. It is only because it becomes clear to the infant that there is more in the world than simply infant and mother that it becomes desirable to achieve some degree of separation and autonomy from the mother. Birth and the cutting of the umbilical cord mark the initial break from the maternal body which envelops the infant in an environment that is immediately responsive to the infant's needs. Repetition and representation of the relationship to the maternal body and this first break are a necesssary basis for achieving separation not just from the mother but from the rest of the world.[6] One emerges from a world to establish oneself as an individual, and one melts back into that world when one dies. How one conceives one's origins and one's end in death has important implications for one's lived experience as an embodied subject with conscious self-awareness. Psychoanalysis suggests that fantasies and desires, both conscious and unconscious, have operative effects within the economy of significance that sustains the subject's socially meaningful identity.

Irigaray believes that the way we represent our own origins to ourselves and others has implications for the way we live our lives. Human individuality is the result of a process by which we create corporeal and psychic boundaries to distinguish ourselves from the rest of the world which are always in danger of collapsing. Death is the ultimate form of this collapse, but it can occur in many forms at any moment and in any place. The creation of a separate sense of self is neither a foregone conclusion nor an ever completable act. As much as we may like to think that we are inviolably separate from the world in order to conserve our sense of separate self, we are in fact immersed in a world of dynamic becoming of which we are an integral part. The way we represent our relationship to the matter out of which we emerge forms the founding structure of an economy that we will continue to reenact at each moment of our lives. Cultural representations of the mother play a key role in the economy of significance that maintains us and makes us possible as coherent subjects. In the next subsection we will see the difficulties created by a masculinist economy for the emergence of feminine subjectivity.

The Feminine Co-opted by the Masculine

According to the psychoanalytic account of subjectivity, the mother/ body must be controlled and defended against in order to maintain the subject's boundaries. This is done in part through representing to oneself how one came to have a body. Initially these representations will be derived from one's own bodily processes. For example, a young child might note her capacity to produce feces, from which she can separate and compare this creative act to that of her mother. This comparison allows her to fantasize participation in a creative act analogous to the creative act that originated her own existence. But as Irigaray comments, the fantasy of the feces-baby is "no solution" to the dilemma of origins.

If you are a boy, you will want, as soon as you reach the phallic stage, to return to the origin, turn back toward the origin. That is, possess the mother, get inside the mother who is the place of origin, in order to reestablish continuity with it and to see and know what happens there. And moreover to reproduce yourself there. If you are born a girl, the question is quite other. No return to, toward, inside the place of origin is possible unless you have a penis. The girl will herself be the place where origin is repeated, re-produced and reproduced, though this does not mean that she thereby repeats "her" original topos, "her" origin. (S 41)

It is through representing oneself with respect to the maternal body from which one emerged that the subject is able to sustain the physical separation from the mother necessary for psychic autonomy. A solution to the problem of one's origins must be found if one is to complete the task of separation from the mother. The path of corporeal and psychic separation is, according to Irigaray, sexually differentiated. Freud's version of the little girl's path of separation puts her at a decided disadvantage. Because Freud imposes the penis as the only desirable replacement for the girl's relation to the place of origin (Freud claims the girl rejects and hates her mother upon discovering her mother's "lack"), the little girl has nothing to make up for the trauma of weaning: "She will never go back inside the mother; she will never give the mother a drink of sperm from her penis, in a substitution-reversal of the lost breast and milk; she will never reproduce her (like) self inside the/her mother, etc. She is left with a *void*, a *lack* of all representation, re-presentation, and even strictly speaking of all mimesis of her desire for origin" (S 42). Woman is thus forsaken and abandoned and is led to submit to the univocal sexual desire, discourse, and law of man. Feminine libido is excluded, and the phallus comes to be the privileged guarantor of sense in a complicated network of representational systems depicting subjects with relationships to the world which are oriented with respect to a specifically masculine paradigm (44).

Irigaray argues, however, that Freud does not tell the whole story and that there are reasons why he represses what could have been the "feminine" version of the representation of desire and one's relations to one's origins. The "feminine" in Freud's masculinist schema is "[a] nothing threatening the process of production, reproduction, mastery, and profitablity, of meaning, dominated by the phallus — that *master signifier* whose law of functioning erases, rejects, denies the surging up, the resurgence, the recall of a *heterogeneity* capable of reworking the principle of its authority" (S 50). The phallus as the master signifier of desire authorizes concepts, representations, and formalizations of language which prescribe an economy of subjectivity premised on "castration." That is, the desire for connection and continuity with one's origins which is really a desire for connection and participation with life processes extending beyond oneself is reduced to the desire for an object one lacks. Reconnecting with one's origins is translated into possession of the maternal body, and only those who have the phallus are entitled to such possession.

A masculine subject can remain fixated on his first love object since he can find a woman to replace her and "go on loving and desiring with the same sex organ the same 'object.'" The little girl, however, "cannot escape the upsurge of sexual *heterogeneity*." Freud evades the heterogeneity of the little girl by insisting that "the girl has always been a boy" and by characterizing her femininity as implicated with "penis-envy" (S 63). He thus perpetuates the sexual homogeneity of a masculine point of view. A feminine subject is left with no consciousness of her sexual impulses or libidinal economy, or for "her original desire and her desire for origin" (68). Her "loss" thus completely escapes representation and so offers no possibility of mourning: "She borrows signifiers but cannot make her mark, or re-mark upon them. Which all surely keeps her deficient, empty, lacking, in a way that could be labeled 'psychotic': a *latent* but not actual psychosis, for want of a practical signifying system" (S 71). The lot of a "normal" woman is "to sustain the penis, to prevent it from drifting into analogical substitutions, from tearing up the anchor it affords for the whole system of generalizations" (79). She does this by remaining unaware of the value of her own sex organs and instead valorizing the penis through penis envy.

The Oedipus complex is resolved for the masculine subject when he renounces the desire for a woman and her sex organ that has no value. In exchange he takes his place as a subject who will derive the benefits accruing to those who appropriately wield paternal law (S 82). In this situation it is no wonder that feminine subjects are forced into a vicarious form of subjectivity that leaves their own possibilities unfulfilled (84). With nothing left to lose, the feminine other becomes fearful not of the loss of her castrated sex organ but of the loss of the love of her owner. It is only through identification with a subject whose relation to his origin is not her own, or through confirmation of her worth with respect to a masculine image of desirability, that she is able to have the identity of one who is attached to the identity of another. Irigaray suggests interpreting castration as "a definitive prohibition against establishing one's own economy of the desire for origin" (83). Without a specific corporeal form and psychic image of self which she can confirm and insure as valuable, the would-be feminine subject has no form of her own. Since she is stripped of the specificity of her own relationship to origins, it is only by affirming the relationship of the masculine subject to his origins that she can take her place in the cultural economy of subjectivity.

Irigaray accepts the psychoanalytic premise that some sort of economy of significance needs to be sustained for a subject to survive as subject. Although she grants that Freud describes an economy of a masculine subject, however, she believes that there might be another form the economy of a subject could take — one that is not bound by the oedipal triangle but that could be equally successful at making possible and sustaining the initial break with the mother. She takes issue with the notion that the only possible form an economy of subjectivity could take is one that prioritizes masculine subjects and sustains feminine subjects only in relation to masculine subjects. The contemporary economy of subjectivity valorizes the phallus as a substitute for lost contact with one's own origins in a reality larger than oneself. Representing this lost contact through valorization of a part of oneself that will somehow entitle one to retrieve what was lost comes to stand in for one's lost contact with a whole world. Femininity, then, comes to represent not simply the place of the mother, but the place of a world larger than oneself that feeds and sustains one at the same time that it may threaten to overwhelm one's identity. Irigaray's project suggests that the mother need not take the full weight of representing lost contact with one's origins. If we reinterpret femininity, we need to reinterpret masculinity and subjectivity in general as well. Confronting sexual difference entails confronting what the current economy which privileges masculine subjectivity tends to deny: that each one of us as an individual emerges from a larger whole. Insofar as we do not need to efface the differences of a feminine other in order to ensure our own value and viability as individuals, we can incorporate a fuller range of differences into our conception of ourselves and others. In the next subsection I consider structures of significance already in existence which could point the way toward such alternative economies of subjectivity.

The Feminine on Her Own

Since the feminine other cannot have the phallus, she becomes it. That is, she becomes the object of desire of an active (masculine) subject — that which fills in the "lack" of a subject who would be whole. By thus sustaining the desire of a "subject," she allows him to love himself through her.

"She is narcissistic, in fact, but only by phallic mandate, for, as we have seen, any narcissization of her own sex/organ(s) is completely out of the question" (S 113). Since the phallus is the guarantor of sexual exchange, and since she does not have "it," she must wish to have "it," but her not having it is precisely what drives up the market value of "it" through her envy. The feminine other is left with no way to represent her own origins and is instead forced to play a supporting role in a sexually differentiated economy of subjectivity which privileges masculine subjects. This means that she has a different relationship to representation and to cultural symbolic systems as well as to her corporeality. Since the relationship to origins specific to her is repressed, symbolic elaborations of subjectivity privilege masculine subjectivity. What the feminine other is unable to say or represent to herself — that is, a relationship to the maternal body that is not symbolized by the penis — is still intimated through the corporeal logic of her body.[7] Although the subjectivity elaborated for her by cultural symbolic systems represents her relationship to the maternal body only through her relationship to masculine subjectivity, she still carries with her the corporeal patternings of her own physical break from the maternal body. Irigaray's work suggests that this corporeal logic could be tapped for alternative representations.

In *Beyond the Pleasure Principle*, Freud describes a little boy's game with a reel and thread (*fort-da*). According to Freud, the reel acts as a substitute for the boy's mother: by pulling in the reel and then throwing it out again, the little boy actively masters the presences and absences of his mother. In order to take up a position as a speaking subject, a boy has to distinguish himself from his mother and her sex and position himself vis-à-vis the phallus and paternal law. The game with the reel and thread entails taking up the position of subject vis-à-vis an object that represents the mother and mastering that relationship by controlling it. Since the father possesses the phallus which signifies that which the mother desires, the boy must renounce immediate gratification of his wish for continued fleshly communion with the mother in order to identify with the father. The father-son genealogy ensures a deferred satisfaction of the son's desire for his mother in the form of a lover or wife.

Irigaray claims that this account does not work for little girls. She argues that the little girl does not have the same need or opportunity to differentiate herself from her mother. She will never be entitled to a substitute mother. Instead, she can only be the phallus — representative of that which will satisfy the desire of a masculine subject. For Freud, the closest she can come to wielding the phallus is through having a son of her own. She can then vicariously possess through her son the power of the phallus, with the satisfaction of desire that represents. But even if women can only vicariously experience satisfaction of their desire for fleshly communion with a substitute for the mother, they still must achieve some form of identity of their own. Irigaray suggests that this sexual difference in identity constitution makes for a different relationship to one's gestation in the body of another, one's birth and separation from the maternal body, and one's sexual identity.

Instead of objectifying the reel and thread as a substitute for the mother to gain control over the mother's comings and goings, girls engage in other forms of play. A little girl might, for example, recreate the space created through the mother-daughter relationship with her own body by whirling around.[8] Instead of insisting on a subject-object split, she engages in an "energetic, circular movement" (S&G 98). Her identification with her mother is not based on a prior subject-object split. It is instead the empathic identification that would simply continue a series of bodily effects. She twirls in circles to continue the intensely immediate sensations of vital contact with her environment. Her whole body is thrown into and involved with this movement. She has no need to absent herself from any part of it or to master the comings and goings of her mother because she has not separated her identity from her mother in a way that leaves her destitute when her mother is gone. Instead, she attempts to participate in the same rhythms as her mother in order to reassure herself that she is still a part of the universe. She swirls in space to feel the living vitality of her own body which is in complete contact with the world around her. And yet, through identification with the mother she is also able to retain some sense of self in this twirling. She makes her world in this twirling, and so makes herself. She both solicits and refuses access to this twirling activity she creates. She becomes the creative mother through her own fleshly contact with her surroundings. Her sexual identity is thus premised on a continuation of creative participation with her surroundings that does not need to insist on oppositional separation or control, but instead works to continue the participation initially felt through communion with her own mother.

Since the possibility of repossessing the mother is unavailable to the girl, she need neither objectify her mother nor satisfy her desire for reconnecting with her by acquiring substitute objects. Unlike masculine desire, her desire does not necessarily take the form of a desire to possess a discrete entity. This allows her other possibilities in desiring, for example, the desire "to reunite the two by a gesture, to touch both perhaps so that birth is repeated, so that no unconsidered regression occurs, so that the self is kept whole or, sometimes, upright. Women do not try to master the other but to give birth to themselves" (S&G 99).[9] By reaching out for the same kind of touch she once experienced with the maternal body, she can once again participate in a mutually nourishing becoming where two are neither subject nor object but come together in a participatory happening which gives birth to both: "The labyrinth, whose path was known to Ariadne, for example, would thus be that of the lips. This mystery of the female lips, the way they open to give birth to the universe, and touch together to permit the female individual to have a sense of her identity, would be the forgotten secret of perceiving and generating the world" (101).

Patriarchal traditions have encouraged men to take over divine power and steal generative potential from women and the cosmic. Whereas feminine subjects would touch one another in order to enter once again into dynamic communion with the world, masculine subjects would find objects to represent lost contact with the maternal body. By possessing this contact in the form of a reified object, they both avoid the risk posed to self-same-identity by participatory transformation and ensure for themselves the illusion of an active subject who has what another desires. But Irigaray hints at another possibility. Woman's lips, unlike the phallus, continually embrace in a mutual touching. It is in communion with the world through a touching that touches back that a feminine subject continues to identify with the mother who provided her first nourishing contact with the world: "To take a woman's lips would be like taking a man's *fort-da*. In fact it is worse. The *fort-da* is already a substitutional mechanism, whereas the lips are the woman herself, the threshold to a woman that has not been distanced by any object. Stealing a woman's kiss is to take the most virginal part of her, the part most linked to her female identity" (S&G 102).

When fixed in one position the feminine other is a prisoner. "A woman can usually find self-expression only when her lips are touching together and when her whole body is in movement" (S&G 102). For a woman to feel herself as a woman, she must be in participatory communion within herself or with others where self and others are not distinct things but processes in which differentiations are made through the exchanges their creative movements entail. She cannot feel alive as a self-same-identical subject because this removes her from such participation with the world. The masculine subject affirms himself as a whole subject by referring himself to an ideal that stays forever the same, untouched by the world of becoming; the feminine subject affirms herself through dynamic contact with an ever-changing world. Because she has never had to displace the vital movement of contact with her surroundings that is a continual becoming in order to identify with an idealized principle that could guarantee her a future satisfaction, her desire is immanent in present becomings.

Symbolic Support for Feminine Subjectivity

The traditional practice of taking one's husband's name is an example of what Irigaray means by a lack of symbolic support for feminine subjectivity. Irigaray claims that this practice is indicative of a whole set of practices that symbolically cut off women from their material links to their own mothers and foremothers, and reduce them to playing the role of corporeal substitute for their husbands (ESD 10–11). A masculine subject can both establish his identity symbolically vis-à-vis his father and forefathers and maintain a sense of corporeal connectedness through physical contact with a wife whom on a corporeal level he does not distinguish from his mother. He is thus able to reify his identity on a symbolic level while relegating possible challenges to that identity to the unconscious or to the "unimportant," "trivial" realm of the corporeal-emotional; that is, he reaffirms corporeal boundaries through interaction with feminine others, displacing sensual and emotional affect onto those others in the process.

Although the masculine subject must renounce the sensual contact by which he initially situated himself in the world in order to be inserted into his genealogy, he is compensated for this loss with a place in time that relates him to men who came before and men who will come after; the narrative of his life has a symbolically marked place within the larger narrative of his family name. His feminine counterpart does not have the same kind of access to such a genealogy. She never fully dissociates herself from the sensual flow characteristic of maternal contact. She is thus more readily associated with what is "primitive" and "closer to nature." She substitutes herself for her mother's body in order to become a mother's body herself and play the part of lost object for those who do have a temporal genealogy. Being cut off from time means that her memories and her histories cannot build in the same way for her as for him. This opens up a different kind of spatiality — a receptiveness to the present that is sensual and full — but it also impoverishes her identity and renders her relationships to other women problematic: "Whereas man must live out the pain and experience the impossibility of being cut off from and in *space* (being born, leaving the mother), woman lives out the painful or impossible experience of being cut off from or in *time*" (ESD 64).

A masculine subject is expected to continue to love himself because it is due to him that history continues; his identity is put into line with the identities of others (ESD 66). It is in upholding the temporal chain of a patriarchal genealogy that his duty lies. For his feminine counterpart, autoeroticism needs to be renounced. She must renounce her mother in order to separate from her and love a masculine subject. There is no need to maintain a temporal link with her mother in order to do this. Instead, she must, in a sense, erase her mother in order to replace her. It is only thus that she can support the illusion of a self-identical subject. Masculine subjects can gauge their movement and activities against the material ground provided by their feminine counterparts. Irigaray protests against this silencing of the feminine other not simply because it privileges men and impoverishes women but also because she believes that it disables other more satisfying possibilities of being. Although she would deny that it is possible to say from where we are exactly what these possibilities might be, her evocative explorations of sexuality and love between the sexes hint at radically different notions of space-time and relations with others.[10]

Sexuality is an important part of what the new form of relationship to others might entail. So long as masculine sexuality is based on a buildup of tension and a release that is blind to the constitutive power of the other, eroticism is returned to a primitive chaos with no hope of furthering the creative engenderment of two loving partners. Instead, all creativity is displaced onto the creation of the child in reproduction. Sexuality in the form of chaotic life drives that operate without relation to the individuation of persons is for Irigaray a form of the masculinist fantasy of self-creation. She insists that masculine sexuality lacks rhythm and the harmony of desires. Because of his inability to come into any kind of attunement with the other, the masculine subject is plunged into a nondifferentiated abyss (TD 97). And because of his refusal to acknowledge that anything other to himself could have creative power, his eroticism fails to contribute to reciprocal creative engenderment, and lovemaking can only plunge him into a fusional loss of identity: "The path to reciprocal love between individuals has been lost, especially with respect to eroticism. And instead of contributing to individuation, or to the creation or re-creation of human forms, eroticism contributes to the destruction or loss of identity through fusion, and to a return to a level of tension that is always identical, always the lowest, with neither development nor growth" (99). Irigaray points to Far Eastern traditions, especially yoga, as an alternative practice that can harmonize body and mind and promote a culture of energy entailing regeneration rather than an energetic discharge. Through the use of such practices, we could foster another kind of sexuality, one in which "the carnal act ceases to be a regression to degree zero for pleasure or words; rather it is the locus for the lovers' revival and becoming. Love is accomplished by two, without dividing roles between the beloved and the lover, between objectival or animal passivity on he one hand, and generally conscious and valorous activity on the other. Woman and man remain two in love. Watching over and creating the universe is their primary task, and it remains so" (ILTY 138).

· Irigaray's descriptions of the sexual act performed with an acknowledgment of sexual difference evoke a mutuality currently unachievable by the masculine subject with his specular other. Instead of a retrogressive descent into infantile fusion, this form of lovemaking would involve a creative shaping, a re-sculpting of bodies in which the subject reconstructs his or her own body as a result of engendering the body of the other: "The sexual *act* would turn into the act whereby the other gives new form, birth, incarnation to the self. Instead of implying the downfall of the body, it takes part in the body's renaissance. And there is no other equivalent act, in this sense. Most divine of acts. Whereby man makes woman feel her body as place. Not only her vagina and her womb but her body. He places her within her body and within a macrocosm, releasing her from her potential adherence to the cosmic through her participation in a microsociety" (ESD 51). The embodied subject's renaissance would be achieved in an activity that would not insist on the repetition of an identical self, but would give new form and thus new birth to the self. Irigaray suggests that the (repressed) feminine subject of our culture has important insights to contribute to such a process.

> Nothing more spiritual, in this regard, than female sexuality. Always working to produce a place of transcendence for the sensible, which can become a destructive net, or else find itself, remain, in endless becoming. Accompanying cosmic time. Between man's time and the time of the universe. Still faithful to the one and seeking to find a rhythm in the other, perhaps?
>
> Unfortunately, the two are often cut apart. Those two rhythms are not only no longer harmonious but are cut off from one another. Does this produce false gods and false hells? To avoid this, an alchemy of female desire is needed. (53)

Man's time is dictated by considerations of subjectivity: he needs to repeat himself at regular intervals as the self-same subject in order to "make sense" according to paternal law. The time of the universe is another kind of time. The cosmic time that feminine sexuality accompanies is a time that follows out the heat of the moment, a time that does not adhere to a preestablished grid, but that follows the rhythm of a sensible that goes beyond the self-contained forms of particulars or individual objects.[11]

The masculine subject of desire can believe that his loving is for objects abstracted out of the sensual realm of infinite becoming. Just as he is contained and containable, so is what he desires. When desire is definitive and for objects that can be substituted for one another, then it is punctual, episodic, and predicated on possession. Desire can thus be both conceptually and physically contained; the objects of the masculine subject's desire have definite properties, and his desire can be satisfied a bit at a time through the possession of these concrete objects. The feminine subject's desire cannot be parceled out in such a manner because she has no preconceived objects of desire. While the infinite for man is set at a distance, the infinite for the woman is here right now in the giving of her body to the variability of unpredictable sensation. What she desires is no particular object but jouissance, a feeling of giving herself in the moment to be shaped in a manner she cannot predict.

> For the female, everything right away is not the equivalent of death. It is more like a quest for the infinite of life. An openness on the infinite in jouissance. Man sets the infinite in a *transcendence* that is always deferred to the beyond, even if it be the beyond of the concept. Woman sets it in an *expanse* of jouissance here and now right away. Body-expanse that tries to *give itself exteriority, to give itself to exteriority,* to give itself in an unpunctuated space-time that is also not orgastic in the limited sense of that word. To give itself in a space-time without end. Or very resistant to definition. (ESD 64)

This alternative approach to sexuality evokes an open-ended and unpredictable response to another rather than possession of a sexual object. Implicit in Irigaray's account is the insistence that such corporeal expansiveness involves profound transformation at both psychic and corporeal levels of identity. Indeed, Irigaray's work argues that these two levels are clearly distinguished only on the basis of an illusion that involves the denial of an other. Both of the lovers involved in mutual lovemaking walk away not just rejuvenated but transformed. Irigaray's insistence on the inevitable corporeality of existence suggests that even less physical encounters have a corporeal dimension with equally significant effects.

Irigaray refuses to diminish the importance of sexuality and love. Her admonition to attend to sexual difference reaches far beyond the sexual act itself; it speaks to the need to acknowledge a kind of sexual division of labor that has allotted the more corporeal aspects of life to the feminine other. The desire of a "masculine" economy of language fails to reflect adequately the porous nature of the body; it refers itself to conceptualized notions of objects of desire and ignores the murky intermediary realm in which desires are not clearly laid out or articulated. The desire that acts on the porous nature of the body takes its cue from the desire that changes and evolves from moment to moment in an unpredictable movement that seeks only to stay in touch with what Irigaray in places calls 'mucous.' This kind of touch respects no shape or previously conceived boundary, but is always in process, remaining in contiguity with membranes, following pleasure as it unfolds. Rather than pursuing objects that can be represented in conventional categories of thought, it pursues that which defies such representation. 'Mucous' is Irigaray's term for the unthought moving toward representation — those strangely uncanny aspects of experience that defy already established self/other and body/mind divisions (see Whitford 1991a, 163). From Irigaray's perspective, this porousness of the body is more subtle than a desire that is always already symbolized. Even if one grants that one's sense of body boundaries, one's very sense of one's embodied experience, is always culturally mediated through the layers of patterned responses built up in one's own lived experience (thus rendering any conception of "immediate" experience or a "pure" experience of the body suspect), this by no means precludes extralinguistic experience, a realm of feeling-sensation that is accessible to the subject and yet not articulable in any clear or straightforward way. Acknowledgment of sexual difference in the sexual act leads not simply to a kind of lovemaking in which both partners acknowledge their corporeality, but to a kind of love that could regenerate a whole culture. Developing various ways of symbolizing, in all their complexity, the subtle interactions of embodied subjects that typically do not emerge into conscious awareness fosters increased recognition and respect for the interdependence of subjectivity.

The Feminine as Subject

When love is seen as creation and potentially divine, then the lover in loving is creating a path between the condition of the mortal and that of the immortal. This divine generation is not the kind of generation that produces a product (for example, a child); instead, it creates the presence of immortality in the living mortal. This, Irigaray suggests, can occur when there is a creative and fecund interchange between two who are radically different from each other coming together in a union in which difference is not eradicated. If Irigaray insists on the importance of sexual difference in particular, it is because of her conception of masculine and feminine subjectivity. Contemporary society, through its practices and meaning systems, supports a kind of sexual division of labor in which the feminine other complements the masculine subject (ESD 15). The masculine subject tends toward self-assertion in his unions with others. Insofar as his partner is the feminine other, she supports and makes possible this self-assertion. For subjectivity to continue, there has to be some form of masculine/feminine at work; that is, there must be an asserting subject and an other who supports that assertion instead of merely asserting her own subjectivity. But if the feminine other is still the supportive other and yet still asserts her own subjectivity — her own memory, her own hopes, her own only semi-articulate desire — then she becomes a living mirror for the masculine subject. When two different subjects attempt to reflect each other, a dynamic interchange occurs in which it is no longer clear who is reflecting whom. Instead of repeating the same movements initiated by one of the two, both develop and mutate their movements in response to those of the other. When the masculine subject is able to affirm the initiating movements of the feminine other with a supportive response, a fecund generation occurs in which both subjects change and yet each remains a subject with a place of her or his own. Both become subjects in a creative interchange which acknowledges mucous and the fluidity of boundaries that have become less than fixed without dissolving: "Perhaps we are passing through an era when *time must redeploy space? . . .* A remaking of immanence and transcendence, notably through this *threshold* which has never been examined as such: the female sex. The threshold that gives access to the *mucous . . .* a threshold that is always *half-open.* The threshold of the *lips*, which are strangers to dichotomy and oppositions. Gathered one against the other but without any possible suture, at least of a real kind" (18). In this interchange in which neither completely loses shape and yet each responds to the other instead of merely repeating herself or himself, a creative process is generated in which both are transformed. Neither active nor passive, the two shape each other without clear distinction between the two, and yet without losing the trace of their difference.

Irigaray refers to a "place for love," or a third term between a pair of lovers. Without this third term, there is no intermediate ground between the two in which difference is acknowledged without needing to be reduced to either the one or the other (ESD 27). Something then becomes frozen in space-time — one or the other of the two subjects casts outward in a loop of desire that returns to himself or herself unchanged. In a double loop of desire there would be a "vital intermediary" and an "accessible transcendental that remains alive." That is, there would be a space between the two that made no reference to a fixed point, but instead was vital and accessible without being predictable or graspable. This intermediary realm is a space-time in which generation-regeneration takes place here and now for both subjects; it is the space of a continual making, a continual generation. The subject in such a space is not the subject who already knows who he is, what his position is, and how to situate himself. It is rather the subject who not only is never complete but also never completes any part of himself; this subject is engaged in a process of evolution which continually puts earlier phases of her or his subjectivity into doubt, both corporeally and spiritually. Social positioning may be rendered problematic by a full acknowledgment of our corporeality, but Irigaray suggests that immortality is one of our tasks as mortals. We must continually transmutate. We need to do more than simply define a position and deny mucous and flux in order to assert definitively who we are without acknowledging ambiguity. The body is always touching upon new ground. It cannot help but be continually feeling and losing itself in the immediacy of experience that it has never already had. In this opening up to thoughts, feelings, and sensations that can never be anticipated, one may lose the illusion that one has a familiar and repeatable shape that has an established place in the social matrix. But one opens up to a new kind of possibility: the possibility that all socially significant possibilities cannot contain one, that one is perhaps not containable, that one indeed touches upon the divine (29): "This person would have then attained what I shall call a *sensible transcendental*, the material texture of beauty. He would have 'seen' the very spatiality of the visible, the real which precedes all reality, all forms, all truth of particular sensations or constructed idealities" (32).[12]

Irigaray points to religion as another instance of cultural symbolism that privileges masculine subjectivity. She argues that the masculine subject's approach to corporeality is to separate his first embodied location in the mother from his spiritual place in the religious scheme of things. He looks for the infinite in a realm from which he removes himself and his corporeality. He is attracted to what Irigaray calls the maternal-feminine (that is, woman reduced to her function of feminine other) because he distances himself from his corporeality despite the fact that it is through embodiment that he has living contact with the world. He projects the corporeality of his existence onto feminine others and the infinite divine onto a

God that transcends corporeality. Continual engagement with the world involves continual response to new sensations and experiences. Irigaray suggests that a feminine conception of the divine would evoke an open-ended receptivity to an infinite expanse of unrepeatable sensations. She invokes angels as the divine intermediaries of the more slippery aspects of embodied existence, passages, and the reworking of boundaries. The body is inert without its relation to mucous. Mucous is its point of contact; by virtue of its ambiguous role vis-à-vis the clear-cut boundaries of intact bodies, it presents a living material that brings one closer to the infinite beyond which exceeds all boundaries. A sexual ethics would treat the body not as a corpse but as something living; angels maintain the body's contact with the divine by mediating between the mortal body and its infinitely variable contact with a sensuous world.

> The mucous should no doubt be pictured as related to the angel, whereas the inertia of the body deprived of its relation to the mucous and its gesture is linked to the fallen body or the corpse.
>
> A sexual or carnal ethics would require that both angel and body be found together. (ESD 17)

Irigaray's theory of subjectivity emphasizes an ongoing process of body constitution. This process, while it may be inflected with experiences of maternal care, is also affected by the whole of the subject's trajectory through time. To treat woman as the maternal-feminine is to deny her feminine subjectivity owing to nostalgia for a regression back to the undifferentiated place of the womb. A subjectivity that presents an alternative to the masculine one would acknowledge the actual maternal body which provided one's initial home in a way that does not eradicate the mother as woman and as feminine subject. It would perceive differently the feminine others who provide masculine subjects with substitutes for that original maternal body. Instead of perceiving them as mother substitutes, providing nurturing confirmation of a self that has already been achieved, such a subjectivity would acknowledge the constitutive role of feminine nurturing. The attentive other that mirrors one back to oneself in an affirming way does not simply confirm one's identity but informs one's identity in an act of mutual transformation that plays out on both symbolic and corporeal levels. Such identity-informing activity could be conceived in terms of a divine immanent in, rather than removed from, corporeality.

Although some have read Irigaray's exhortation that sexual difference is the question of our age as an exhortation to specify the crucial features of a femininity that leaves intact the binary opposition of male and female, I would argue that she instead pushes us to a notion of difference and embodied specificity that would ultimately undermine the very notion of sexual difference with which she starts.[13] On Judith Butler's reading, Irigaray's project goes beyond the denigrated term of a traditional binary. Irigaray's notion of the feminine is not simply "matter" (as opposed to masculine form); it entails an unnameable feminine beyond the masculine/feminine oppositions it supports. The feminine figured within an intelligible philosophical binary is the specular feminine, but the "excessive" feminine that is unrepresentable is that which must be excluded for the binary to operate at all (Butler 1993, 39). Butler claims that Irigaray distinguishes an unthematizable materiality from the category of matter. This inarticulable materiality is the site for the feminine within a phallogocentric economy; it is what must be excluded from that economy so that the latter can present the illusion that it is internally coherent (38). The excessive, unrepresentable feminine cannot be contained within current systems of representation. If Irigaray evokes such a feminine, she can do so strategically only by articulating the blind spot that is required for the phallogocentric economy to function in a specific context. This means that this notion of the feminine (if indeed we can call it a notion) is always in movement. In the context of reading philosophical texts, for example, it is that which is excluded by a particular text. Since what is excluded from a particular philosophical text shifts from text to text, so does the category of the "feminine." Such a feminine is an excessive materiality that resists materialization and cannot be reduced to a maternal body or anything representable. It is "a disfiguration that emerges at the boundaries of the human both as its very condition and as the insistent threat of its deformation" (41). Rather than simply reinstating or reifying a traditional dichotomy, Irigaray's notion of sexual difference thus opens up the specificity of the material and the possibility of moving beyond dichotomies in understanding the body, and in particular the sexed body.

Irigaray suggests that contemporary society sets up a hierarchy of maternal and paternal functions, thus instituting a sexual division of labor in which the maternal reproduces the child and the work force and the paternal reproduces society and symbolic and cultural capital. Irigaray would have us challenge this hierarchy: "Even today, bodily tasks remain the obligation or the duty of a female subject. The break between the two produces rootless and insane thinking as well as bodies (women and children) that are heavy and slightly 'moronic' because they lack language" (ESD 87). Love should be sensual and should involve the self-love of both lovers; one lover should not be disincarnated and the other reduced to carnality.

Instead, both should fully experience their carnality. Symbolizing feminine subjectivity is a crucial step in the process of challenging the contemporary sexual hierarchy. Women need to establish new values that correspond to their creativity and self-intimacy for a woman needs to be established through a feminine divine that would symbolize mother-daughter and daughter-mother relationships which she could replay for herself. Symbolizing the submerged feminine in the process of constituting and reconstituting identities at both the symbolic and corporeal levels would have two important benefits. First, it would disable a masculine subjectivity that denies the subjectivity of the feminine other. And second, it could open up new alternatives for subjectivity in which corporeality on the part of both self and other could be fully acknowledged.

Increased interest in the body on multiple disciplinary fronts is arising at an opportune time. Irigaray's work implicitly develops a theory of embodied subjectivity that works toward breaking down mind/body dualisms. It simultaneously develops a theory of sexual difference that shows how the latter is crucial to contemporary subjectivity. Irigaray's exhortation to acknowledge sexual difference, far from trapping us in stereotypes we would rather discard, can lead us to rich exploration of our corporeal consciousness and thus enable us to touch upon the divine right here on earth. This exploration can take many forms. For Irigaray, one form that it has taken lies in the reading of philosophical texts in ways that render their gender bias more evident. Her purpose is twofold in these readings: she wants to manifest the operation of the feminine other in the philosopher's text, and she wants to create through this symbolic reworking a viable symbolic position for a feminine subject that is more than the negative counterpart of a masculine norm.

According to Irigaray's reading of psychoanalysis, the cultural imaginary and symbolic are crucial to subjectivity but need not be predicated on the phallus or castration. That is, one need not be an oedipalized subject to be any kind of subject at all, and indeed her work indicates that there may already be another kind of subject lurking in the wings. This subject that is currently not much more than the shadow of the oedipal subject operates according to a different kind of economy. Irigaray's project suggests that this economy could be given further symbolic support, and that this reworking of the symbolic in support of a subject who is more than the negative counterpart of the masculine subject, who is the subject that must be contained in order to perpetuate the illusions necessary for the masculine subject's survival, could transform the cultural imaginary and prepare the way for a different kind of subject not premised on lack.

Irigaray's Reading of Philosophy

In an interview first published in 1975, Irigaray explains her readings of philosophical texts.[14] The philosophical logos stages representation according to "masculine" parameters that constitute a phallocratic order. This phallocratic order presents a difficult problem for Irigaray in her project of fostering acknowledgment of sexual difference and creating symbolic support for feminine subjectivity. If she were to follow the traditional rules of conventional language, she would foreclose the possibility of transforming the cultural imaginary. Thus, giving coherent characterizations of the feminine subject in readily accessible language cannot change the structures through which we conceive of the feminine. Fostering the kind of recognition of sexual difference Irigaray is after entails undermining the structures that ensure that words have coherence and meaning. She cannot, then, simply make use of this language to posit an alternative, feminine reality. But Irigaray is not interested in relegating the feminine to the realm of the unconscious, the irrational, or the psychotic. She wants to symbolize the feminine underside of conventional language in a way that will have meaning to socially recognizable subjects. She is therefore willing to run the risk of unsettling the contemporary structure of language in order to open up a space for new possibilities in thinking, speaking, and living.

Irigaray's project in rereading philosophical texts is to "reopen" the figures of philosophical discourse "in order to pry out of them what they have borrowed that is feminine, from the feminine, to make them 'render up' and give back what they owe the feminine." She says that there is more than one way to do this. One is to interrogate "the conditions under which systematicity itself is possible" (TS 74). A discursive utterance is coherent only by virtue of concealing the conditions under which it is produced. Speaking subjects draw nourishment from "matter" in order to produce and reproduce themselves. This "matter" involves the workings of a theatrical apparatus that enables a specific form of representation to emerge. Interventions on the scene of representation must remain uninterpreted in order to ensure the coherence of discursive utterances. To reveal these behind-the-scenes conditions and so challenge the domination of the philosophical logos, one must interrogate "the *scenography* that makes representation feasible, representation as defined in philosophy, that is, the architectonics of its theatre, its framing in space-time, its geometric organization, its props, its actors, their respective positions, their dialogues, indeed their tragic relations, without overlooking the *mirror*, most often hidden, that allows the logos, the subject, to reduplicate itself, to reflect itself by itself." Interrogating the conditions of coherent utterances cannot be carried out straightforwardly in the language structured by those conditions. Instead, the interventions on the scene must be reenacted "in each figure of discourse, in order to shake discourse away from its mooring in the value of 'presence.'" For each philosopher, Irigaray would use this method to "point out how the break with material contiguity is made, how the system is put together, how the specular economy works" (75). Irigaray insists that any significance that language has for us must be found in the messy, chaotic multiplicity of actual living rather than an ideal realm of eternal, unchanging ideals far removed from the contingencies of sensuous existence.

Irigaray indicates the sources of language in embodied experience in various ways. There is, of course, her famous evocation of Plato's cave as the womb. The womb represents not only the feminine but the roots of conceptual thought in sensation and the flux of the body as well. Irigaray also evokes language of the elements to make a similar point: "And you would remember that the elements still originate outside your language" (ML 58). There is something beyond language, something connected to language, but which the masculine subject in his use of language denies. This something is "the sea, sun, air, and earth" — something that is extralinguistic, that speaks of the material nature of reality and yet cannot be captured in the words with which we try to describe this reality. These elements motivate language in that language attempts to incorporate them through representation, but language inevitably fails to represent them fully. Margaret Whitford suggests that Irigaray uses the vocabulary of the elements as a kind of alternative vocabulary for evoking the body and its sensations.

> The elements allow Irigaray to speak of the female body, of its morphology, and of the erotic, while avoiding the dominant sexual metaphoricity which is scopic and organized around the male gaze; she can speak of it instead in terms of space and thresholds and fluids, fire and water, air and earth, without objectifying, hypostatizing, or essentializing it. These terms are not so easily reduced to the body of one sex or the other. They are more pliable, accessible to the imagination of others and available for their private mental landscapes. They have both an individual and a collective dimension. (Whitford 1991a, 62)

Irigaray grants that returning to the roots of language in the sensuous is bound to carry the risk of untenable confusion, but she also believes that the alternative to such a risk is a kind of living death in which our passions wither and our thinking becomes sterile. We are embodied creatures living in a world that incessantly impinges upon us, and any self that we are able to stabilize out of this ever-changing movement of which we are but a part is completely implicated with what surrounds us.

Irigaray takes the feminine as her point of departure for the "outside" to phallocratic language that could destabilize that language and open up other possibilities in representation, perception, and meaning. For Irigaray, masculine subjectivity and a language based on the economy of the same are impossible without the exploitation of the feminine. To make the feminine speak according to that economy would be to assimilate her to masculine subjectivity and so to perpetuate the exploitation that denies her her specificity. To show the roots of masculine discourse, the material ground from which it emerges, and the mechanisms by which it denies that ground in order to maintain its coherence, Irigaray makes use of the strategy of mimesis.

> To play with mimesis is thus, for a woman, to try to recover the place of her exploitation by discourse, without allowing herself to be simply reduced to it. It means to resubmit herself — inasmuch as she is on the side of the "perceptible," of "matter" — to "ideas," in particular to ideas about herself, that are elaborated in/by a masculine logic, but so as to make "visible," by an effect of playful repetition, what was supposed to remain invisible: the cover-up of a possible operation of the feminine in language. It also means "to unveil" the fact that, if women are such good mimics, it is because they are not simply resorbed in this function. *They also remain elsewhere*: another case of the persistence of "matter," but also of "sexual pleasure." (TS 76)

Thought cannot come from nowhere. Speculation is about life and emerges from life. It cannot exist in a vacuum. Words must be removed from the things they represent if they are to refer to anything at all; but the gap between words and life entails a whole set of material conditions that, once unveiled, cast doubt on the self-purported truth of those words. "Woman" in her role as the human other is associated with the maternal body from which the infant must separate, the body from which man must remove himself in order to think properly, and the fecund realm of nature over which he must have control. She is therefore relegated to the side of "matter" and the realm of conditions that must be covered up if masculine subjectivity and thinking are to function. But the feminine function that Irigaray wants to reveal is not simply the one necessary to this masculine economy; it is the excess of the feminine emerging from this structure. The feminine others that play their part in this economy are not simply the conditions of its perpetuity. They also remain elsewhere and have another kind of pleasure unknown to the masculine economy: "Mother-matter-nature must go on forever nourishing speculation. But this resource is also rejected as the waste product of reflection, cast outside as what resists it: as madness. Besides the ambivalence that the noruishing phallic mother attracts to herself, this function leaves woman's sexual pleasure aside" (77).

The feminine pleasure derived from the function of feminine other cannot be articulated without threatening the masculine economy because this pleasure is specific to the feminine — it is hers apart from any role she may play vis-à-vis masculinity. Insofar as desire follows the dictates of phallocratic law, sense and sensibility go on as usual. Insofar as feminine desire is freed up and given new forms of expression, then the masculine economy is undermined, and new forms of life and human beings would have to emerge.

> That "elsewhere" of feminine pleasure can be found only at the price of *crossing back through the mirror that subtends all speculation.* For this pleasure is not simply situated in a process of reflection or mimesis, nor on one side of this process or the other: neither on the near side, the empirical realm that is opaque to all language, nor on the far side, the self-sufficient infinite of the God of men. Instead, it refers all these categories and ruptures back to the necessities of the self-representation of phallic desire in discourse. A playful crossing, and an unsettling one, which would allow woman to rediscover the place of her "self-affection." Of her "god," we might say. (TS 77)

The feminine other acts as the "matter" that provides the masculine subject with a reflection without excess that ensures his self-representation as a subject with a coherent, unified identity. This self-same subject may act in a world that is constantly changing, but feminine "matter" ensures that he can experience himself as a calm center from which he can respond to and initiate change under his own direction. The masculine subject wants to maintain his distance from the world of movement and change so that he can retain this mastery. For the feminine other to cross back through the mirror she provides would unsettle this economy. Her pleasure is not located simply in the pleasure of providing the masculine subject with pleasure, although there is pleasure to be had in such reflection. Neither is it simply to be found in the pleasure of actively mimicking masculine subjectivity. Her pleasure is not located solely in the sensuous realm beyond linguistic description, nor in the realm of eternal ideals or a self-sufficient God. The "elsewhere" of feminine pleasure lies somewhere in the playful crossing through the different realms of this economy — a crossing that would ultimately undermine the economy and open up the possibilities of another kind of economy.

Irigaray would jam "the theoretical machinery itself" so as to suspend "its pretension to the production of a truth and of a meaning that are excessively univocal." Rather than ask what a woman is, she would repeat and interpret "the way in which, within discourse, the feminine finds itself defined as lack, deficiency, or as imitation and negative image of the subject" (TS 78) in order to demonstrate the possibility of a disruptive excess in language which emerges from its feminine side.

This "style," or "writing," of women tends to put the torch to fetish words, proper terms, well-constructed forms. This "style" does not privilege sight; instead, it takes each figure back to its source, which is among other things *tactile*. It comes back in touch with itself in that origin without ever constituting in it, constituting itself in it, as some sort of unity. *Simultaneity* is its "proper" aspect — a proper(ty) that is never fixed in the possible identity-to-self of some form or other. It is always *fluid*, without neglecting the characteristics of fluids that are difficult to idealize: those rubbings between two infinitely near neighbors that create a dynamics. Its "style" resists and explodes every firmly established form, figure, idea or concept. (79)

What Irigaray calls the "specular make-up of discourse" organizes the self-reflecting subject of that discourse and maintains, "among other things, the break between what is perceptible and what is intelligible, and thus maintains the submission, subordination, and exploitation of the 'feminine' " (80). The feminine other is associated with matter, nature, and the body, while masculinity is associated with concepts, ideal forms, and reason. The separation between the two allows the stabilization of a self-same masculine subject at the expense of a feminine other who carries the excess that overflows masculine identity. Preservation of perceptible objects, of a realm of nature on which he can act without self-annihilating submersion in a continually shifting, senuous world, and of a body he can recognize as his, all depend on maintaining a gap between the empirical world and the intelligible world and his privileged relationship to the latter.

Thus, for Irigaray, the feminine is a crucial feature of an economy that constitutes subjects in a specific way and ensures that those subjects can have coherent experiences and knowledge of the world. But this coherence is bought at a high cost. It requires the exploitation of the feminine which translates into exploitation of real women, natural resources, and marginalized others. Articulation of what is specific to the feminine would destabilize the phallocratic order and "put the torch" to rigid concepts and sterile categories. A new way of thinking would emerge that would privilege the sense premised on material contiguity — the sense of touch. In privileging this sense over sight, Irigaray evokes a sensual encounter with the world premised on immersion and participation rather than separation and control. A subject focused on tactile sensation is less able to distinguish himself as an active subject acting upon passive objects. Instead of perceiving blank space around chosen objects of sight, he is more likely to be absorbed in a world in which it is difficult to abstract either himself or other objects. Irigaray sees the project of opening up space for another style of living as crucial not simply for the women that she would empower, but for men as well and for a new kind of ethics that would go with a new way of thinking, speaking, and being.

In the next chapter I explore Irigaray's reading of Nietzsche in *Marine Lover*. In this book her "mimicry" of Nietzsche's work both echoes what she most admires about it and elicits the feminine other who would break free from his texts. By demonstrating the ways in which what Nietzsche is unable to see (or hear or touch) about the feminine other he evokes is linked to what he can see of her, Irigaray gestures toward an economy that could include both masculine and feminine subjectivity.

2
Irigaray's Nietzsche

Mimicry and the Feminine Other

Irigaray titled her dialogue with Nietzsche *Marine Lover* because if she chose to initate a dialogue with him, it was because she was enamored with his work. In an interview in which she was asked about *Marine Lover*, she says that it is a book not *on* Nietzsche, but *with* Nietzsche, "who is for me a partner in a love relationship."[1] Like Irigaray, Nietzsche engaged in a project of "placing the discourse of the philosophical tradition 'on trial', by a passage to another type of language" (Oppel 1993, 92). When the interviewer implies that this was a love-hate relationship, Irigaray responds that her relationship to Nietzsche was that of a lover who, rather than wanting to be Nietzsche's double, wants him to listen to her call coming from beyond the circle created by his work. "This is a call and a refusal," she comments; "I don't believe that it's necessary to call it hate."[2]

While the works in which Irigaray uses the third person render her own voice a subversive echo, in *Marine Lover* she demands acknowledgment from Nietzsche and lays out in more positive terms what he is missing in ignoring her. Through this dialogue, or rather attempt at a dialogue, the feminine "I" not only tries to shatter the mirror of Nietzsche's circle in order to get the Nietzschean "you" to perceive something he had not perceived, but also struggles for a voice of her own. She is no longer an echo, yet she is not yet quite a subject. Although it is, of course, a response written by a specific woman, the voice in which she puts this response evokes and plays with the feminine other that emerges from Nietzsche's texts. Instead of simply refusing the position he assigns her, she gives voice to the universal feminine depicted by him. As many commentators have pointed out, Nietzsche's depiction of women and the feminine is complex; although he exalts virile masculinity and denigrates "weak" effeminacy, he also affirms the creative power of a feminine becoming.[3] At the same time that Irigaray mocks Nietzsche for his representation of the feminine by evoking the fears that a fuller recognition of her would release, she also hints at rejuvenating possibilities for this positioning.

Nietzsche's feminine other, according to Irigaray's reading, is lost in becoming; she is the sea, the moving flux of waves, the tendrils of seaweed dancing at the bottom of the ocean, the cyclic ebb and flow of the tides on the shore. She is whole and entire at every instant because the whole is what endlessly comes into life at each moment without repetition. She cannot lack because she does not refer herself to the totality of a subject she is trying to be. She simply responds and pursues her pleasure. She goes where her desire leads her, as it leads her. This desire is premised not on filling in some hole but rather on the vibrations that set her humming, the motions that set her dancing, the tastes and touch that call for more tasting and touching. This feminine other neither identifies with nor completely distinguishes herself from what is "not-her." The ebbs and flows of her movement "set the rhythm of time," and yet each "moment is worth absolutely no more than the other, for the whole is present in each" (ML 14).

Irigaray contrasts the feminine image of the sea with Nietzsche's world, which she characterizes as "always hot, dry, and hard." According to Nietzsche, "what is great in man is that he is a bridge and not an end" (Nietzsche 1966, 15). Irigaray mocks this metaphor, asking, "Are you truly afraid of falling back into man? Or into the sea?" (ML 13). The image of the bridge suggests a need for distance and separation from the sea which for Irigaray represents the feminine other and sensual becoming. If a masculine subject were to fall into this sea, his boundaries would become blurred. He would no longer be able to repeat himself. He would experience both space and time differently. The masculine subject must arrest the movement of this incessant becoming in order to present himself as a "man" — a recognizable social subject who maintains self-identity. Nietzsche challenges this self-identity and his manhood in the process; he contests the stable ideals of Western thought and embraces sensual becoming. But if Nietzsche at times identifies with rather than distances himself from feminine becoming (as we will see in the next section), Irigaray finds this identification as problematic as Nietzsche's disidentification with "effeminacy." Whether reduced to specular mirror or affirmed as creative process, whether Nietzsche's other or image of Nietzsche's own creative power, Nietzsche's depiction of the feminine, according to Irigaray, obliterates the passage between self and other and so arrests the living movement of fleshly encounter.[4]

When she is positioned as specular other, Irigaray claims that the feminine other becomes a "stranger in her own body" in order "to join in your [Nietzsche's] game . . . [S]he speaks the 'yes' dictated to her by your latest movement, your latest will" (ML 36). The feminine other "sub-tends" the logic of predication which posits stable subjects with attributes by reflecting back to the masculine subject — who is himself a process of becoming just as she is — reiterations of an "identical" self-image which confirm his illusion of stable continuity. Although Nietzsche's work challenges conventional subjectivity, Irigaray's reading suggests that the feminine as specular other still plays this role in his texts. Since this feminine other receives no reassuring image of herself in return, and since her role in fact depends on her not being invested in demanding such a self-image from the other, woman also ends up representing the horror of the abyss, loss of identity, and death: if she were to "wise up" and abdicate her role, masculine identity could not continue. Irigaray's emphasis on embodiment and the world of material flux makes it impossible to forget that despite the stability of certain structures of life, ultimately life is about change, flux, and the breaking down and building up of various material forms. The body is no less subject to this flux than everything else. The notion, then, that we are the same person with the same self throughout our lives is, on the one hand, an obvious lie and, on the other hand, an illusion of masculine subjectivity that is crucial to it. Repetition of both corporeal and psychic identity is dependent on the specular other who mirrors back a reassuringly familiar image.

Irigaray charges Nietzsche with wanting the feminine other to be no more than a "looking glass eternally set opposite you" (ML 33). It is as if

Nietzsche's words would fragment and disperse without her, and with and through her they are fed back to him so that he can hear them again. Like an echo chamber, she provides him with confirmation of his voice as well as a delayed feedback loop that allows him to hear what he has said.

I was your resonance.

Drum. I was merely the drum in your own ear sending back to itself its own truth. (ML 3)

Although Nietzsche denigrates the role of feminine other, it turns out that without this other, Nietzsche would not be able to hear himself think.[5] She is the material medium for his voice, the perpetual relay between his mouth and ear. Without her, Nietzsche would lose touch with himself. She sings his memory so that he does not "fall into some abyss of forgetfulness" (3). The masculine perspective is invested in denying not only the active, constitutive role that the feminine function plays in the masculine economy, but also the possibility of the emergence of a feminine subject. Thus the feminine other is reduced to "an exemplary echo chamber. An enclosure, sealed off of course, for admirably appropriate resonance. A physical setup that goes into vibration, amplifies what it receives all the more perfectly because the stimulating vibration comes close to the system's 'natural frequency' — that is obviously constructed as a function of a model. A labyrinth whose internal cavities are always already limited, directed, speculated for the re-production of whatever should come into it. A simulacrum without a hint of deceit" (109–10). Femininity deprived of touching herself plays with "acting the figure of death." She is "all in webs. She spins all day long, all night long. And never undoes. The woman of your dreams. Perfectly absent 'from herself'." Absent from herself, she makes the perfect echo because she tirelessly repeats "the master's words and desires. Wholly in the air. Giving herself endlessly out to be — be for him. Eternal — without body. Pure mechanism" (110).

This feminine other is a sounding board or echo system for a process of material mediation. Without such mediation the ebbs and flows of the body would simply dissipate, leaving no trace. Speaking without being able to hear the sound of one's voice, looking into a mirror that does not reflect one, or pushing ahead into space that never resists one's movements would make the formation of a coherent self-image impossible. That one can form a coherent image that develops stability over time is due to the form that material mediation takes. The masculine subject selectively attends to the information he picks up. First, he assumes that all the sounds he picks up from a sounding board originate with him and him alone. Second, he excludes from the sounds he picks up the reception of anything "foreign" to the sound image so crucial to the continuance of his own sense of stable self. The feminine other is highly attentive and responsive not simply to the whole range of vibrations from the masculine subject's ever-changing body but to the desire of the masculine subject for a specific image. Thus, she provides a kind of tuning system that can highlight and diminish the vibrations she picks up in ways that the masculine subject finds satisfying and desirable. Without this focusing activity — to which the masculine subject contributes through a further screening system which displaces dissonant noise back onto her — he would be confronted with images of himself that he would find bizarre and disturbing, never mind threatening to his sense of continuity.[6]

The feminine other does not expect to be able to receive this kind of attunement from the masculine subject. First, she does not need it because her pleasure comes from contact and response without any worries about a framework that structures repetition of the same. Second, the masculine subject is too concerned with reaffirming his own image to be able to relinquish it long enough to trace any pattern in her movements. This is why Irigaray suggests that the feminine other is not conscious in the way the masculine subject is. Consciousness is not possible without an ego to which one can refer experiences. The danger for the feminine other is that she is never gathered back into herself. Her pleasures and pains are not memorable in the way the masculine subject's are. They are experienced, and then they are gone, never to return. No self is developed, no memory is retained, and no feedback loop is established that could resonate her back to herself so that her self-identifications could become ever more complex. Indeed, without the need or the desire for identification, the feminine other is "free" to travel with the intensity of each moment, but without the benefit of building these moments into a more stable structure.

Thus the feminine other is a kind of "prime matter" (ML 92). She is part of a flux of forces with no stable pattern. She may exchange herself within herself, just as she may exchange herself with others. She follows movements where they are without respecting boundaries or worrying about what might be lost or gained in the process. She is not "strictly speaking" marked with predication because there is "strictly speaking" nothing to mark. Without a feedback loop, she can develop no repeating formation of a "same" self. Without a sounding board to assist her in the process of gathering up and focusing her effects into a unity, she cannot "be" anything in particular at all.

This failure of the masculine economy to provide suport for feminine subjectivity leaves her in a state of dereliction. Without adequate cultural support in symbolizing feminine specificity, the feminine other is highly vulnerable to the loss of identity and the melancholy effects of having no home of her own. Just as masculine subjects are apt to view the world in terms of objects they can control or possess, feminine (non-)subjects are apt to lose themselves in others in their desire to communicate with subjects. Nietzsche's marine lover wants to share a conversation with Nietzsche; Nietzsche — despite the passage to another kind of language his work presents — shuts out her voice.

A New Way of Thinking: An Elemental Logic

Irigaray, like Nietzsche and Deleuze, is suspicious of traditional philosophical thought: "Philosophy teaches the eyelids to close tighter and tighter to bar anything still presented by the senses, teaches the gaze to turn inward to the soul, that screen for the projection of ideal images. The horror of nature is magicked away: it will be seen only through the blind of intelligible categories, and the weaknesses that ultimately will lay man low will be laid at the door of an insufficiently lofty point of view" (ML 99). By turning us away from sensation, philosophy promotes an artifical relationship to reality which impoverishes our understanding of ourselves and our experience. Nature is horrible because it is threatening. It renders our ideal images suspect and threatens death to the selves we have worked so hard to create. Irigaray, like Nietzsche, attempts a passage to another kind of language in order to return language to its roots in a sensuous world that is here-right-now rather than referred to some transcendent beyond. Like Nietzsche, she would make words dance with earthly intensities. Her language evokes rhythms of natural elements in constant movement and the fluid passage of forms that emerge from this flux only to dissolve. The feminine other to which she gives voice is more comfortable with this realm of incessant movement because she has no stake in maintaining her own form as fixed. Instead, she can enjoy the flow of the elements as they come together and fall apart in ever-changing patterns. If Nietzsche is also able to celebrate this flow and mark its movement with his notions of force and will to power, he is still unable, according to Irigaray, to release himself to the rhythm of these swiftly changing forms.

Dionysus is the god of immanence who celebrates the dissolution of individuation in order to embrace sensual participation in the dance of earthly forces. Irigaray is sympathetic to Nietzsche's conception of Dionysus. If she takes on Dionysus in the final section of her book, "And the Gods . . . ," it is not because she does not find in Nietzsche's work riches for her own project. But Dionysus, like Nietzsche, is plagued with a blind spot that leads to his refusal of the feminine other. And this refusal thwarts Nietzsche's project of creating a language that will free the body so it can sing of the earth. To create oneself out of the matter of this world requires, for Irigaray, coming into contact with one's irreducible other — the opposite sex. In failing to recognize this other, Dionysus becomes vulnerable to fusion in a world from which he cannot distinguish himself. And so, despite his attempt to rejuvenate himself through opening his body to the sensual, he ends up putting himself into another kind of tomb.

In affirming the Dionysian over the Apollonian or Christian moment in religious thought, Nietzsche initiates the return to the sensuous roots of language so important for Irigaray's own project. Irigaray's genealogy of gods from Dionysus to Apollo to Christ traces a growing divergence between gods and men, and between reified conceptual thought and the sensual realm of embodied existence.[7] Dionysus is still a god who acknowledges both the realm of embodied flux as well as the conceptual realm. Apollo turns us further away from the former realm toward a realm where harmony is preserved through a stricter bifurcation of embodied flux and the concepts through which we understand it. Christ, as we will see in the next section, comes yet further along in this history. All these gods in one way or another obscure the realm of sensuous experience, the realm of "prime matter," the stuff of life that then gets reified and structured so that we can have conscious experience. This level of sensuous experience may be inchoate and ultimately ineffable, but that does not mean that this experience is not real or completely inaccessible. Indeed, Irigaray suggests that this level of inchoate experience already has a certain degree of structure and form that is implicated with, but not constrained by or reducible to, articulable experience.

The feminine that Irigaray would evoke in *Marine Lover* turns out to involve a kind of differentiated becoming far more nuanced than that of a fusional void. For Irigaray, Nietzsche's Dionysus represents an impoverished form of femininity. The Dionysian is closer to the primordial "feminine" because it more fully acknowledges the realm of the senses and the body, but Dionysus, as Irigaray points out, does not know the passage out of a mother's womb. And so also lost to him is "the doubling of their bodies, the difference of their boundaries — the coming into appearance in one's own skin." The Dionysian moment lacks the differentiation of the feminine, the special form of differentiation that is not predicated on subject/object distinctions and yet that does not precipitate one into an undifferentiated abyss. Dionysus may have the benefit of a kind of immediacy of experience lost to Apollo, but "the only skin he knows is a dead skin." The body offered him to dwell in "suffers the most extreme violence and survives only a short while" (ML 123). In other words, Dionysus partakes in a sacrifice of the feminine analogous to that of Zeus and Apollo: he may be more willing to risk the outlines of a reified self, but he still plunders the feminine without acknowledging her constitutive role, and he ends up losing himself and his own living body in the process. Although he can receive nourishment from his embrace with the feminine, his drunken ecstasies turn out to be another form of detachment from the body. He summons dance and music, but his ecstasies both recall and forget the flesh "as it remains in the movement of its becoming": "The rhythm is too fast and goes beyond the natural beat. Exaltation that tears away from the roots. Attracts one out of the self, upward. Finding a place high up, on the very peak. Coming up to it by moving away from it. Having no element but the one drunkenness opens up at the end of its surge. Always ecstatic. Always beyond one's own body. Always in exile from one's own comleteness" (137).

Irigaray contends that in appropriating all creative power to himself, Dionysus replicates the illusion of masculine self-sufficiency. Although Dionysus identifies with sensual becoming, he loses the passage between self and other of truly feminine becoming. Dionysian ecstasy dissolves the boundaries of social convention without permitting the differentiating contact of creative energies that are distinguishable without being distinct. Dionysus attempts to become both the feminine sea and an immortal god and gets torn apart in the process. Instead of flowing in living movement in responsive contact with what is other and yet not other to him, he wants eternity and longs for deathly self-sameness (ML 129). At the same time that he embraces the becoming that dissolves stable forms, he wants to be that becoming. He thus displaces the totalization of masculine subjectivity to the totalization of becoming: if he is becoming, he is self-sufficient becoming through all eternity that admits nothing foreign to his own process.

Despite Nietzsche's recognition of the interconnectedness of the forces that make up both people and the rest of the world, he replicates the perspective of one who must exclude becomings that do not originate from within that perspective. Although he is willing to risk the dissolution of stabilized forms of life, he has yet to invent a language that invites participation and the mutually constitutive production of a dialogical text. In attempting a dialogue with Nietzsche, Irigaray attempts to open up the representational system of Western thought to its unrepresentable other. For Irigaray, this attempt constitutes part of the project of permitting the living movement of contact between the sexes in more fleshly encounters as well. Human others are active subjects who, despite all the impersonal forces of which they may be made, have still achieved something out of the pluralities of which they are a part — a face, a body, a self, with more or less defined boundaries that may dissolve or reconfigure in keeping with present becomings. Achievement of human subjectivity is, according to Irigaray, a creative act that is inevitably collaborative and never finished, an act that leads one out into the vast multiplicities of life. Irigaray would have us remember to acknowledge this act as an achievement and to give gratitude to those around us who not only provide us with the support we need to continue but also challenge us to continue to live and change form.

Christian Flesh

Dionysus still gets drunk on the confusing array of sensual forms through which perception manifests itself. He has not made the shift to emphasis on sight that will come with Zeus and Apollo. He is not satisfied by appearance; he has to experience life with all his senses. "And these doings are horrible in the eyes of the gods to come. A necessary passage, to be wiped out" (ML 135). Dionysus, who is already phallic and one step removed from feminine sensuality, is left behind in favor of gods who further reduce and restrain sensual experience. The new gods summon living things out of their immediate surroundings and separate each man from the whole, creating a void "between each and every man" (139). Now when men open their eyes, they no longer feel in contact with their surroundings. There is a space between them and the rest of the world. Irigaray suggests that the ability to distance oneself from the rest of the world, to think of oneself as separate, is premised on a loss in perceptual richness.

And today they can no longer see what was apparent to them yesterday. Opening up their eyes, they feel separated from the immediate that surrounds them. Opacity and insignificance cover and dwell in all things. And the gaze, closed to the mystery of natural growth, enters into slumber and weaves a dream garment that carries the whole far away from its earthly blossoming. All is shrouded in an appearance that gives it a more striking and glorious aspect. Beauty shines in the face. Is laid over the face, like the mask of desire. (141)

Irigaray's genealogy from Zeus to Christ traces an ever-widening divergence between a sensuous realm of corporeal becoming and a transcendent realm of reified concepts. Although Irigaray and Nietzsche are in agreement that cultural regeneration requires overcoming this gap, Irigaray finds rejuvenating possibilities in a radical reinterpretation of Christianity which Nietzsche does not.[8] Traditional Christianity's reduction of Mary, the virgin-mother, to the "sensory-substrate" (ML 179) of the love between God, the Father, and Christ, His son, replicates the cultural matricide of the tradition from Zeus to Apollo. Christ attempts to bring the divine into corporeal life by being the embodied god. Instead of closing each individual up in the tomb of her or his own body, he would open the body — but "not through or for the mother's passion, but by identification with the Father's Word. He would go from the Father to the Father, without a backward look at his birth into the body" (165). Christ does not have the kind of relations Dionysus does with women because he is already "bound to his heavenly Father." If he acknowledges the "fulfillment of carnal exchange" (166) in any way, it is through its deferment to a time after death. Mary, according to Irigaray, is a "sort of mimetic representation" of the murder of Christ. Just as Mary "dies to her generation in order to become merely the vehicle for the Other," so must Christ be sacrificed "in his living body, if he is to accede to a transfiguration worthy of the Kingdom" (166–67). Her "yes" to the annunciation that made Christ and Christianity possible was a no to her own life, "to her conception, her birth, her generation, her flowering. No to everything, except the Word of the Father" (167).

Irigaray points to another reading of Christianity by speculating about the meaning of the phrase "the word is made flesh." The word made flesh in Mary might mean the advent of a god who, unlike the god of Greek desire, does not violently burst in and "does not simply rule the world from a heaven of dreams, and does not remain closed in a text of law either" (ML 181). The divine for Mary might be "so near that it thereby becomes unnameable. Which is not to say that it is nothing. But rather the coming of a reality that is alien to any already-existing identity" (171). If Mary is the one able to give flesh to god, it may be because she is still able to listen silently and give new flesh to messages that other people cannot perceive: "Can she alone feel the music of the air trembling between the wings of the angels, and make or remake a body from it?" After the loss of a more materially present god and the arrival of a God who dispenses His truth from a great distance, woman is called upon to incarnate divinity: "A virgin-mother would give God back to God. A tardy, and quickly neglected, recognition of woman's share in creation? Cocreation of a divine nature? The presence that had been buried and paralyzed in the text of the law is made flesh once more in the body of a woman, guardian of the spirit of the divine life" (176).

If the virgin-mother is reduced to a sensory-substrate, if the father-son relationship is reified and referred to a distant realm, if Christ is set up as an idol of incarnation, these things have been done in keeping with the narrative from Dionysus and Apollo — a narrative Irigaray insists is premised on the denial of the feminine and the refusal to acknowledge sexual difference. On Irigaray's view, one can read the desire of the divine to dwell in the flesh in aspects of Christ's persona that are covered over by the traditional reading of Christianity: "That the Christic symbol might be decoded as an invitation to become shared flesh, still causes an uproar. That 'multiply' might not simply mean 'make children' for the Father, but rather create oneself and grow in the grace of fleshly fulfillment, is sheer blasphemy!" (ML 170). Perhaps Christ did not have to die on the cross to be perceived as divine. Perhaps Mary's ability to incarnate divinity speaks to an ability to listen to what is beyond the conceivable and the perceivable which we all share. Touching on the divine in our fleshly encounters entails welcoming contact with that which thwarts the comfortably routine patterns of life. Appropriating such contact in order to preserve the illusion of self-originating agency not only impedes the creative fecundity of fleshly encounters but also disallows a new possibility in stabilization: the differentiating movement of living mirrors who transform one another in mutually constitutive reflections.

Although Nietzsche does admit multiplicity, it is a multiplicity without a face. Matricide dooms even this masculine subject to a bottomless chasm. The refusal to acknowledge the feminine other's role in his birth and incarnation, the willful appropriation of feminine creativity that only veils the uneasiness caused by his blind spot, does not simply perpetuate his masculine identity but closes off the possibility for another way of experiencing life.

The sacrifice he makes to the Idea is inscribed in this — that he preferred the Idea to an ever provisional openness to a female other. That he refused to break the mirror of the (male) same, and over and over again demanded that the other be his double. To the point of willing to become that female other. Despite all physiology, all incarnation. Hermit, tightrope walker or bird, forgetful of her who gave him birth and company and nourishment, he soars up, leaving everything below him or inside him, and the chasm becomes bottomless. (ML 187–88)

By abandoning the project of overcoming everything, Nietzsche could plunge into the sea without fear and with gratitude for the others that will light up the shadows of the depths and provide him with perspective — perhaps not the perspective of a god who has overcome all, or who has incorporated all other perspectives into himself, but the limited perspective of someone who is grateful to the perspectives of others and their constitutive effects in providing him with the limits and boundaries he needs to have any kind of perspective at all.

Irigaray's Critique of the Eternal Return

Just as Nietzsche's conception of Dionysus turns out to entail its own form of matricide, so does Nietzsche's conception of the eternal return, on Irigaray's reading, turn out to entail an appropriation of feminine becoming which does not acknowledge the passages between self and others. The sea of feminine becoming is whole at each moment because each moment is taken in its singular freshness rather than referred to an ideal totality. Like Dionysus, Nietzsche is torn between the realm of sensual becoming and the desire for immortality. Although the Nietzschean subject may embrace the continual dissolution of forms of sensual becoming, he also affirms "something that can only take place after you, and without you: the being of your becoming" (ML 41). According to Irigaray, this constitutes nostalgia for lost contact with the feminine; rather than risk immersion in the sea of becomings, the Nietzschean subject recapitulates all life in himself and becomes dead "so that that moment may be through all eternity" (54). Rather than acknowledging the passage between himself and the other, this subject reproduces himself twice over: "as subject and effect of your will, as will to power and eternal recurrence" (35).

The eternal return, on Irigaray's reading, turns out to be a ploy, perhaps at one or two steps removed, of masculine subjectivity. The notion that all events are inextricably linked and that the affirmation of any one event thus means affirming all of life in all its contingent interconnectedness allows the Nietzschean subject to turn the whole world around himself. He makes himself the fulcrum of this tightly linked set of events, and he rejoices in the eternal return because it means the eternal return of himself with himself at the center. Irigaray takes what Nietzsche considered his greatest achievement to be no more than an indication of his failure to escape the masculinist dream of autoproduction. The creative power attributed to Nietzsche's subject involves assuming that everything turns around him and that nothing moves "except by him and according to his strength." Nietzsche may have the strength to say yes, but this is "a sign of turning in the void, when nothing comes from the other to keep the movement going" (ML 16).

Irigaray's feminine other can also say yes — yes to life, yes to movement, yes to the subject who appeals to her for response without knowing that that is what he is doing. That Nietzsche says yes to life is therefore important to her — perhaps a topic of conversation that they could have, something that they share. How bitter the disappointment, then, when his yes still refuses her her difference: "And your whole will, your eternal recurrence, are these anything more than the dream of one who neither wants to have been born, nor to continue being born, at every instant, of a female other? Does your joy in becoming not result from annihilating her from whom you are tearing yourself away?" (ML 26–27). Although the Nietzschean subject can let in more than perhaps the typical masculine subject, and although he is receptive and affirming, saying yes to life and sensual becoming, it turns out that he can do so only if all this movement turns out to be ultimately self-originated. Nietzsche breaks out of the tombstone of specular masculinity only to replicate it at the cosmic level of the eternal return.[9]

Irigaray claims that Nietzsche's emphasis on overcoming is the dream of a god; it weighs down the child whose first duty should be to "run after his mother, and away from her, and back again, weaving threads so that his world keeps hold of that creative female presence." This means retaining "the innocence of a will that is still free of the burden of a memory. Of a: you must overcome" (ML 16). Without the burden of overcoming exalted by the notion of eternal return, a child could live in the moment, allowing permeable boundaries between self and other where there was no "I" and no "you." Childhood would then involve projecting into the other and receiving the other "without the one ever becoming separate from the other. Without the other being preferable to the one" (17). Living in innocence of memory and the childhood of one's fathers leaves one more open to "a passage and a sharing in life and death" (18). The eternal return fosters an image of revolving around a fixed center and a yes to life that secures oneself and denies the movement of the other; the image of feminine becoming suggests that the yes to life is a yes to passages and sharing, the movement of others as well as one's own movement, and a creativity which evolves in the textures woven by one's to and fro among others.

The Nietzschean notion of eternal return involves a repetition that for Irigaray makes of the body an "imperceptible illusion" (ML 22). The being of becoming can never be anything more than an idealization of life; to refer to life through this notion is to turn away from the living body of a corporeal subject in order to play god and engender life "from a language-body alone" (65). Thus, despite all Nietzsche's references to the body and his attempts to listen to it, Irigaray claims that Nietzsche has failed to reclaim the body; he may evoke the body, but he succeeds only in throwing it back into the chasm because he refuses to explore its living boundaries. Irigaray's implication is that such exploration would inevitably entail a kind of recognition and contact with an other that would jeopardize stable body boundaries. Furthermore, this kind of contact is constantly occurring despite Nietzsche's failure to acknowledge it. Thus Nietzsche, despite his challenge to traditional conceptions of the subject, by failing to acknowledge the material constitution of the body and thus the interdependency of self and others in a realm where boundaries become undecidable, has failed to follow out the implications of his exploration of the self. Despite his call for honesty with respect to the body and the earth, Nietzsche enacts another version of the masculinist evasion of the body: "Neither to suffer from nor even to imagine the matter from which life is made, and unmade" (29).

At the same time that the Nietzschean subject refuses to acknowledge the other, he craves sensuous experience, living contact, and being brought up against what is not him, what brings him to himself by not being under his control. It is this other that orients him and "gives him back his weight." And yet he is also afraid of her and so wants to "find his place back in the tomb" (ML 29) where there is no longer any question about who he is because he is already finished and summed up: "And the fact that your unique necessity is death is what keeps us apart. Whereas you finish all (female) things off by wrapping them in an airy shroud, I leave them open so that they can go on breathing and respond to the sap that feeds them. So they can flower over and over again" (30). Irigaray objects to this wrapping up of all female things. She cries out against Nietzsche's impetus toward death and the way his lack of recognition and acknowledgment closes off the passage between the masculine and feminine and veils feminine creativity. She also cries out against the feminine other's tendency toward enslaving herself by subordinating her own creativity, innocence, and play to his projects. Despite the feminine movement that refuses to turn around an axis, it is still she who "at the end of your hour" carries the load of what the masculine subject has created. This may break her back, but Nietzsche does not care "as long as she still has the strength to give that present back, in the shape of a sounding echo that the voice of her flesh fills out" (32). In a way, then, she does turn around an axis; she continually returns to the masculine subject who calls her, she does not abandon him, she is there when he calls. He may withhold acknowledgment and refuse to see her sacrifice — the sacrifice of her own becoming, her innocence, her play — but she also participates in this partnership. She plays the blind mirror and gives the present back to him through the material mediation of her own flesh. If Irigaray creates a feminine subject who spends the entire book trying to talk to Nietzsche, it is not just to tell him what he is missing; it is because she craves and needs his recognition. "Why are we not, the one for the other, a resource of life and air?" (31), she cries, implying that being such a resource to each other would prove fruitful for her as well as him.

Irigaray characterizes the contemporary paradigmatic relationship between the masculine subject and the feminine other as based on an illusion: if the active subject were to acknowledge what "really" happened, he would see that in the other he is changed and becomes other without recurrence. If he can get away with the illusion that he is a living subject who remains self-identical, it is because she perpetuates his becoming and gives it back to him, "or not, variously deformed." A trace of his passage into her "leaves a mark, in the flesh" (ML 69), but it escapes him because he refuses to look for it. He refuses to acknowledge the passage between the two, refuses to acknowledge that it is only because the feminine other responds to his becoming by echoing back an image with which he can identify that he can maintain the illusion of his separateness. And if he does not notice the mark he leaves on her, it is because he refuses to see that there is any passage at all involved in this process. Irigaray suggests that Nietzsche's notion of woman at a distance, far from depicting woman in a positive light, floats women "into death." If women are kept at a distance in this way, it is so they can "give themselves up to be" supple canvases against which masculine activity can represent itself.

As Kelly Oliver points out in her reading of *Marine Lover*, Deleuze's conception of the eternal return is that of the eternal return of difference rather than the eternal return of the same.[10]

The eternal return [for Deleuze] is the return of forces that multiply life rather than diminish life; only active forces return. The eternal return operates as the mechanism for the *self-overcoming* of reactive forces. In this way, the eternal return makes a gift of oneself possible insofar as self-giving is also always a process of self-destroying. Through the eternal return a new "self" is continually emerging. Through this process of continual self-destroying and self-creating, the never-ending process of othering takes place. The self becomes other. (Oliver 1995, 106)

From this perspective one could argue that Nietzsche, by engaging in a project that entails the self-destruction of the subject, paves the way for an unselfish receptivity and generosity to the other.[11] Oliver asks why Irigaray's reading is so compelling when at the same time Oliver herself is more sympathetic to Deleuze's reading as more in keeping with Nietzsche's texts.[12] She makes the intriguing suggestion that Irigaray strategically refuses to see difference in Nietzsche in order to mimic Nietzsche's resented woman: "This lament is powerful because it is not only addressed to Nietzsche but also to all of the patriarchal traditions in philosophy" (114). She thus gives birth to a woman who, through the selective principle of the eternal return, engages in a self-overcoming of resentment which will lead to the feminine subject who no longer needs to take a reactionary position. This reading suggests that Irigaray takes up a Nietzschean stance in making her discomfort with Nietzsche's appropriation known. By interpreting and evaluating Nietzsche's valuing of woman, she does not enact the resentful stance of slave morality, but instead carries out the evaluation of those values that have defined her, thus preparing the way for her own self-overcoming.[13]

Sexual Difference and Reading Nietzsche

Nietzsche's sea lover would like to think of the feminine other as being in the distance.[14] He can then use "her to fashion his highest reveries, to weave his dreams of her, and spread his sails while remaining safe in port" (ML 51), but he never truly has to risk the identity he has worked so hard to secure. Irigaray implies that even though the feminine other is actually in the closest proximity imaginable — providing masculine activity with the specular alchemy that is the living fodder he requires for a continuous and yet living identity — he puts her at a distance and then exploits her. He denies the actual role she plays in his material existence, and then, even when he has decided to acknowledge her to the extent that he does, he says that she is at a distance, thus preserving his boundaries intact. If she is a living presence, it is a presence so far away that she could not possibly threaten his boundaries or his self-centered sense of power and agency. By thus displacing her creative powers, the masculine subject can appropriate them without truly granting them their real power to shape him. The lengths to which Nietzsche goes both to recognize and to contain feminine creativity become truly self-serving. If Nietzsche acknowledges the feminine, it is only in order to plumb her depths from a safe distance in order to add extra vitality to his own process of self-centered self-aggrandizement: "Between you and me, me and me, you want me to make a dam. You want me to confirm you endlessly in your form so that you can lose yourself over and over again, becoming other while giving a pledge of recurrence" (56).

Irigaray claims that the feminine other does not need the pledge of gold in order to engage in exchange: "She needs only to embrace herself. Women need only to embrace each other for their truth to have a place — matter and form intertwined in the instant, without abyss or eternity" (ML 85). It is Nietzsche's marine lover who can embrace herself. The feminine other who would yet have her own voice — even if she can achieve it only through a kind of echo. The feminine other who has no stake in the masculine economy has a special skill: she is able to respond attentively and with subtlety to the movement of another. She is able to give herself up to be what he needs her to be. This feminine other is not provided with a reciprocal mirroring effect by the masculine subject. She thus has no need of him for her truth; there is nothing returned to her, no truth to be received from him. He does not even notice the traces he makes in his passage into her. If she continues to play her role vis-à-vis this self-centered masculine subject, it is because she enjoys movement for the sake of movement. She plays in the instant without concern for repeating the same. She can do so with or without him. Her truth, then, can be found in an embrace with herself as well as with him. And since embracing herself imposes no repetition of an alien sameness, it provides her with greater freedom of movement: "If the female sex takes place by embracing itself, by endlessly sharing and exchanging its lips, its edges, its borders, and their 'content,' as it ceaselessly becomes other, no stability of essence is proper to her. She has a place in the openness of a relation to the other whom she does not take into herself, like a whore, but to whom she continuously gives birth" (86).

Some have complained that Irigaray places undue stress on the maternal role. It is true that Irigaray does draw from maternal imagery in rethinking forms of relationship. For example, she gives compelling accounts of the intrauterine experience.[15] Her notion that the feminine other can be both one and yet two — self and other in exchange without either losing itself —

finds vivid depiction in the imagery of the relationship of the mother to the fetus. But if Irigaray goes to this metaphor, it is to make two crucial points: (1) that it is due to a kind of matricide that we forget or belittle our origins in the mother; and (2) that this matricide is due not simply to our reluctance to remember our messy confusion with our own mother (in a literal sense) back in the womb, but also, and more important, to a whole symbolic system that replicates this matricide in countless ways on multiple levels. What the matricide comes down to is not merely refusal to acknowledge the mother as a person in her own right, but refusal to acknowledge our own corporeality and the ongoing constitutive effects of encountering a world as an embodied being always in process.

Irigaray starts off a discussion of Nietzsche's association of woman with truth by noting how, after initially suggesting that "nothing is more foreign . . . to woman than truth," Nietzsche drops the word 'foreign' and instead associates woman with falsehood. She points out that the latter is not foreign to truth but is rather its counterpart. What "beckoned toward an outside" is lost in this transition. Here she suggests that Nietzsche's notion of woman is caught up, for the most part, in the notion of a masculine subject's feminine other, and that despite the suggestion that the feminine could be used as a category from which to trouble such "proper" oppositions, he loses this opportunity by forgetting it. Forgetting is, for Nietzsche, an active process that enters into the creation of the present. If Nietzsche chooses to forget in this way, it is perhaps because he has had a glimpse of something too disturbing to what he wants to perpetuate. Nietzsche's representations are thus returned to the "echonomy" of sameness. Just as Nietzsche's notion of eternal recurrence would seem to take us out of the traditional system of representation only to return to it, so does Nietzsche's play with the connection between woman and truth.[16] So long as the masculine subject denies the constitutive role the feminine other plays for him, subjectivity will proceed as it always has, feminine others will be denied access to an "echonomy" that would enable them to be pulled out of their own kind of labyrinth, and reciprocity among people will be sadly impoverished.

In the next chapter I further explore Irigaray's evocative characterization of the sensible transcendental which opens the corporeal and conceptual logics of embodied subjects to what is always beyond and yet contiguous with conscious experience. An art of perception can bring about a spiritualization of the flesh in which the specular economy of subjectivity is transformed and two subjects can become living mirrors engendering mutual transformation.

3
Irigaray's Sensible Transcendental

Living Mirrors and Corporeal Logic

In *Speculum*, Irigaray presents a scathing critique of Freud's characterization of human subjectivity: Freud's blind spot leads him to valorize and perpetuate an economy that privileges masculine subjectivity. In the middle section of the book, titled "Speculum," she makes a whirlwind tour of metaphysical texts throughout the history of Western philosophy. She starts with a piece titled "Any Theory of the 'Subject' Has Always Been Appropriated by the 'Masculine'," which begins with the announcement of the title and proceeds: "When she submits to (such a) theory, woman fails to realize that she is renouncing the specificity of her own relationship to the imaginary. Subjecting herself to objectivization in discourse — by being 'female'. Re-objectivizing her own self whenever she claims to identify herself 'as' a masculine subject. A 'subject' that would re-search itself as lost (maternal-feminine) 'object'?" (S 133). In this essay Irigaray makes the connection between Freud's theory of subjectivity and the metaphysical implications of such a theory for key texts chosen from throughout the history of Western philosophy. Although Freud has done us the service of rendering the "symptom" of the masculine blind spot visible and thus making it available for analysis, rereading earlier texts in the history of philosophy in light of this symptom reveals to what lengths masculinity goes in order to sustain itself. Through the readings she gives of Plato, Aristotle, Plotinus, Descartes, Christian mystics, Kant, and Hegel, Irigaray explores different forms the masculine blind spot has taken in the Western tradition. If the masculine subject "can sustain himself only by bouncing back off some objectiveness, some objective," and if this sustenance depends upon "opaque matter [i.e., the feminine other] which in theory does not know herself," then if "the earth turned and more especially turned upon herself," then "the erection of the subject might thereby be disconcerted and risk losing its elevation and penetration. For what would there be to rise up from and exercise his power over? And in?" (S 133).

In her reading of texts from the history of philosophy, Irigaray demonstrates the resonance between the feminine other of Freud's subject and the "natural" other of a subject invested in completing a fully rational representation of the world. The form that that representation should take shifts from philosopher to philosopher as the conception of truth and the problems that go with it shift in response to the metaphysical problems presented by each conception of truth. But, as Irigaray demonstrates, each ideal of a totalized representation of the world depends on displacing that which the representation cannot contain onto a feminine other and perpetuating a whole system of ploys and decoys which ensures that this feminine other is maintained at a safe remove from the masculine economy: "She is the reserve of 'sensuality' for the elevation of intelligence, she is the matter used for the imprint of forms, gage of possible regression into naive perception, the representative representing negativity (death), dark continent of dreams and fantasies, and also eardrum faithfully duplicating the music, though not all of it, so that the series of displacements may continue, for the 'subject' " (S 141). So long as the feminine other abides by the imperative of the masculine to maintain his value and his desire, she has no need to contest the "decent modesty" that man demands of her. But once she feels the need to "get free of fabric, reveal her nakedness, her destitution in language" (143), she will tune her ear to another music and deliberately thwart the scene of representation.

If masculine subjectivity has a blind spot for feminine specificity, if this blind spot is detrimental to feminine subjects, and if removing that blind spot would create serious problems for the maintenance of specular masculinity, then what would/could happen if the mirror started to speak? What possibilities and what risks does such a moment hold, and what can we do to facilitate such a possibility and minimize the risks? Irigaray starts from where we are; by symbolizing the feminine other that has not been allowed to speak, she both challenges masculine specularity and engages in a project of creating another economy that could also sustain a viable form of subjectivity.

In the last chapter we saw how Mary could be seen to represent a capacity to incarnate divinity by listening for a message that comes from beyond the conventional forms of lived experience. Although Irigaray does not use the term 'sensible transcendental' in *Speculum*, the hints of an alternative subjectivity, especially as they emerge in "Mystérique" and "Volume-Fluidity," resonate with the notions of a feminine divine, a horizon for the feminine gender, and the sensible transcendental which emerge more fully in her later work. Irigaray contends that the masculine approach to the divine posits it as a transcendental ideal set at a distance from sense experience in a time and place untainted by the corruption of the ever-changing states of material reality. The sensible transcendental is Irigaray's term for a feminine divine which always touches on and yet exceeds whatever sensible reality the subject may be experiencing. Margaret Whitford suggests that the sensible transcendental is "the flesh made word (in an audacious reversal of the New Testament)" (1991a, 48). Full cultural recognition of the body would entail symbolization of the body in relation to masculine as well as feminine subjects. If women were not relegated to the position of primary guardians of the corporeal in our cultural representations, masculine as well as feminine subjects could incorporate their corporeality into their sublimations (142). Such a project of recognition and symbolization would entail undoing the sexual division of labor which allows masculine subjects to displace their corporeality onto feminine others and excludes the latter from the transcendental functions of culture (122). Whitford presents the sensible transcendental as an imprecise concept "referring to all the conditions of women's collective access to subjectivity" (47) and emphasizes its symbolic aspect; it is through the open exchange of embodied communication in discourse where "one's deep unconscious feelings are mobilized" (48) that the symbolic can be transformed and women can create a different place for themselves in the social order (144).

Whitford argues that Irigaray attempts to avoid the dangers of a God created in the image of man by conceiving of the divine as a multiple becoming incarnated in sensuous bodies (1991a, 144). The feminine divine is not the counterpart to a male God, but rather an immanent approach to the divine premised on communication which cuts across the traditional dichotomies of masculine/feminine, self/other, and mind/body (140–47). Through the embodied encounters in which women and men transform language in order to articulate a genuinely intersubjective dialogue, new possibilities for subjectivity and self-other relationship will be created (cf. Deutscher 1994). In this chapter and the next I explore the various strategies Irigaray enacts for fostering such communication. No conscious experience is adequate to reality. Whatever our conscious experience may be, it cannot reveal the mystery of life; it can never adequately represent the full richness of the living present. Even when we draw back from this realization in our specular dreams of capturing the world in a completed system of reified ideals, these dreams unravel in the flow of unrepeatable, unanticipatable moments. Irigaray suggests that to refer the flow of life to a transcendent ideal removed from sensibility and all the "messiness" of material existence corporeality entails is to attempt to cut life off at the source in order to control it. A lover of beauty who is able to contemplate the beautiful in sensible things in such a way that she becomes united with it and so attains " 'authentic reality' . . . becomes dear to the divine and is made immortal" (ESD 32). The person who can experience life in its "authentic reality" is the person who is open to a sensible transcendental. This person is the lover of life who refuses to entomb herself in a sterile body and who instead encourages the ceaseless transmutation of a self and world in living contact.

For Irigaray, the otherness crucial to creative engenderment is to be found not in a transcendent realm of the divine or in mystified notions of Being but here-right-now within and through our relations with concrete others (ESD 128–29). It is in the corporeal and conceptual exchanges of ourselves with others that we create — through contact with that which always exceeds ourselves and so exceeds any corporeal or conceptual patterns we may have already established — new ways of being in the world.

Mystical Language and the Fire of Becoming

Irigaray appeals to the mystical writings of female saints to suggest some of what has been lost in and by the masculine economy of language. Although the language of mystics is also ruled by the specular economy of a masculine logic, the cracks in its logic evoke an alternative sensibility. Irigaray explores and elaborates these breaks in mystical language in her pursuit of an economy of language and subjectivity that would provide symbolic support for a feminine mode of being.

La mystérique: this is how one might refer to what, within a still theological onto-logical perspective is called mystic language or discourse. Consciousness still imposes such names to signify that other scene, offstage, that it finds *cryptic*. This is the place where consciousness is no longer master, where, to its extreme confusion, it sinks into a dark night that is also fire and flames. This is the place where "she" — and in some cases he, if he follows "her" lead — speaks about the dazzling glare which comes from the source of light that has been logically repressed, about "subject" and "Other" flowing out into an embrace of fire that mingles one term into another, about contempt for form as such, about mistrust for understanding as an obstacle along the path of jouissance and mistrust for the dry desolation of reason. Also about a "burning glass." This is the only place in the history of the West in which woman speaks and acts so publicly. What is more, it is for/by woman that man dares to enter the place, to descend into it, condescend to it, even if he gets burned in the attempt. (S 191)

Mystical language evokes the underside of consciousness, a realm of processes in fiery motion. The identities of subjects and others are quickly lost in this realm as they merge and diverge in participatory communion with other processes. The fire of a becoming unimpeded by the divisions of specular logic continuously transmutes the elements of the world into new forms.[1] These ephemeral forms are never in isolation, but emerge in the creative heat generated by elements in constant contact. "She" is more attuned to this realm because "she" has been relegated to the role of tain of the mirror which allows her a better vantage point on both sides of the mirror; it is due to her reflection that the masculine subject perceives recognizable forms rather than the endlessly differentiating movement of life processes in which no form remains the same.

The mystic senses that "something *remains to be said* that resists all speech, that can at best be stammered out," a something that defies any form yet created (S 193). The masculine subject confers being upon himself by denying what would disturb the clarity of his vision and thus walling himself off into a "prison of self-sufficiency" (192). It is the mystic who, by abstaining from all discourse, or by uttering inarticulate sounds "all the while keeping an attentive ear open for any hint or tremor coming back" (193), is able to break out of this prison. "The 'soul' escapes outside herself, opening up a crack in the cave so that she may penetrate herself once more. The walls of her prison are broken, the distinction between inside/outside transgressed. In such ex-stasies, she risks losing herself or at least seeing the assurance of her self-identity-as-same fade away" (192). Like the masculine subject, the mystic has created corporeal and psychic selves which can be maintained only by the exclusion of open participation with processes that would sweep those selves away. In the fire of becoming, where all forms are in continual transmutation, no identity can remain; even the mystic must allow cracks in the structures, thus preventing her complete dissolution. Because of the various representations that ground her in a social existence shared with others, the mystic will likely not lose herself all at once. Instead, she will have to wander randomly in the dark, fleeing the logic that frames her. She will have to explore the shadow of her gaze since her eye "has become accustomed to obvious 'truths' that actually hide what she is seeking." She will have to "push onward into the night until it finally becomes a transverberating beam of light, a luminous shadow. Onward into a *touch* that opens the 'soul' again to contact with divine force, to the impact of searing light" (193).

In her reading of texts from the history of the Western tradition of philosophy, Irigaray demonstrates different forms of what she calls the "imaginary retreat into pure objectivity": Plato retreats into mirrors and the realm of ideal forms,[2] Aristotle affirms man's active ability to take full possession of his humanity in contrast to woman who is closer to matter, Plotinus defines Matter as a mere shadow that receives the active power of the Ideal Principle,[3] Descartes recreates a world of his own making.[4] "Pure objectivity" in all these cases entails a retreat to various versions of a realm that is protected from the ceaselessly transmutating forces of life as process. The mystical language of the female saints willing to risk self-loss burns away this objectivity.

We must reach the final dispossession of the last imaginary retreat into pure objectivity: the "I" calculated and therefore still knew *where* it stood. Reference points, drafting plans to survey this extension, this mother-matter — all these are henceforward taken from mastery. All surfaces and spatial constructions also collapse in a conflagration that pushes further and further back the depths of a gulf where now everything is burning. Fire flares up in the inexhaustible abundance of her underground source and is matched with an opposing but congruent flood that sweeps over the "I" in an excess of excess. Yet, burning, flowing along in a wild spate of waters, yearning for even greater abandon, the "I" is *empty* still, ever more empty, opening wide in rapture of soul. (S 195)

Irigaray describes the imperceptible void opened up by the mystic as relentlessly immediate and yet unified. Despite the dissolution of self-same-identity that the mystical state entails, it is not dismemberment that results.[5] The unity to which Irigaray refers is clearly not the wholeness of a self-sufficient subject with coherence and nothing missing. It is rather the wholeness of an experience with no lack because there is no ideal form to which the experience is referred.[6] The unity this wholeness entails is not the unity of a totalized self nor a fusion without differentiation but the unity of an experience that is immanent and not referred to anything else. In a touching open to the imperceptible sensible, one is opened out onto what surrounds one in a form of differentiation that makes no reference to ideals or the recognizable forms of past experiences. Thus, nothing can be missing from the experience, and the experience is not fragmented but extends out onto what comes next and next and next without grid or system of reference.

Everything is relentlessly immediate in this marriage of the unknowable, which can never be evaded once it has been experienced. In a deeper unity than the still, already, speculative unity that underlies the sense of these wrenching contradictions. The bottom, the center, the most hidden, inner place, the heart of the crypt to which "God" alone descends when he has renounced modes and attributes. For this most secret virginity of the "soul" surrenders only to one who also freely offers the self in all its nakedness. This most private chamber opens only to one who is indebted to no possession for potency. It is wedded only in the abolition of all power, all having, all being, that is founded elsewhere and otherwise than in this embrace of fire whose end is past conception.

Each becomes the other in consumption, the nothing of the other in consummation. Each will not in fact have known the identity of the other, has thus lost self-identity except for a hint of an imprint that each keeps in order the better to intertwine in a union already, finally, at hand. Thus I am to you as you are to me, mine is yours and yours mine, I know you as you know me, you take pleasure with me as with you I take pleasure in the rejoicing of this reciprocal living — and identifying — together. In this cauldron of identification will melt, mingle, and melt again these reversing matrices of our last embraces. (S 196)

In this encounter, self-same-identity is lost, but one is not thereby rendered completely without form. Instead, one feels oneself out through contact with another. In this openness to the sensible transcendental that exceeds the perceptible and conceivable supporting self-same-identity, one is opened up to a transformative experience that is rejuvenating rather than annihilating. Irigaray's remark that the road the mystic will have to take in fleeing the logic that has framed her is "not nothing" (193) speaks to the layers of representations that constitute the ideal form she attempts to resemble and provide the basis for her unity. In fleeing this logic, the mystic achieves an awareness informed by what lies beyond all representations of a deeper unity which takes no stable form as its reference.

In her later work Irigaray refers to the horizon of one's gender as one's transcendental reference that helps to give one a past, present, and future. But in the case of the feminine divine, this horizon is the horizon of a sensible transcendental and entails receptive encounter with what nourishes the familiar forms of conscious awareness and yet always exceeds them — the imperceptible and inconceivable at the limits of the perceptible and conceivable.[7] In opening up to this touch, one dissolves one's perceptions and one's self-same-identity, but in deference to an immanent transcendental that leads one out onto what is contiguous with that conscious experience. Irigaray claims that such contact will not place one in the abyss of dismemberment and fusional regression, but instead will open one out onto the unknown and the inconceivable in the context of differentiated contact. Thus, by attending more closely to corporeal experience rather than leaving it behind in order to spin out metaphysical fantasies in abstraction from the sensual, one grounds a perception that goes back to one's roots in life. That is, one attempts to attend to the limits of perceptual awareness as well as the limits of conceptual thought, and in the gap between the two find the point of contact that will make possible new formations of both.[8]

What if matter had always, already, had a part but was yet invisible, beyond the senses, moving in ways alien to any fixed reflection. What if everything were already so intimately specularized that even in the depths of the abyss of the "soul" a mirror awaited her reflection and her light. Thus I have become your image in this nothingness that I am, and you gaze upon mine in your absence of being. This silvering at the back of the mirror might, at least, retain *the being* (l'être) — which we have been perhaps and which perhaps we will be again — though our mirage has failed at present or has been covered over by alien speculations. A living mirror, thus, am I (to) your resemblance as you are mine. We are both singular and plural, one and ones, provided that nothing tarnishes the mirrors that fuse in the purity of their exchange.

Provided that one, furthermore, does not exceed the other in size and quality. For then the other would be absorbed in the One (as) to infinity. (S 197)

The notion of a living mirror invokes a different kind of specularization than the masculine specularization from the feminine other. Whereas matter's active role is denied in masculine specularization, a living mirror invokes participatory creation. There is no sexual division of creative labor into active and passive, subject and object. Instead, two transmuting subjects mutually engender each other in living contact with a world in which they are immersed. The sensuous immediacy of this encounter is not the immediacy of a metaphysical present, but the immediacy of an encounter in which old perceptions and conceptions melt away and each subject recreates herself and what surrounds her through a nuanced dance of collaborative response. This encounter cannot be spoken; it may perhaps be inarticulately hinted at. But the mystic who would attend to such an encounter is nonetheless listening to the hints and echoes of something real, something at the limit of the perceptible and the conceivable.

Harmonizing Corporeal and Conceptual Logics

Irigaray's characterization of a sexual division of labor suggests the formation of distinct logics appropriate to the distinct functions of two forms of cultural practice. We could say that the undersymbolized practices associated with the body are informed by corporeal logics and the practices associated with the mind are informed by conceptual logics, both of which can vary in keeping with specific cultural and historical contexts. The latter has clearly been more available to analytic scrutiny and elaboration than the former. Irigaray's conception of the feminine as a category of excess for contemporary forms of representation renders any clear bifurcation of the two logics highly problematic; as the "feminine" is symbolized, it becomes informed by conceptual logics even as it transforms "masculine" labor practices in the process. It is useful shorthand, however, for indicating a pervasive bifurcation in the development of two kinds of logics produced by the relative lack of integration between two kinds of labor. In what follows I use the two terms to indicate the benefits of symbolizing corporeal logics, thereby facilitating integration of cultural practices that have tended to evolve in relative isolation from one another.[9]

Habits of the body allow one to form a determinate morphology and a corporeal logic that organize sensuous happenings. Habitual patternings can provide reference points for the repetition of sensation by grouping sensations according to basic corporeal categories. These categories can then become more or less loosely correlated with the categories of conceptual thought. Corporeal and conceptual logics can become more removed from each other — but only at the cost of a sense of alienation from one's own body. Corporeal boundaries can be transformed just as conceptual boundaries can be transformed. Unfortunately, one can lose the flexibility of the possibility of both transformations: insofar as one adheres to rigid conceptual categories, one can become ever more distanced from the corporeal boundaries that originally inspired them; insofar as one adheres to corporeal boundaries, one can remain stuck in conventional perceptual structures. Corporeal logic as well as conceptual logic is contiguous to a region that surpasses both logics. Irigaray refers to contact with this region with her notion of the sensible transcendental. This region does not constitute a space unto itself — either transcending us or internal to us (for example, in a region of the unconscious) — but is immanent to our lived experience. That is, it is an "outside" that is integral to the "inside" of our actual experience in the sense that it is implicit in the logics of our experience; without it we would have no experience at all. It is this region, the horizon of the sensible transcendental, that provides the impetus for conceptual as well as corporeal forms of organization.

Irigaray encourages us to pay attention to what may lie beyond and yet inform the perceivable. This receptivity will have implications for any attempt to maintain a self-same-identity as well as for any corporeal boundaries we may already have established. But Irigaray's work also suggests that such receptivity need not be chaotic. Because it is premised on boundaries already established, and because it entails a kind of responsiveness to what impinges on those boundaries, new boundaries can form that are a felt response to something "real" — that which impinges on the boundaries we have already formed. It is by remaining anchored in corporeal logic that we can reshape that logic rather than simply leave it — and all basis for coherent subjectivity — behind. Insofar as conceptual logic takes its impetus from corporeal logic, Irigaray implies, it is based on "reality"; insofar as conceptual logic perpetuates a dream and an illusion of nonembodiment in order to perpetuate its self-identity, it refuses to attend to the nuances of the impetus of "real" or "natural" forces that could rejuvenate it. Although corporeal logic is less able to detach itself from these larger "natural" processes, it can stifle itself and entomb the body through a preference for the repetition of familiar sensations and perceptions. The "real" is unrepeatable. The mystic can free herself from both corporeal and conceptual logics in order to allow this "real" to impinge anew in ways that will prompt corporeal as well as conceptual transformation. This process — as opposed to merely conceptual change — constitutes a transformation not only of the mind but of the body as well.

Prior to any corporeal or conceptual ideal to which she might refer herself, the feminine other feels herself through contiguity with herself and her surroundings. To be "(the/a) woman is already to feel oneself before anything else has specifically intervened" (S 230). Her limits are experienced through localization in space and time. Although her corporeal boundaries are undecidable and not nearly as definitive as her conceptual self would like to believe, the sensual limits she can feel in open receptivity to a world that is always impinging on and permeating her allow for ever-changing points of contact. Although the line dividing inside and outside becomes undecidable when we take into account the full receptivity of embodied contact with a world without reference to an ideal corporeal shape, these points of contact are still felt points of intensity that speak of the encounters of matter that is engaged in a process of participatory engenderment. The forms that emerge from this contact are nonrepeatable. They emerge only to fade away in the wake of new forms. But they are real nonetheless. They hint of elements coming together only to fall apart from one another in order to come together again in inconceivable formations that never adhere to any regular pattern. Insofar as a subject allows her corporeal and conceptual logics to be superseded by what can never repeat, that subject experiences the influx of novel sensation that cannot be "perceived" in the conventional sense of the word, but that speaks to the beyond of what can never be articulated in conscious experience (230–31).

Given the gendered division of labor that allots the responsibility for corporeal logic to the feminine and responsibility for conceptual logic to the masculine, and given the privileging of the masculine and the greater emphasis on symbolization of conceptual logic with its specular ruses, conceptual logic is more likely to be defended against the unknowability of the sensible transcendental. The masculine defense against self-dissolution and the void of unrepeatable matter is the displacement of corporeal logic onto the feminine other and the appeal to a masculine symbolic system that distances ideals into a transcendental noncorporeal beyond removed from sensuous matter and the material disintegration of mortality. The feminine other's defense against self-dissolution is to attach herself to masculine subjectivity. Attention to conceptual logic alone is apt to perpetuate masculine specularity, with its fear of touching on the unknown that would transform conscious experience. Since conscious experience is inevitably conceptual (save, perhaps, in certain mystical states), heightened attention to corporeal logic is apt to bring both corporeal and conceptual logic to its point of contradiction, and so force the gap between the two that would allow both to be transformed through an influx of that which provides the motivating impetus for both. Because we are speaking subjects who need self-same-identities, we are wedded to conceptual logic. This logic assumes a corporeal logic that will maintain us as coherent bodies. Insofar as we attend to corporeal logic, we put into question not only the shape of our bodies but our conceptual selves as well.

Irigaray's conception of a successful psychoanalytic cure indicates how psychoanalysis can constitute an opportunity for integrating words and symbolization with sensation and perception. For Irigaray, concepts and perception can become out of balance; corporeal logic and conceptual logic can fall out of synchronicity, thus upsetting an individual's relationship with the world. For Irigaray, it is the task of psychoanalysis to harmonize concepts and perceptions and thus bring mind and body into a balanced whole.

A successful analysis would be the one that successfully restores the balance and the harmony of the perceptional economy. Pathology can often be explained by the fact that certain past events and affects are crystallized in the present of the subject, and their energy is no longer available. These residues must be brought to the patient's perception, they must be made fluid again, put in perspective so that creativity can again work freely. This means, for example, that we need to give back to each sense the objective and subjective speeds of its current perceptions and facilitate harmony between these and the past, present, and future history of the subject. (S&G 156)

A psychoanalysis that does not respect corporeal logic is a failed analysis as far as Irigaray is concerned. As she puts it, "If the patient runs the risk of turning into an idiot through psychoanalysis, it is as a result of sense deprivation and the spiritual dearth that results from the word's inadequacy vis-à-vis sensation and perception" (S&G 154). Experience goes beyond the conscious perceptions of the subject; imperceptible becomings are involved which then emerge in conscious awareness in a particular form owing to the organizing structures of the subject. One's perceptual economy can become unbalanced if one disallows certain configurations of perception that may allow energy to run more freely. Because certain feasible organizations of perceptual experience are disallowed in past experiences, these become disallowed in present experiences, thus closing out certain patternings. If these restrictions become too severe, the individual is left with an increasingly restricted range of conscious experience. Although some restriction of the perceptual possibilities open to the embodied subject must occur for the subject to be able to experience anything at all, this restriction can become narrowed to the point of a sterile repetition of past patternings that allows nothing new to enter. In this eventuality, the individual has become calcified to the point of a kind of living death.[10] The problem for Irigaray is how to allow an openness to what is new in experience without completely dissolving all possibility for subjectivity. Irigaray emphasizes the creative power needed for developing new forms of organization of conscious experience in response to the infinite array of sense stimuli; both "receptive affect or sensoriness" and "imagination as synthetic faculty" (S&G 163) are necessary in order to achieve some level of coherence as a self.

I feel that subjective liberation and development mandate a method that is still ill defined because we lack an imagination capable of creating the sex, the flesh. To fill that lack, we need to put perception and creation into relation with art, with aesthetic perspectives, forms, colors, and especially with the play of contrasts.

We need to have two in each sex, not one sex divided between two. Perception and creation differ from one gender to the other. When we divide perception and creation between the two genders we impoverish both and destroy the identity of each. This false division ends up by changing human faculties: perception becomes sensation and the imagination becomes an imaginary that correponds to a *pathos* of the senses. (S&G 163)

The sexual division of labor which relegates reproduction of bodies to feminine others and symbolic production to masculine subjects creates a strange bifurcation between body and mind. Symbolic production becomes cut off from the realm of sense experience; imagination develops its symbols in a transcendent realm only erratically answerable to the corporeal realm. Thus, cultural symbolism of various forms, like religious symbolism, does not attend to the fleshly aspects of our existence in all its rich detail. In this situation we fail to develop a full range of symbols for the corporeal aspects of living, and the symbolic systems we have developed fail to integrate important aspects of our experience into conscious awareness.

For Irigaray, it is reference to a transcendental ideal removed from the sensual realm of matter (rather than receptivity to the sensible transcendental) that produces a gap in our experience that can either alienate us into a reified realm or plunge us into regressive fusion. The sensible transcendental that "comes into being through us" opens us up to imperceptible differentiations made through mutually engendering interaction among the various specificities of material processes. It thus entails neither fragmentation nor immersion into a nondifferentiated abyss.

According to Freud, the founding act of society is the murder of the father. It is the desire to murder the father in order to take the father's place vis-à-vis the mother that fuels the oedipal structure of subjectivity. Irigaray claims that in the oedipal ambivalence toward the father with whom the masculine subject would identify and whom he would murder so that he can replace him is already a displacement of "an even more ancient murder, that of the woman-mother" (S&G 11). The ambivalence aimed at the father is "projected retroactively upon the primitive relation to the mother's body." Partial drives "seem to refer especially to the body that brought us *whole* into the world" (13). For Irigaray, it is the umbilical cord that marks the primal link to the mother and one's initial birth. The phallus comes after the umbilical cord: "All that had taken place within an originary womb, the first nourishing earth, first waters, first sheaths, first membranes in which the *whole* child was held, as well as the *whole* mother, through the mediation of her blood. According to a relationship that is obviously not symmetrical, mother and child are linked in a way that precedes all dissociations, all tearing of their bodies into pieces" (14). Unless we find an image for representing the placenta, we are "constantly in danger of retreating into the original matrix, of seeking refuge in any open body, and forever nestling into the body of other women" (15).[11]

In the womb one is completely surrounded by an environment that is in fundamental synchrony with the needs of the fetus. In thinking about this space, one can conceive of it as a home, as a space in which one's connectedness with one's surroundings is not antithetical to one's own survival as a separate self. It is an environment meant to nourish, and also meant eventually to expel the fetus into a place of separateness. In this sense it presents a kind of originary paradigm and model for our relationship to the world and to human others. Contemplating our own origins in a natural environment that nourished us and initiated separation is a rich source for conceiving our relationship to the world. The symbolization of intrauterine experience could provide a paradigm for retroactively conceiving of the interpenetration of self and other in which neither is dismembered and in which the integrity of each with respect to one's later identifications is preserved.

The contemporary cultural imaginary construes the womb as a nostalgic place in which the environment is centered on the fetus in a way that is analogous to the way in which masculine subjects continue to represent the world. The maternal-feminine as feminine other surrounds, encompasses, and supports one in a home that is designed specifically to nourish the fetus. Irigaray points out that the fetus does not encounter the mother during pregnancy and that the special relationship of fetus and womb is destroyed in the expulsion of the infant into the world.

Within her womb, an amnion and a placenta, a whole world with its layers, its circuits, its vessels, it nourishing pathways, etc., a whole world of invisible relations that adheres to her womb, that takes place in her womb, that gives him pain and gives her pain when the time comes for her to push him out and be delivered. But this world is not to be confused with her. It is destroyed forever at birth and it is impossible ever to return to it. All kinds of veils may claim to take its place, seek to repeat it, but there can be no return to that first dwelling place.

In fact she was never there, except in that ceaseless transfusion of life that passed from her to him, by a hollow cord. She offers the possibility of entry into presence but has no place in it. No encounter is possible with her during the pregnancy.

The son, obviously, always wants to go back there. And, if he can't, doesn't he tear away bit by bit the whole membrane that separated him from her but created an inconceivable nearness that he can never cease to mourn? She is so close, invisibly penetrating him, and she remains an unmasterable presence, if such a word can still be used in this way for a relationship in which she flows into him and for him, without face or form. (S&G 33)[12]

The world of the mother cannot be inferred or extrapolated from the sense experience of the fetus or infant. Whatever the mother experiences is not accessible through a mere reversal of what the fetus or infant experiences. The other who provides the all-encompassing space of the womb is beyond the infant. She is radically other to the infant without being, for all that, completely transcendent. The other of sexual difference is not the maternal-feminine, the container or place that provides one with an origin; it is the other who has a place in her own right. Immersion in this other is so complete that one can neither escape the all-encompassing presence of the other nor separate oneself from that other. In addition, any sense of one's own existence is predicated on the living response of this other. She provides the amorphous grounds of the subject and yet feels and responds to that subject from a place of her own — a strange place of envelopment and mucous contact. Her relationship to the fetus is creative and yet neither active nor passive; sensations of pregnancy involve tactility, but not the tactility of an active touching or being touched. Instead, it is the kind of touching of two lips, or of the hands in prayer.

Since in the contemporary cultural imaginary the feminine represents a veiled desire for the creative space of the original matrix, and since there is no adequate symbolization of the relationship of human subjects to their origins in this matrix, this space becomes a space of undifferentiated fusion. Instead of representing the creative forces at work as coming from multiple points at once, undifferentiated fusion — in which one is one with the maternal-feminine and in which the singularities and differences of mother and child are denied or lost — overwhelms any current claims to identity. Irigaray suggests that the womb was never a place of undifferentiated fusion but a place of a nonsymmetrical relationship among forces that could be distinguished, albeit differently from the personal distinctions we make based upon oedipal subjectivity. In veiling our fascination with this place and refusing to symbolize it, we lose opportunities for creating symbols deeply rooted in our own lived experience of body confusion with another which could open up new possibilities in the present. There are natural limits to each individual that are encountered in the encountering of material others in one's environment. It is precisely in those material limits to our own creativity where we run up against others and come into contact with a world that impinges on us and that shapes and informs us that we come to have any kind of self at all: "The problem is that when the father refuses to allow the mother her power of giving birth and seeks to be the sole creator, then according to our culture he superimposes upon our ancient world of flesh and blood a universe of language and symbols that has no roots in the flesh and drills a hole through the female womb and through the place of female identity" (S&G 16).

Phallic erection as the masculine version of the umbilical cord would represent the source of life.

If phallic erection respected the life of the mother — of the mother in every woman and of the woman in every mother — it would repeat the living bond to the mother. At the very place where there once had been the cord, then the breast, would in due time appear, for the man, the penis which reconnects, gives life, feeds and recenters the bodies. The penis evokes something of the life within the womb as it stiffens, touches, and spills out, passing beyond the skin and the will. As it softens and falls, it evokes the end, mourning, the ever open wound. Men would be performing an act of anticipatory repetition, a return to the world that allows them to become sexual adults capable of eroticism and reciprocity in the flesh.

This return to the world is also necessary for women. It can take place only if woman is released from the archaic projections man lays upon her and if an autonomous and positive representation of female sexuality exists in the culture. (S&G 17)

For Irigaray, we need to refuse desubjectivized social roles. The role of the mother is dictated by a social order premised on a division of labor between the producing masculine and the reproducing feminine. In refusing to obliterate the mother's desire in deference to the law of the father, we give her the right to pleasure, sexual experience, passion, and speech. In translating the bond to the mother's body, we discover a language that can accompany bodily experience rather than erase it: "It is crucial that we keep our bodies even as we bring them out of silence and servitude. Historically we are the guardians of the flesh. We should not give up that role, but identify it as our own, by inviting men not to make us into body for their benefit, not to make us into guarantees that their body exists" (19).

The realm of the sensible transcendental opens up corporeal logic to what is beyond it and yet informs it. Because we all experience some kind of break from the sensuous realm of intrauterine experience, we all have the corporeal logic of a break between the inside and the outside of our mothers within our corporeal experience. Whether or not we consciously remember our births, we all went through a period of radical break between two kinds of environments that we can retroactively describe and imagine and that, from a psychoanalytic perspective, we can assume we have fantasized about in our early childhood musings upon our own origins. The question of origins is important because we base our present experience of ourselves on a corporeal and conceptual account of who we were, where we are now, and who we are going to be. Psychoanalytic theory has the advantage of attempting to describe this trajectory in the context of a corporeal account of ourselves. Who we are and who we are going to be is implicated with our material forms, our origins in the bodies of a maternal other, and our future as corporeal forms with a specific shape and our ultimate dematerialization in death. Desire, which seems to relate more immediately to our corporeal forms since we associate emotion and desire with the "irrational" and so, perhaps by default, embodied part of ourselves, speaks of our corporeal logic. Conceptual logic, by contrast, speaks to what we have been able to distance from the realm of the embodied.

Angelic Passages and the Feminine Divine

In "Belief Itself" Irigaray elaborates the theme of the angels who facilitate the passage between different realms. Various veils between the individual and that individual's first dwelling in the womb need to be put in place in order for the passages between the subject and the mother necessary for the representation of the subject to occur. But angels can transmit messages from beyond the horizon, beyond the ultimate veil.[13]

> Awesome call or recall that circulates so swiftly and lightly, an annunciation of more weight than any coded message, moving to and fro between the first and last dwellings that are withheld from present visibility or readability, to be deciphered only in the next world. From beyond the angel returns with inaudible or unheard of words in the here and now. Like an inscription written in invisible ink on a fragment of the body, skin, membrane, veil, colorless and unreadable until it interacts with the right substance, the matching body.
>
> We have to search back very far to find it, assuming it (*ça*) can be found, far beyond and deep within the language, in its first bed or nest or cradle of beliefs. There, always undecipherable and undeciphered, unless one passes-passes back through God and his angels, bent and folded up within every message and every code, forming the basis for every potential inscription, is this *veil*, through which there once took place and perhaps will again take place the sympathy between two bodies capable of mutually decoding one another. (S&G 36)

The message the angels transmit is one that has "more weight" than a coded message. It moves between the first dwelling of the womb prior to all personal identity or subjectification on either a corporeal or a conceptual level and the last dwelling of death, in which the individual's subjectivity once more dissolves into complete interpenetration with the rest of the world. The angel thus brings messages of the imperceptible. And this message can be received only by the body prepared to hear it. The realm of the imperceptible evoked here is one with which we are or can be in contact through the passage of angels. It is always there "beyond and deep within language," and although it can never be deciphered, it provides the basis for every "potential inscription." The veil provided by the womb — the place of first nourishment of the fetus in preparation for the separation of the infant from the mother's body — is the first veil between the elemental becomings of the potential subject and the rest of the world, the veil that will establish the possibility of further veils and passages that will enable a subject to emerge. Without such veils there could be no subject, no way of separating oneself from the world.

Masculine subjectivity as it is currently structured depends on obscuring this first veil. It is not such separation to which Irigaray objects but the form the separation takes. In reducing the mother to the intrauterine space of the womb, we not only deny her a presence as a subject in her own right (since this would destroy our illusion of controling our first dwelling space), but also provide ourselves with the further illusion that this space is readily available to us again through contact with feminine substitutes for the mother.

The main problem with this scenario is that it deprives us of an opportunity that would open us out onto the realm of the sensible transcendental. The angels that pass messages to us from beyond can also open us up here-right-now to possibilities for the same kind of sympathy between two bodies capable of mutually decoding each other that occurred in the harmonious and nourishing interaction in the womb. This interaction was not informed by the subjectivity of the mother any more than it was by the subjectivity of the child-to-be. It occurred at a level beyond personal identity and the reduction of elemental forces to the corporeal and conceptual schemas that stabilize recognizable social subjects. But, Irigaray's analysis suggests, it is this level of material interaction that informs whatever follows. And it is to this imperceptible realm of elemental becoming that we need to return if we are to revitalize ourselves and our words. Although the relationship between mother and fetus is nonsymmetrical, the level of material interaction that permeates the perceivable and thinkable realm of our conscious interactions is always there and available to us if only we care to listen to the angels as they mediate the passages between the here and the beyond (S&G 36–37).

Mediation takes place, according to Irigaray, in "every operation of language and representation." This "almost undecipherable mediation" involves "skin and membrane that can hardly be perceived, almost transparent whiteness," and evokes that "first dwelling place in her" which links "the lowest earth and the highest heaven" (S&G 38–39).

But the angel mediates by keeping space open and marking the trail from the oldest of days to the farthest future of the world. Serving as active memory, even if it remains unconscious, this mediation is turned by the diabolical will to reproduce the relation to light into an inscription that makes the rules, or at times into a writing that hides the source.

There's only one chance: the angel goes before the devil. He takes place earlier. If one can manage to clear a way past the devil's obstructive workings, sometimes one comes upon this awesome destiny, this daunting encounter. Otherwise, the whole stage is taken over by the devil, the devils, who turn everything upside down to make the leap and make us leap into dark, hidden, sulfurous beyond. (40–41)

Capturing angels and domesticating them brings on a "diabolic paralysis that freezes movements and words" (42). It is to take something that "has always flowed uncontained" into skeletons and death masks. If we want to find a home for the angels, we need to rebuild the whole scene of representation. The angels that provide passage to the beyond also provide "the advent of flesh itself, which in its most airy, subtle rapture might go beyond or before a certain sexual difference, once that difference has first been respected and fulfilled" (45). The angels that transmit messages from the imperceptible can spiritualize the flesh if we attend to their messages. Irigaray, throughout her later work, insists that the spiritualization of the flesh must come through an acknowledgment of sexual difference — the recognition that there are two genders, and the creation of symbolic means for each gender to achieve its own perfection. This is necessary so that feminine and masculine subjects can come together into a couple and create a relationship premised on more than procreation. A loving relation between two differently gendered subjects could create more than a child; it could foster the spiritualized becoming of both.[14] This becoming would not situate itself in a transcendent realm removed from material becoming, but would instead be the becoming-spiritual of embodiment. Although Irigaray does not here call this spiritualization of the flesh the sensible transcendental, we can see how the angels that bring messages of the imperceptible beyond bring us to a heightened awareness of a sensibility that unfolds into an infinite expanse of always material becomings.

Irigaray's sensible transcendental evokes something "buried beneath logic and indeed beneath all existing language" (S&G 52) that yet inspires language. Trusting in this beyond brings on a crazy speech that breaks with social coding and the rules of logic in order to return to that beyond for inspiration. Just as investigation of the womb reveals itself to be the first veil that makes possible the passage from complete immersion in a world from which there is no separation to the separation necessary to subjectivity, so does poetic language hint at a nonlogical, nonrepresentable beyond which yet nourishes the language that allows for a stable representation of things. Irigaray prioritizes touch as a sense that can hint at the sensible transcendental and this divine beyond. This emphasis brings us back to our own bodies in a very personal way. Touching upon the world brings into awareness not just the world's proximity but the world's proximity to us. It leaves us no room for situating ourselves at one step removed, and it confronts us with a form of participation in which we are no longer clearly the agent of what transpires (59).

Horizon of Gender

Continual becoming extends into an infinite space and time without closure. Lacking some guideline, some horizon to which she can refer her becoming, the feminine other is vulnerable to the guidelines dictated by others. Then this becoming is no longer her own but subordinated to the becoming of another. Irigaray suggests that this is the case in contemporary culture with its privileging of masculine subjectivity. Forming a relationship with a "horizon of accomplishment" for one's gender allows one to protect one's own process of becoming and yet permit sharing with others. In other words, it allows one to retain some degree of individuation despite one's interrelationships with others. The masculine subject, in referring himself to a transcendent God, retains individuation by distancing himself from others via reference to a transcendent ideal. A feminine divine, on Irigaray's view, would not distance the subject from the world or others by referring her to a transcendent divine, but would instead symbolize a divine that is of this world and yet provides a reference point for the spiritualization of flesh in communion with others (S&G 63). Exploration of these dimensions of existence that refuse to reduce the feminine subject to the maternal-feminine would transform our understanding of traditionally feminine social functions and of the nature of the subjectivity involved in performing them. The shift in such understanding would have radical implications for the relationships involved within these dimensions as well. Thus, mother-child relationships, as well as the relationships of lovers, would have to change. Irigaray hints that a feminine divine would encourage another form of becoming.

Irigaray claims that Far Eastern traditions provide resources for fostering embodied awareness that could open Western culture out onto other possibilities in being and thinking. She is particularly interested in the notion that the body could be cultivated to become "both more spiritual and more carnal at the same time."[15] Through Eastern spiritual practices that lead one to an attentive awareness of movement, nutritional practices, and breathing and a respect for cosmic rhythms, "for the seasons and years as the calendar of the flesh . . . [,] the training of the senses for accurate, rewarding and concentrated perception," the body could be brought to a carnal and spiritual rebirth. This rebirth would go beyond a psychoanalytic regression to one's corporeal origins in relation to one's embodied parents. In such a rebirth "the body is thus no longer simply a body engendered by my parents; it is also the one I give back to myself." Through this corporeal training of sensibility, the individual would be able to integrate multiplicity and "remedy the fragmentation associated with singularity and the distraction of desiring all that is perceived, encountered, or produced" (ILTY 24). One could then cultivate the sensible to the point where it becomes spiritual energy rather than renounce it or sacrifice it to the universal.

Irigaray maintains that history should not conceal cosmic events and rhythms. We should respect the universe as "one of our most vital and cultural dimensions, as one of the macrocosmic keys to our microcosm" (S&G 60). This means that feminine others must explore their femininity rather than resist exploitative hierarchies only to promote the reversal of those hierarchies. Just as Irigaray appropriates language characterizing the elements to evoke a material level of existence of which we may not be aware, so does she turn to this language to evoke natural processes and the cosmos. Earth, air, fire, and water, universal rhythms, and cosmic time are words that evoke a macrocosm of which we are a part.[16] They are larger processes from which we, as microcosmic processes, are inseparable. Just as we need to acknowledge the material contribution of the womb to our own existence, so we need to acknowledge our environment as an ongoing part of our living. Insofar as we abstract ourselves out of this ever-present background of processes larger than ourselves, we not only delude ourselves into thinking that we are separable from them but also cut ourselves off from what nourishes us.

A training in perception, then, is important to spiritual development. Such an art of perception would pass from innerness to outerness. It would be a nuanced perception of the individual's experience of herself or himself as well as a "copulative" perception that comes together in a mutually transformative space with the perception of another. In the latter form of perception the subject does not attempt to dictate perception or define it solely from her or his own perspective in the attempt to maintain self-identity. Instead, she or he would allow the other to shape her or his experience through open receptiveness and response to the other without reference to the guidelines of a repeatable self. That is, the individual would not reduce her experiences to the already familiar, already established boundaries of her corporeal and conceptual selves but would instead allow those boundaries to be transformed. This kind of process would engender rejuvenating transformations of the self in keeping with the vivid sensations of open and unrepeatable contact with the world. Although such contact holds risks for human identity — the feminine risk of vulnerability to exploitative subjects as well as the risk of complete loss of self — Irigaray is suggesting that the anchor of self-same-identity is not the only possible guideline for human identity. Her alternative is the guideline of mutually nurturing self/other. One does not respond to absolutely everything in one's environment without discrimination, but one can create copulative spaces — for example, within the space of the couple — in which one can openly receive and engender rejuvenating transformation with a loving other.

For a dialectic of the couple to occur, we need an art of perception that cannot be reduced either to a pure innerness or a pure outerness but passes ceaselessly from one to the other. This art requires that concrete perception be detailed and attentive, a perception that as autoaffection is individual, is copulative as the privileged space of heteroaffection, and finally is collective. This training in perception requires a time frame that passes not through destruction or sublation but through heeding and knowing a culture of the senses as such. Finally we achieve access to progressive levels of intensity and to a contemplation of nature in itself, of itself and of the other, which philosophy has disregarded as a stage in spiritual development and fulfillment. (S&G 144)

In the next chapter I turn to Irigaray's strategies for "shattering mirrors." She continues the project of providing symbolic support for feminine subjectivity by further developing concepts of mutual engenderment. I explore her refiguration of Hegelian negativity and intersubjective communication in order to elaborate further the differentiating contact of subjects who can creatively encounter one another as living mirrors.

4
Shattering Mirrors

Mirrors, Rights, and Cultural Change

Irigaray is very sensitive to the difficulties of a touch in which sub-ject-object distinctions break down. If one is not structured according to masculine subjectivity, one is in danger of having no subjectivity at all. The masculine subject distinguishes himself by displacing corporeal and conceptual boundary confusion onto feminine others who reflect him back to himself as identical. This structure, according to Irigaray, is fur-ther supported with reference to a transcendent realm of God or ideas that is safely beyond the realm of corporeal confusion. For the one who has tra-ditionally played the role of feminine other, what form of subjectivity could be available? The feminine other is immersed in the world. She does not have the same need for displacing corporeal and conceptual confusion; her traditional role has been to allow herself to be immersed in such confusion rather than maintain strategies for displacing it. And yet Irigaray has no desire to leave her in this space of confusion, this realm of the unconscious, where she is so vulnerable to the machinations of masculine subjectivity with the exploitation it entails. But how to invent another structure that can incorporate corporeal confusion without complete loss of identity? Irigaray's answer is to turn to symbolization. Just as the masculine subject's subjectivity has symbolic reference points to support him, so could symbolic reference points be created for another way of being. Irigaray's notions of the sensible transcendental and a feminine divine are designed to fulfill this kind of symbolic function.

Because women have traditionally played a different role in the cultural schema from which Irigaray works, they form a distinct gender. Turning women into men would not just be a tragic loss of an alternative possibility in subjectivity, according to Irigaray, but would ultimately be impossible, since the feminine other is required for masculine subjectivity to work. Given the impracticality of asking a culture simply to abandon masculine subjectivity — especially with no viable alternative available — Irigaray insists that we need to acknowledge two genders and work on providing the hitherto impoverished gender with the symbolic support it needs to become more than the counterpart of masculinity. If the feminine other were given the support of a gender in its own right, then feminine subjectivity could fully emerge, an alternative to masculine subjectivity would be available, and the whole cultural imaginary would shift so dramatically that it is impossible to say in advance what kind of subjects we would be. Although Irigaray makes it clear that she thinks women have a crucial role to play in cultural rejuvenation, this is by no means an automatic contribution. She believes that there are specific dangers to women's attempts to establish their subjectivity in relation to one another. In addition, she believes that it is through interaction between two different genders that the most radical cultural transformations can be brought about. Irigaray is quite critical of what she calls "between-women sociality" (ILTY 3). She cautions against the dangers of "a genealogical division of roles that side-steps the labor of the negative" among women (4). Women need to learn to mediate, and they need symbolic support for such mediation. Otherwise they will project their own contradictions onto other women and avoid real debate. Women need to be awakened to the identity specific to them and to the rights and responsibilities that correspond to their gender identity: "Immediacy is their traditional task — associated wih a purely abstract duty — but it places them back under the spiritual authority of men. And so to grant a woman what she wants without teaching her the detour of mediation boils down to behaving like a patriarch, against her interests" (5).

Although Irigaray advocates creating a genealogy of women, creating a women's culture, and fostering positive images of mother-daughter relations, a feminist agenda that refuses to look at women's relations to men seems to be, on Irigaray's view, as limited as a masculinist agenda that refuses to recognize feminine subjectivity. It is the relationship between the two genders and ways of fostering recognition between the two that constitute the focal point of Irigaray's later work. Irigaray is most interested in the transformation that would emerge from a genuine encounter between two genders. According to her, it is only then that engendering would have to take different forms because it is only then that masculine subjectivity could no longer carry out its ruse of self-sufficiency and femininity could no longer reduce itself to unconsciousness. In a genuine encounter between the two genders, both genders would have to transform and contemporary structures of subjectivity would have to change.

Irigaray's criticism of contemporary feminism needs to be read in the context of her own disappointment at the way her attempts to work with men to bridge the gender gap were greeted by feminists who thought she had betrayed their cause.[1] Still, it is surprising that she does not also acknowledge the many steps that may need to be taken in order to bring about the kind of cultural transformation she looks for. It is not clear, for example, how one is supposed to implement the kinds of genealogies among women she advocates before these genealogies are created in spaces free of masculine intervention. Also, her own program for new values seems impoverished. She advocates putting up public pictures of mothers and daughters to counter negative publicity surrounding this relationship, and she strongly advocates implementing laws that acknowledge sexual difference. Rights should be for gendered subjects, she insists, and not some quasi-neutral subject which veils a masculine norm. But she does not say much about the problems and the difficulties of creating such sexually differentiated legislation. In her later work she has attempted to be practical and programmatic; it is this work, derived from public lectures addressed to actual women and men, that is most vulnerable to the charge of biological essentialism. In these lectures Irigaray delineates steps that we can take right now that can implement in quite practical ways the kind of acknowledgment of sexual difference that she advocates. The sometimes simplistic slogans of her public lectures, however, belie the subtlety of her engagement with philosophical texts.

I suggest that to take this later Irigaray seriously, we need to read her in the context of her earlier work, bearing in mind her own characterization of her project, for example in 1994, as that of finding a new language adequate to two different subjects without subordinating either subject to the other. If we do this, sexual difference cannot have the stereotypical nature that some of her claims sometimes suggest. Thus, I read her sloganistic suggestions as practical interventions that are meant for the specific historical situation in which we find ourselves rather than universal notions about sexual differences that are transhistorical. I believe that in giving a positive characterization of femininity and rights for a feminine gender to be protected in a sexually differentiated legal code, she is speaking to what she sees as a pervasive sexual division of labor in which women bear the brunt of "corporeal" labor while men bear the brunt of "cultural" labor. For Irigaray, both forms of labor are cultural. It is due only to a masculinist blind spot that one could think otherwise. Irigaray's direct descriptions of woman and man in these lectures renders my formulation of her views in terms of a masculine subject and feminine other somewhat unwieldy. Although in places I adopt the terminology of 'woman' and 'man' in the development of her views for the sake of consistency with quotes from her work, it is my belief that translating her views into a theoretical framework that posits a division of labor between active (masculine) subjects and supportive (feminine) others would illuminate other forms oppression can take as well. On my view, acknowledging sexual difference can be only one step toward acknowledging the multiple differences among human beings and the way these differences play out in the interdependent economies of subjectivity on the social field of contemporary cultures.

In *Thinking the Difference*, Irigaray advocates redefining rights appropriate to the two sexes and promulgating legislation protecting these rights. She considers the rights that are currently protected to be the rights of "non-existent neutral individuals" (TD xv), and she believes that women's rights such as the right to virginity of body and mind, to motherhood "free of civil or religious tutelage," and "women's right to their own specific culture" are rights that women should be working for. She also believes that a politics of sexual difference must involve cultural change on two levels: forms of symbolic mediation such as rules of speech and cultural representations of women and men must be changed in order to reflect acknowledgment of and respect for women, and civil law must be changed "to give both sexes their own identities as citizens" (xvi). I am sympathetic to the notion that legal codes can be detrimental to an ethical project of fostering respect for the specificity of individuals. I am skeptical, however, that encoding a feminine alternative to the "neutral" (masculine) code of current legal practices will produce the kinds of effects Irigaray seeks. In keeping with my own project of providing a model of subjectivity that would foster new nondualistic ways of living, thinking, and speaking, I emphasize Irigaray's project of symbolic transformation. Through her project of re-reading philosophical texts in order to reveal what in those texts has been appropriated from the feminine and to articulate a voice for that feminine, Irigaray attempts to symbolize a new kind of subjectivity. Symbolization of such alternatives can be a powerful tool for fostering the individual and collective experiments of those committed to overcoming oppressive cultural dualisms. Because these experiments go beyond intellectual argument by engaging us at the level of affective fantasies about ourselves and evoking the nonsignifying intensities of corporeal rhythms, they can affect us on more than the conceptul level and so provide us with opportunities for harmonizing the corporeal with the conceptual and creating new styles in ethical living.

Feminine Culture

Irigaray claims that man needs to deny his embodiment in order to maintain his separation from the matter that produced him (TD 17–18). Since our conception of human nature tends to take the masculine subject as its norm, what is called human nature "often means forgetting or ignoring our corporeal condition for the sake of some spiritual delusion or perversion" (18). Women, by contrast, provide another possibility.

> Woman's subjective identity is not at all the same as man's. She does not have to distance herself from her mother as he does — by a *yes* and especially a *no*, a *near* or a *far*, an *inside* opposed to an *outside* — to discover her sex. She is faced with another problem entirely. She must be able to identify with her mother as a woman to realize her own sexuality. She must be or become a woman like her mother and, at the same time, be able to differentiate herself from her. But her mother is the same as she. She cannot reduce or manipulate her as an *object* in the way a little boy or a man does. (TD 18)

Unlike the little boy with his *fort-da* game, the little girl — and the woman she becomes — has a directly intersubjective relationship with her mother (cf. Chapter 1). "Hers is more an *inter-subject* economy than the economy of subject-object relations" (TD 19). The opportunity this differing relationship to her mother provides cannot be fulfilled without the creation of symbolic support. A feminine economy, according to Irigaray, is crucial not only to the emergence of feminine subjects that can provide cultural alternatives to a masculine norm that has resulted in nuclear warfare and a devastated environment, but also for a nondestructive relationship between women and men (20).[2] The denial of constitutive others has important implications for women. In the gap left by any relationship to themselves, women cling all the more to whatever symbolic support is given to feminine subjectivity. Since motherhood is the primary form of feminine subjectivity in our culture, it is to motherhood that women often return. To save the earth "from total subjugation to male values (which often give priority to violence, power, money)" (112), Irigaray suggests that we need to restore respect and symbolic support for the mother-daughter relationship as well as feminine speech and virginity. There are certainly many women who resolve the conundrums presented by the problems of being the feminine other by taking up the position of "masculine" subjectivity. These women become as specular as men, denying their corporeality and their mothers and the constitutive work of the feminine others around them in the same way that men do. Given that women's traditional role has been to bear the brunt of reproductive labor, and given that masculine subjectivity has traditionally displaced corporeality onto the feminine other, women are closer to the broader processes within which we inevitably find ourselves and over which we have no control. If, as I suggested in "Harmonizing Corporeal and Conceptual Logics" in Chapter 3, corporeal logics are more attuned to the broader processes in which human life-processes participate, and if women are the keepers of the corporeal, then women could be said to be more attuned to the "natural" owing to their cultural position. It then makes sense to turn to women in order to speak to the inadequacy between corporeal and conceptual logic that has led to some of the contemporary difficulties in which we find ourselves: "We need regulation that is in keeping with natural rhythms; we need to cultivate this natural filiation, and not destroy it in order to impose upon it a split, dual nature of our bodies and our elemental environment. Women are affected more fatally by the break with cosmic equilibria. It is therefore up to them to say *no*" (26).

Irigaray's references to a natural, cosmic rhythm point to the broad range of background processes against which and within which human life plays out. That is, processes that always go beyond any human intervention into life, and any specific cultural form that human life may take, are always much larger and more complex than the human processes they encompass. As much as we may wish that we could put them at a distance or somehow establish our autonomy from them, it is within these larger processes over which we have no control that we live out our lives. Given Irigaray's views on the contemporary sexual division of labor, as well as her reticence about what could come from what would be an inevitable and radical transformation of both genders in the full emergence of feminine subjectivity, the kind of sexual difference with which we are currently familiar, and which Irigaray herself must characterize in her historically specific interventions, would have to change if her program for recognizing sexual difference were actually carried out. Whatever we may say about reproductive processes and how close they may bring us to life cycles of a more "natural" sort, this relationship is still culturally mediated. If women's reproductive cycles bring them "closer to nature," it is within the specific cultural situation in which we find ourselves. There is nothing to militate particularly against men being equally close to such rhythms through full acknowledgment of their own corporeality and mortality. For Irigaray, the project of equalizing opportunities so that women are equally able to become masculine subjects would constitute a huge loss of an important cultural resource that might provide a way out of a stultifying and life-threatening situation for us all (TD 39–40).

One of the most important things that would be lost in the equalizing of women and men would be what Irigaray terms the "culture" of the sexual subject: "Becoming a man seems to correspond to distancing oneself from oneself, from one's concrete, living environment, entering into a coded universe that more or less accurately duplicates reality, acquiring the skills to compete, wage war, etc." (TD 48). This process leads to an economy of exchange in which self-identical subjects quantify the objects they exchange according to rules of equivalence. Objects — women, goods, and money — can then be passed from one subject to the next without endangering the identities of the subjects engaged in the exchange. Relations are thus maintained through the fluid circulation of various kinds of objects without threatening either the stability of social subjects or the structures through which those subjects are related. To avoid an alienating economy in which people become identified with their property and relationships come to be premised on how much one owns, we need to introduce feminine subjectivity with its alternative model for relationship with others.

Civil society, in our time, requires public relationships to be places of reciprocity between individuals. It is not satisfactory that the only civil mediator should be money. It is not satisfactory that relations between persons should be incessantly conflictual and made hierarchical by powers associated with property ownership rather than people's qualities and experience. This undemocratic social structure, which is necessarily individualistic and conflictual, has its origins in the relations between the sexes. (TD 86)

In order to avoid the further impoverishment of culture to the sad state of a masculinist order which prioritizes money and economic exchange over genuine communication, as well as to empower women who are unable or unwilling to take up positions of "equal" power, Irigaray proposes reevaluating the right to sexual identity and insists that sexual identity be recognized as part of civil identity. In *I Love to You*, Irigaray elaborates a form of Hegelian recognition that would go beyond the civil recognition of masculine subjects in the public realm, and gives a critical rereading of Hegel's notion of negativity designed to aid in the reconceptualization of civil identity.[3] According to her rereading of Hegel's notion of recognition, each subject would acknowledge her or his limits in concrete encounter with another. Here she evokes a situation of energetic interaction in which neither subject is overwhelmed by the other or reduced to the schema of the other, but in which a generative encounter occurs in the realm of sensibility itself. Returning "to ourselves as living beings who are engendered and not fabricated" (ILTY 14) involves exploring "the resources of the natural universe with which the cultivation of sensibility opens up more subtle and gratifying exchanges" (13).[4] In the next section we will see how Irigaray connects an acknowledgment of sexual difference with this process.

Negativity

On Irigaray's critical rereading of Hegelian negativity, the negative can never be overcome in the final sublation of Absolute Spirit; the material flux of life will never achieve the rational form of a completely articulated concept. The negative in sexual difference that Irigaray has in mind would involve accepting the limits of gender and recognizing the irreducibility of the other. It would thus facilitate a cultivation of the sexed dimension without ever providing it with closure. Once the illusion that enables masculine subjects to displace their corporeality onto the feminine other was disabled through recognition of the feminine role in masculine subjectivity, negativity would operate differently.[5] Each would have to recognize her or his own limits. For the masculine subject to accomplish the labor of the negative, he would need to take into account the limit inscribed in nature: he cannot appropriate the natural in order to proclaim that he is the whole. Neither the feminine other nor the masculine subject can accomplish the whole in herself or himself. Sensibility is neither as simple nor as unitary as people think. Although tradition usually attributes sensibility to a single subject, it is often divided between two subjects (ILTY 56–57).

Irigaray cautions against promoting a dream of dissolving identity. We need to construct a positive alterity between feminine and masculine subjects. To evade this task in a dream of identity-dissolution would leave us vulnerable to the masculine economy that would reduce individuals to their relationships vis-à-vis property. It would relinquish the potential in femininity for developing another way of being and relating to others, and it would abandon both masculine subjects and feminine others to a gender hierarchy that labels the latter as inferior. She claims that a revised Hegelian notion of recognition could facilitate our attempts at overcoming the hierarchical domination between the genders. In "You Who Will Never Be Mine" Irigaray elaborates her form of Hegelian recognition — one that would go beyond the civil recognition of masculine subjects in the public realm and would instead acknowledge sexual difference. This form of recognition would acknowledge the limits of the subject in her or his concrete encounter with an other. It would provide a new kind of model for intersubjective relations — one that moves from a subject/object dichotomy to a sharing between two subjects, neither of whom needs to exchange objects (ILTY 103). Through transformative encounter with the other, each one continually becomes in the ebb and flow of concrete contact. Because each respects the history and intentionality of the other, each cannot assimilate the other to her or his own history or intentions. This respect provides limits on one's own becoming, and these limits provide the material for further becomings. Insofar as this process anchors the subject in a natural reality that does not allow for transcendent flights of fantasy, each subject is forced to harmonize her or his corporeal and conceptual logics. Each one's words must find some adequation in the roots of language in corporeal experience, and corporeal experience must push its way into conceptual thought. It is in the fecund encounter of two embodied subects, neither of whom displaces her or his embodiment or effaces the other, that this kind of harmonizing, integrative process can occur. It is thus through the encounter of two genders that are different that Irigaray feels we might enable each gender to accomplish its specific identity in relation to individual and collective history. It is through a special kind of relationship in which one no longer appropriates all creative movement to oneself, but instead focuses on the creative movement provided by another, that one can come up against one's own limits and so anchor one's conceptual flights in a natural reality.

According to Irigaray, we live out our individual lives not as neuter individuals but as women and men, girls and boys. Upholding the rights of abstract citizens is not sufficient; since there are no neuter individuals, we need rights for real persons — that is, sexed persons. Despite certain exceptions and anomalies — the occasional hermaphrodite who may escape surgical correction and who refuses either gender designation — it is certainly the case that the vast majority of us designate ourselves and/or are designated as she or he rather than both at once or neither.[6] However one negotiates one's positioning vis-à-vis gendered pronouns, we cannot escape such negotiation. Human beings in our place and time are thus not able to escape taking up some sort of position vis-à-vis the question of gendered identity. Thus, the generic 'he' with its implication of a neutered individual who stands in for a human norm can only be a delusion. Whatever our race, class, religious affiliation, or cultural identity, we cannot fail to take up some sort of stance vis-à-vis our sex. For Irigaray, this renders sexual difference the most fundamental difference of all. It is precisely because there is no way to escape this differentiation that it provides the opportunity for escaping a regime of subjectivity that would erase all differentiation.

Insofar as we elaborate, rather than elide, sexual difference, we are opened out onto a way of thinking and being that refuses to elide difference in general. Because sexual difference is actually, in our culture, impossible to evade, despite the cultural ruses that would obliterate feminine specificity, it is the culturally specific opportunity we have for opening up human subjectivity to an open-ended infinity of differences. The alternative is the regime of masculine subjectivity with its emphasis on a logic of the same. In the Hegelian regime in which an abstract civil subject is interchangeable with any other subject, personal subjectivity is lost. Specificity is displaced onto a feminine other who has no identifiable subjectivity of her own. It is insofar as this schema is disrupted that the opportunity for a more personalized individuality emerges. Symbolization of sexual difference, a gendered horizon specific to two sexes rather than one, provides a means for further specification of all individuals as well as a personalized form of love that goes beyond the exchange of feminine others as objects to a space of genuine love and communication among truly differentiated subjects.

Irigaray accepts Hegel's definition of love as relevant to patriarchal cultures, but claims that Hegel himself was unable to "resolve the problem of the lack of spirit and ethics he observes" (ILTY 20). In the Hegelian scenario, love of woman for man is reduced to the duty of a servant to man while love of man for woman is reduced to a regression to natural immediacy. The woman's role as wife and mother is "a function of an abstract duty"; her universal tasks as wife and mother can be performed only if she renounces her singular desires and if her singularity is reduced to the natural immediacy attributed to her by men. The love of a woman for her husband and children is thus reduced to "a labor of the universal, in the sense that she has to love man and child without loving *this* man or *this* child" (21). A citizen is expected to renounce sexed singularity in order to realize the universal task of service to the community. In this context, love for one's wife grants one a permissible lapse into primitive fusion within the safety of family life.

This absence of two in the couple forces the intervention of other limits deriving from the labor of the negative on man's terms: death as the rallying place of sensible desires, the real or symbolic dissolution of the citizen in the community, and enslavement to property or capital.

This division of tasks between home and the public realm could not be sustained without depriving woman of a relationship to the singular in love and of the singularity necessary for her relationship to the universal. The home — the couple or family — should be a locus for the singular and universal for both sexes, as should the life of a citizen as well. This means that the order of cultural identity, not only natural identity, must exist within the couple, the family, and the State. (ILTY 23)

Irigaray would have all of us remain ourselves in our process of becoming. Each gender needs a model of such becoming that would enable us to accomplish our task of being a specific individual in corporeal as well as spiritual aspects of our being. Each gender needs to take responsibility for its own becoming rather than dividing the task of such becoming so that one gender can perpetrate the illusion of being whole unto itself. It is only the two genders together that represent the whole. Recognition of this fact involves "respecting natural reality as constitutive of the subject" (51) and can lead to a negative limit. Recognizing that one is sexed implies recognizing that one is not everything. Recognizing one's identity as gendered then allows one to enter the world of mediation in which one can recognize the existence of another gender. Sexual difference is "at one and the same time the most particular and the most universal model, a model in relation to which genealogy is a secondary, though necessary, paradigm" (52). For the full flowering of democracy to occur, negativity must play out in the mediation of each citizen in her or his singularity, and this can happen only when each woman and man is a full citizen from birth. Such citizenship would be protected by the state, and civil society would temper the authority of the family. Civil identity would then be related to one's natural identity as a woman or a man, and social models "organized in accordance with the reality of living persons" could then foster an exchange of energy that served the life and growth of all (55).

Owing to the sexual division of labor vis-à-vis corporeality and the sensible and to the differing relationships to genealogy and the divine, feminine others and masculine subjects experience corporeal morphology, religion, and genealogy differently. The "passivity" of feminine others is not simply that but a complication of any dichotomy of active/passive. The complication of such a dichotomy could lead to a different understanding of that relationship that would have important repercussions for our understanding of the subject-object relationship as well.

Woman's receptivity would not be restricted to her relation to man alone but would extend to the natural economy, especially the cosmic one, with which her equilibrium and growth are more closely associated. Her so-called passivity would not then be part of an active/passive pair of opposites but would signify a different economy, a different relation to nature and to the self that would amount to attentiveness and to *fidelity* rather than *passivity*. A matter, therefore, not of pure receptivity but of a movement of growth that never ultimately estranges itself from corporeal existence in a natural milieu. In which case, becoming is not cut off from life or its placing. It is not extrapolated from the living nor founded in a deadly character. It remains attentive to growth: physiological, spiritual, relational. In this way it masters nothing in a definitive fashion, and reason is no more than a measure, not an appropriation. As a measure, it is different for man and woman. Denying their difference(s) leads to the excess of the unmeasured. (ILTY 38–39)

It is due to Irigaray's sensitivity to the specular subject who appropriates the creativity of the other that she is so keen to ensure a form of subjectivity that is continually open to creative interaction with another. She suggests that it is only through coming up against the limits presented by the other that one can guard against the specular tendency to identify with the all. For Irigaray, any leap to identification with the all leads to a lack of attentiveness to present sensibility and thus an abstract conception of wholeness that leaves the corporeal behind. One's gender as a universal exists prior to oneself in one's singular embodiment of a gendered individual. Dialectical creation between two gendered individuals makes possible a new definition of values grounded in a natural reality. Insofar as I refer myself in my gendered singularity toward the horizon of my gender, I accomplish my gender by becoming with respect to something beyond me. This becoming takes place in the concrete encountering of myself with others in their singularity.

In coming up against my own limits through contact with what is not me, I am confronted with negativity. Because these limits are always shifting and defined in the singularity of unanticipatable encounters, I must always work and rework these limits. In doing so I refer my becomings to a horizon and am thus able to live my present out of a past into the future toward an infinite divine. Because the feminine form of this divine is a sensible transcendental, as the feminine other striving to achieve feminine subjectivity, I am not placed in some transcendent realm removed from the realm of the sensible. Instead, my becomings are referred to a horizon of infinitely extended sensible contiguity. Open receptivity to the other who is irreducibly other prevents me from too easily abstracting this realm of the sensible transcendental into a realm beyond the concrete specificity of my present becomings. It is only through the continual transformation brought on by these contacts with what is other to me that I continue to reform and refigure in direct confrontation with my own limits. It is precisely such limits that allow me to experience myself rather than simply posit myself as an abstraction. It is through such encounters with what is not me that I confront gaps in psychic coherence and bodily integrity and am able to engage in the creative labor of harmonizing corporeal and conceptual logics. If we consider Irigaray's rereading of negativity in the context of the multiple forms active subject–supportive other relations can take — in their less benign as well as more positive manifestations — we can apply this concept to other axes of difference as well.

Irigaray relates the encounter with the other to an ability to think. Insofar as one is plunged into the natural immediacy of someone who has not been forced to confront his limits, he has not defined his form in relationship to a reality that goes beyond him. It is a crucial fact of our existence, for Irigaray, that we are not self-made but engendered by two and born of another. We are thus irretrievably always in relationship to others. It is due to a patriarchal mythology that "becoming on the basis of *one* has been inscribed as origin" (ILTY 40). For Irigaray this means that the masculine subject has never really awoken to find himself in a world not of his own making. The masculine subject refers himself to a horizon of the divine that is all about him and the subject he is and wants to be. Western philosophy has supported this mastery of one's own form by reiterating the refusal of interaction with the other (45). It is important to break free from the masculine economy of subjectivity because the latter promotes delusions of self-sufficient wholeness, fosters the need for control over self-image, and alienates us from the roots of our experience in the natural world and the world of processes that extend beyond ourselves. Symbolizing the traditional role of the feminine other in a way that would give her voice and render her a subject in her own right could suggest a radically different kind of economy — one that moves beyond the need to repeat a highly controlled form of self-identity, the need for a feminine other for specular confirmation at the expense of that other's own subjectivity, and the need to exchange objects in order to confirm one's activity as subject. This alternative economy would make possible a subject that could both give and receive, be passive as well as active, and achieve an exchange that would be a communion and a genuine communication rather than the passing on of objects (45).

Defining a culture of the feminine would have important repercussions not simply for women but for the possibility of another kind of communication. A masculinist model of communication relies on a hierarchical transmission of established language and law. Such a model transmits dependency and risks enslavement to the past and is a model of information rather than communication. Irigaray proposes a second model, one that would open up the present to construct a future through reciprocal listening and "the exchange of a meaning between us here and now" (ILTY 46). Such a model would be horizontal rather than hierarchical, intersubjective rather than parental. In the next section I explore this alternative model of communication.

Feminine Language and Intersubjective Communication

Irigaray claims that her linguistic research shows an imbalance between the two genders that provides further indication of a sexual division of labor when it comes to the cultural production and reproduction of human subjects: "Men use *I*, women *you/the other*, but these *I* and *you* are situated within one single problematic where there are not two subjects but rather the workings of the incomplete economy of a single subject" (ILTY 65).[7] Although little boys tend to talk about possessing objects and then later possessing ideas and engaging in erotic, romantic, or social exploits with no thought to sharing between persons, little girls "still dream of accomplishing intersubjective communication." They want to share carnal and spiritual love with their lover, and they "dream of the communion of body and spirit, of exchanging words and social activities" (131). The cultural horizon that posits the masculine gender as the human norm manifests itself in myriad ways throughout culture. Religious symbolism is one important way, but another crucial way this imbalance is manifested is through language.

Irigaray seems to think that there is a time in early childhood when the little girl is able to have genuine intersubjective communication with her mother; because she does not have to objectify her mother as the boy does, she is able to share communication with another subject like herself. This form of communication is soon disrupted with the little girl's introduction into a patriarchal world in which the model for human subjectivity is masculine and where masculine subjectivity objectifies the mother in order to posit itself as an active subject. The masculine economy of subjectivity does not simply entail objectifying the mother so that the masculine subject can take up a position of possessing or not possessing cultural substitutes for the mother; this economy of objectification and exchange, an economy that exchanges things as well as women, is also permeated within the larger social context of capitalism by the value given to money.

The masculine economy of language, then, privileges a masculine subject who objectifies his mother and concerns himself with his position among a community of active subjects who exchange both things and feminine others. Irigaray finds that this situation is borne out in sexual differences between women and men with respect to their use of language. Women crave communication — the kind of intersubjective communication they once had with their mothers. But because the norm for subjectivity is masculine, women can no longer say "I" and "you" with a feminine subject in mind; thus their language becomes oriented toward "he" and "they," with "they" assumed to be generically masculine.[8] Because the mother has already been put into this situation, she "orders her daughter around and subjugates her just as she is ordered around by and subjugated in the cultural universe" (ILTY 76). Thus "the relation between two persons, which was, so to speak, co-natural to the feminine, becomes a process that has to be reconquered. Woman has to seek out the values of exchange and communication, as does man, but for different reasons. He has to overcome the priority he gives to the accumulation, possession, or at best the exchange of objects, while she must avoid the risks of hierarchy and submission, of fusion between persons, of losing her identity in the impersonality of *one*" (76). The Western tradition for the most part "represents living energy as sacrificed to spirit, to a truth assimilated to immutable ideals, beyond growth, beyond corporeality; celestial ideals imposed as models so that we all become alike — our sensible, natural and historical differences neutralized" (99). To regulate and cultivate energy between human beings, we need a language that facilitates intersubjective communication rather than one that simply transmits information.

Irigaray explains that the title of her book, *I Love to You*, invokes a strange use of grammar in order to indicate an address by a subject to another who does not take the other either for a direct object or for an indirect object by revolving around the other: "It is, rather, around myself that I have to revolve in order to maintain the *to you* thanks to the return to me. Not with my prey — you become mine — but with the intention of respecting my nature, my history, my intentionality, while also respecting yours" (ILTY 110). The masculine subject takes the feminine other as a direct object to be possessed. This renders him an active subject vis-à-vis a passive other who reflects him back to himself without contributing anything of her own to the relationship. Of course, owing to the displacement of his corporeality onto the feminine other, she seems to emanate emotional confusion and inchoate affects, but these are dismissed by the masculine subject as superfluous residue rather than incorporated into the relationship through a process of attentive recognition which engenders creative transformation.

The feminine other has a tendency to define herself vis-à-vis a masculine subject. Instead of situating herself as an active subject with respect to an object, she situates herself with respect to the other who acts as mediator between herself and herself. That is, she refers her subjectivity to the other; it is only through the other that she feels she has existence. Although Irigaray would say that masculine subjectivity is actually dependent on a nurturing other despite the male's delusion that he can maintain himself as a self-sufficient whole, the feminine other who defines herself through the masculine subject is so dependent on the mediation provided by the masculine subject that she is not able to acknowledge her own contribution to her subjectivity. Thus, in either case there is a kind of effacement of the feminine. It is only when both can revolve around themselves without effacing the other, thus allowing a self-aware subject to incorporate the contributions of both subjects to the relationship, that a generative form of love can occur. Irigaray explains that the "to" of "I love to you" is the guarantor of the intentionalities of both of the subjects involved. "And so: you do not know me, but you know something of my appearance. You can also perceive the directions and dimensions of my intentionality. You cannot know who I am but you can help me to be by perceiving that in me which escapes me, my fidelity or infidelity to myself.

In this way you can help me get away from inertia, tautology, repetition, or even from errancy, from error. You can help me become while remaining myself" (ILTY 112).

It is through a relationship in which neither subject is effaced that two subjects can help each other practice a form of negativity that anchors one in natural reality. Through the other, one discovers one's limits in the concrete here and now. Listening, understandably enough, is an important part of the kind of respectful mutual encounter that Irigaray would like to foster. In listening in order truly to communicate rather than simply waiting for a break in the conversation so one can transmit more information, the subject needs to listen to another as if the words of the other subject were irreducibly unique and as yet unknown. Instead of treating words as familiar objects of exchange, the listener should hear the words of the other as the manifestation of an intention that has implications for the human and spiritual development of the other. It is this special kind of listening that can bring about a transition of thinking and being into a new dimension of consciousness. It is through a special kind of relationship in which one no longer appropriates all creative movement to oneself, but instead focuses on the creative movement provided by another, that one can come up against one's own limits and so anchor one's conceptual flights in a natural reality.

I am listening to you not on the basis of what I know, I feel, I already am, nor in terms of what the world and language already are, thus in a formalistic manner, so to speak. I am listening to you rather as the revelation of a truth that has yet to manifest itself — yours and that of the world revealed through and by you. I give you a silence in which your future — and perhaps my own, but *with* you and not *as* you and *without* you — may emerge and lay its foundation.

This is not a hostile or restrictive silence. It is openness that nothing or no one occupies, or preoccupies — no language, no world, no God.

This silence is space-time offered to you with no a priori, no preestablished truth or ritual. To you it constitutes an overture, to the other who is not and never will be mine. It is a silence made possible by the fact that neither *I* nor *you* are everything, that each of us is limited, marked by the negative, non-hierarchically different. A silence that is the primary gesture of *I love to you*. Without it, the "to," such as I understand it, is impossible.

This silence is the condition for a possible respect for myself and for the other within our respective limits. It also assumes that the already existing world, even in its philosophical or religious form, should not be considered complete, already revealed or made manifest. (ILTY 117)

Irigaray's notion of the different other emphasizes the impossibility of identification with the other and an irreducible difference, but in the context of a horizonal transcendent. That is, rather than placing this irreducible difference in a realm removed from the sensible realm of conscious experience, she places this difference in a realm that always transcends conscious experience but is not at a remove from that experience. Rather than distance between the subject and the irreducibly different other, there is always contact, and this contact always leads to further fecund encounters which generate further transformations. The other, then, is transcendent to me not in the sense of inhabiting a realm that is different from my own, but in the sense that there is no way that I can exhaust the novelty of the other. No matter what my experience of the other, no matter how much contact with the other I have, there will always be something new in each encounter, something beyond me, something I could not possibly anticipate. Openness to the freshness of each encounter opens me onto the realm of the sensible transcendental, which is infinite and reaches out onto the divine. Instead of referring oneself to 'Thou' in one's attempts at communication, Irigaray suggests that we instead refer ourselves to "*He* or *She*, the ideal representations of my own and the other gender's becoming" (ILTY 119).[9] By thus opening out our relations onto two horizons, we overcome the contemporary tendency to assume that one horizon with one gender ideal can encompass all aspects of human life, and we thus maintain an ongoing and open-ended encounter on the material plane between two who are different.

In "A Breath That Touches in Words" Irigaray points out that only a mother breathes for her child. After we are born, we all must breathe for ourselves. She claims that our language usually stifles breath more than it cultivates it. Because the ideals our culture presents to us "act like a sort of drug promising us ecstasy beyond ourselves" (ILTY 121), our messages are generally suffocating. Language referred to an ideal transcendent to the sensible realm is a language that has been "uprooted from its engendering in the present, from its connections with the energy of my own and the other's body, and with that of the surrounding natural world" (123). Irigaray elaborates a language that involves attentiveness to the breath, to silence, and to ourselves and the other with whom we speak by proffering the notion that intersubjective communication should involve what she calls "*touching upon.*" In attending to the words of another, we need to proffer a carnal attentiveness that touches upon the other. Such touching attends to more than the information communicated by the words. In attending to the words of the other, I attend to tone of voice, modulation and rhythm, semantic and phonic choice of words, and the determinate form breath takes in the breathing out of words. Attending to the informative content of words can often lead us to abstract those words from the embodied subject who sits or stands before us and who has an embodied relationship to those words and to the listener. It is only through attending to the full range of effects produced by the speaker in a concrete setting that we can really touch upon the other as a subject with a natural reality, an intentionality, and a history of her own. Insofar as we strip those words of the natural reality of the other, we render them assimilable into our own history, and lose the possibility of a more fully embodied response of our own in a form of communcation that has become a genuine encounter.

> The intention of the *touching upon* would not be to tear the other away from the intimacy or interiority of his/her own self, from his/her temporality, nor to make him/her fall back into the natural immediacy of simple touching. In this *touching upon*, there is nature and spirit, breath, sensibility, body and speech.
> Rather its intention would be to draw the other to the site of communication *with*, the site of the heart and the still sensible word. (125)

When speech involves a *touching upon*, it can stay word and flesh, language and sensibility. In such speech, sensibility and intelligence are no longer divided, and thus there is no need for a hierarchically ordered division between active and passive, sensible and intelligible, body and mind, feminine and masculine. When speech involves such touching upon, the tactile does not become alienated in possession, and truth is not elaborated in terms of a disincarnated beyond. With such speech there is no "production of an abstract and supposedly neuter discourse" (ILTY 126). When there is genuinely intersubjective communication with a particular kind of listening and touching upon, neither subject can remain solipsistic, and intentionality is mutually informed. The subject addresses herself or himself to another, but also receives herself or himself back from the other in the form of a a further engenderment of her or his own becoming. The subject becomes engendered on the basis of the other rather than being reduced to the image or ideal or illusion of the other.[10]

With genuine intersubjective communication between two different genders, man can no longer be "a sort of abstract equal-to-all individual whose generic and specific qualities are both concentrated in and abolished by the institution of the family," and woman can no longer be "a potential substitute for another woman, an object for use and exchange whose properties and functions, both natural and abstract, are determined by the needs of a given society, of a cultural era and its commerce." Then community can be made up of real persons "organized in terms of and through the economy of their differences" (ILTY 127).

Respect for the negative, the play of the dialectic between us, would enable us to remain ourselves and to create an *oeuvre* with the other. And thus to develop, building a temporality instead of believing in eternal promises.

. . . Flesh itself becomes spiritual while remaining flesh; affect becomes spirit while remaining love.

This alchemy needs measures, words, and ways which bring together while distancing, elevate while incarnating, individualize while universalizing. It implies a culture of breath, a becoming between earth, fire and water that overcomes inertia, submersion, ice, fire, and void, one where air subsists as indispensable matter for life and for its transubstantiation in spirit. (148)

Irigaray provides a compelling model of interaction between two subjects, neither of whom displaces her or his corporeality onto the other. Instead of the specular economy of masculine subjectivity, this interaction evokes the creative communion of two, each of whom acts as a living mirror for the other. A living mirror cannot reflect an image back to the subject without adding something of its own to that image. In the process, such mirroring inevitably becomes a dance in which both subjects are transformed. An economy of subjectivity premised on participatory communion and recognition does not need to anchor identity to a "lack" translated into an object of desire that structures (oedipal, masculine) identity. Instead, personal identity is formed and transformed in living contact with reciprocating others.

Deleuze, and Deleuze and Guattari, also create models of interaction in which active/passive, subject/object hierarchies are rendered undecidable and desire flows from point to point rather than fixating on what it can never have. In the next four chapters I turn to the work of Deleuze, and Deleuze and Guattari, to elaborate their model of nomadic subjectivity and to indicate the resonance as well as the disparities between Irigaray's project and theirs.

5
Deleuze's Project

In the preface to the English edition of *Difference and Repetition*, Gilles Deleuze claims that the difference between writing history of philosophy and writing philosophy is that while in the former case the writer studies "the arrows or the tools of a great thinker," in the latter case the writer tries to speak in her own name "only to learn that a proper name designates no more than the outcome of a body of work" (D&R xv). Writing philosophy in one's own name turns out to be what Deleuze and Félix Guattari describe in *What Is Philosophy?* as a process of creating consistent concepts which will take one beyond the commonsense perspective of a personal self. We will find that the theme of opening up the constraints of a commonsense perspective to a reality that lies beyond resonates in a remarkable way with Irigaray's theme of spiritualizing the flesh in order to experience a sensible transcendental that defies the conventional forms of perception and conception.

According to Deleuze, the philosopher's body of work expresses the concepts she discovers in the process of thinking and writing philosophically. *Difference and Repetition* is the first book in which Deleuze believes he was "doing" philosophy rather than simply writing history of philosophy, and he declares that everything he has written since, including what he has written with Guattari, is connected to this book. The title of the book proclaims Deleuze's preoccupation with the problem of difference and repetition. For Deleuze, thinking difference and repetition without subordinating them to identity or to the same involves breaking free from the classical image of thought; the discovery of genuine concepts of difference and repetition requires liberating thought from a model of recognition premised on referring representations to already established identities. Like Irigaray, Deleuze would have thought break free from the representational model of traditional philosophy in order for us to think the unthinkable.

In the original preface to *Difference and Repetition*, Deleuze mentions various areas of modern thought which have discovered "a power peculiar to repetition, a power which also inhabits the unconscious, language and art." Heideggerian philosophy, structuralism, and contemporary fiction explore the difference that haunts any present repetition: present beings are ontologically different from Being; words have meaning only with reference to other words from which they differ; human beings differ from the substantial selves they wish they were. Representation is premised on the primacy of identity. Identities — phenomena such as Freud's conscious ego, Marx's bourgeois reality, Nietzsche's god, authorial intention, and the speaking subject — are put into doubt by various theoretical perspectives of modernity. In the wake of a generalized anti-Hegelianism in which "difference and repetition have taken the place of the identical and the negative, of identity and contradiction," one can no longer take identity at face value. Modern thought emerges with the loss of identities and the failure of representation. Now, "all identities are only simulated, produced as an optical 'effect' by the more profound game of difference and repetition" (D&R xix).

In this chapter I explore the philosophy of difference and repetition that Deleuze creates in the context of my project of developing a pragmatically useful model of subjectivity. In the chapters on Irigaray I developed a critique of masculine subjectivity with its economy of the same: masculine subjectivity, according to Irigaray, is premised on a need to be blind to the constitutive other who is different from oneself in order to perpetuate the illusion of a self-identical self. With Deleuze, I continue to develop this model. There are certainly other approaches to reading Deleuze, but for the purposes of this book I focus on the implications of his philosophy for human subjectivity. Although much of the perspective I attach to Deleuze's name in the next four chapters derives from my reading of his books written with Guattari as well as books written under his own name, I have presented my reading as a reading of Deleuze's work primarily because I have read the collaborative books through the lens of Deleuze's books. I emphasize the theme of incorporating the imperceptible encounters of unconscious processes into conscious awareness. Just as Irigaray's exhortation to attend to the feminine and feminine subjectivity speaks to the unspoken underside of a cultural representation of the subject, so does Deleuze's exhortation to let living and thinking emerge from imperceptible encounters speak to the underside of contemporary forms of representational thought. Both would have us change the image of thinking in order to encounter difference and repetition in a new way. Both would have us change not only the content of our thinking, but also the very way we think and live our lives in order to enounter the differences within ourselves as well as in others.

I approach the work of Deleuze, and Deleuze and Guattari, from a perspective informed by Irigaray's project of overcoming mind/body dualisms. Like Irigaray, I believe that we cut ourselves off from the corporeal aspects of life at our peril; the tendency to ignore or trivialize our participation in a sensual world of process constitutes a form of alienation that has dangerous repercussions for ethical living with human others as well as within the world of which we are a part. Irigaray's concepts of spiritualizing the flesh, the sensible transcendental, negativity, and a listening that entails 'touching upon' all work toward symbolizing aspects of life that we have tended to ignore or take for granted. I have used the term 'corporeal logics' in contrast to 'conceptual logics' as shorthand for the patterns of organization that inform corporeal practices. I use the former term to suggest that the embodied aspects of human living are not natural but culturally mediated, and to emphasize that they require a form of labor that often goes unrecognized.

The nurturing, affective labor of providing attentive support for the embodied aspects of human living has traditionally fallen to women. Styles of perception, like styles of thought, are developed in the interdependent setting of social life. Our perceptions of the world can undergo radical transformation as we become more attentive to them and the processes that constitute them. Irigaray develops a vocabulary for attending to sensory experience and points to sexual difference as the key to overcoming the mind/body dualisms that privilege the former over the latter. I agree with Irigaray that such dualisms work with and through economies of subjectivity that privilege an "active" subject vis-à-vis a "passive" supportive other. I also agree that sexual difference is one thread by which we could begin to unravel detrimental mind/body dualisms. I do not, however, agree that sexual difference is the only thread.

I have used the term 'corporeal logic' in my development of Irigaray's project in order to indicate formations of the extralinguistic material and psychic flux of existence which informs sensation and emotion. In discussing the work of Deleuze, and Deleuze and Guattari, I also use this term to indicate extralinguistic processes of which we are for the most part unaware that both nourish and threaten the sensations and emotions of "commonsense" experience. Irigaray's reference to the body and its wisdom is more explicitly located in the lived experience of an embodied individual.[1] She wants us to deepen our embodied encounter with what is contiguous to our ordinary experience so that we can transform consciousness in keeping with "natural" rhythms that pertain to aspects of our embodied experience of which we are typically not aware. Although she remains more firmly within the psychoanalytic paradigm of familial relations in characterizing the origins of human subjects in the body of another, the work of opening up the category of the feminine, on my reading, could be extended to include a realm of difference beyond that of sexual difference.

Deleuze, and Deleuze and Guattari, are even more critical of the psychoanalytic framework than Irigaray; they are leery of its normalizing tendencies and, like Irigaray, insist on theorizing the possibility for change at the level of broader social processes as well as at the level of the individual. Their break with psychoanalysis enables them to propose models that challenge familial positioning and suggest postfamilial forms of subjectivity. Their approach emphasizes the transformations that occur in the dynamic interactions of day-to-day living and develops a vocabulary for describing and fostering such transformations. The vocabulary they develop articulates some of the same kind of interactions in which Irigaray is interested: interactions that occur among processes rather than substances, that entail mutual transformation rather than one agent acting on another, and that challenge the conventional forms of perception and conception. Deleuze and Guattari draw from a broader and more eclectic array of disciplines — many of them scientific (mathematics, geology, chemistry, biology, physics) — than does Irigaray. This has the advantage of permitting the articulation of interactions that defy conventional norms regarding personhood, since the fluxes and flows of molecular processes cross the personal boundaries of bodies and selves. But this language can also become perhaps dangerously abstract when considered from the perspective of fostering ethical relationships. Deleuze's conception of the transcendental field of the virtual (which we could compare to Irigaray's conception of the sensible transcendental) entails "bracketing" the self/other structure of alterity in order to think the impersonal and preindividual singularities out of which the human world is constituted.[2] Although I argue how and why this move can be risky given contemporary power relations — in particular, for the purpose of my own project, those entailing a division of labor with respect to the "cultural" products of the mind and the "perceptual/affective" products of the body — I also welcome the rich resources their work provides in opening up new possibilities in being and suggest strategies for mitigating its dangers.

There are various ways of understanding what corporeal logic in the work of Deleuze, and Deleuze and Guattari, might be about. In *Difference and Repetition*, Deleuze attempts to create a logic of difference that would move thought from a representational model to one in which encounters with imperceptible forces could be integrated with encounters with perceptible ones. One could refer to the realm of becomings and encounters as one that suggests a realm of corporeal logic that is not completely without organization but that typically eludes our conscious awareness. In *Anti-Oedipus*, Deleuze and Guattari describe a subject's organization in terms of what they call 'molecular' and 'molar' processes. Molecular processes occur at a level below conscious awareness. Molecular desiring-machines are akin to Kleinian part-objects; they constitute the elements of the fluid processes of the unconscious. Molar machines are stabilized aggregates of molecular elements. The partial objects of the molecular unconscious form multiplicities which produce rather than repress flow (A-O 295); molar machines invest in determinate formations of these multiplicities which exclude other formations (ATP 287). Deleuze and Guattari prescribe a practice of schizoanalysis that would destabilize or deterritorialize molar organization and integrate an expanded range of molecular becoming into conscious existence. In *A Thousand Plateaus*, Deleuze and Guattari describe this practice in terms of a process of destratifying from the various strata of human existence.

For Deleuze, as for Irigaray, the realm out of which our conscious experience emerges and of which we are not consciously aware is very real, but not in the traditional sense of conforming to established norms of perception and conception. It is a realm that we not only can but should access more fully if we are to live ethical and vital lives. In the reading I give here,

I emphasize those aspects of Deleuze's work, as well as his collaborative work with Guattari, which develop an image of thinking as an integrative practice meant to bring about a transformation of consciousness at both the corporeal and conceptual levels. Deleuze's critique of representation and the project of creating a new image of thinking — one that would allow us to think difference differently — entails a subject open to the chaotic flux that challenges any perceptual ordering or conceptual system which is in place. Instead of investigating what had to be the case for conscious experience to be as it is, Deleuze attempts to describe the dynamic conditions that generate not only the perception and thought of familiar experience but that of unprecedented experiences as well. His project develops a conception of sensibility open to that which defies "commonsense" perception and the traditional categories of representational thought. It thus promotes not simply a transformation in perspective upon our experiences but a transformation in those experiences themselves. This transformation involves our challenging the boundaries of body and mind by opening them onto multiple connections with the world.

In the chapters to come I explore the possibilities Deleuze's work provides for reconceiving human subjectivity as an undecidable and heterogeneous mix of body and mind, and for theorizing those bodies and minds as processes that form an integral part of life as process. As we will see, Deleuze does not share Irigaray's concern for the (feminine) supportive other. His attention to what defies familiar forms of conscious perception and conception, however, provides further details for my project of characterizing human subjectivity as a nondualistic, interdependent process, much of which occurs behind the scenes of representational consciousness. I draw upon Deleuze's work and his work with Guattari in light of Irigaray's project of fostering forms of subjectivity that are no longer contingent on a division of labor that relegates the body to a (feminine) supportive other and the mind to a (masculine) active subject. Their work provides a rich resource for giving symbolic support to new forms of subjectivity able to integrate simultaneously the flux of material as well as conceptual existence into conscious awareness. Such forms of subjectivity could move us beyond the collective need to exploit specific others by displacing corporeal dissonance upon them and allow us more flexibility in transforming ourselves in response to the dynamic becoming that is life without completely losing ourselves in the process.

In the first section of this chapter I give an account of the various layers involved in the production of subjectivity as it emerges in *Anti-Oedipus*. My account is informed by my project of finding an approach to the inarticulable, imperceptible levels of our own embodied processes of subject constitution that will enable new forms of subjectivity to emerge. I give a reading of *Anti-Oedipus* designed to highlight crucial points of convergence and divergence with Irigaray's critique of Freudian theory. In the next section I characterize Deleuze's project in light of the book's theme of creating anoedipal possibilities in subjectivity. And in the final section I discuss Deleuze and Guattari's characterization of philosophy as an art of creating concepts in *What Is Philosophy?* in anticipation of Deleueze's reading of Nietzsche.

In *Anti-Oedipus*, Deleuze and Guattari object to the psychoanalytic account of (masculine) subjectivity.[3] While they believe that this account has descriptive power for subjects of contemporary capitalism, like Irigaray, they also believe that it is blind to alternative economies of subjectivity that would subvert what it describes. But whereas Irigaray believes that psychoanalysis is blind to sexual difference, Deleuze and Guattari believe that it is blind to anoedipal desire. Not only is anoedipal desire more variable and open than desire constrained by the oedipal triangle of mommy, daddy, and me, but it is productive as well. Whereas oedipal desire is defined through castration and lack, anoedipal desire produces itself in immanent structurings of molecular fluxes and flows. We will see that Deleuze and Guattari's description of the schizo who is able to access anoedipal desire resonates with Irigaray's conception of a fledgling feminine subject. Both present risky and yet enticing possibilities for an alternative economy of subjectivity that could break out of the logic of the same governing the oedipalized (masculine) subject. Both posit a different kind of desire and pleasure that entails a new way of thinking, speaking, and being in the world.

Anoedipal desire in its immanent operation has striking similarities to Irigaray's presentation of a feminine desire premised on touch and contiguity rather than possession. In Chapter 8, we will see how productive desire creates 'lines of flight' out of the chaotic forms of what Deleuze and Guattari call the 'virtual'. A line of flight is a flow of movement that breaks with conventional social codes in the creation of new forms of life (ATP 204).[4] The virtual could be read as Deleuze and Guattari's rendition of the reality that always exceeds our perceptual and conceptual grasp — the realm of the infinite, or what Irigaray calls the sensible transcendental or the divine. But at the same time that they uphold the transcendent quality of such a realm, like Irigaray they insist on an immanent reading of this transcendence. The realm of the infinite is never at a remove from us, but is always with us here-right-now in our every earthbound experience of the "ordinary" world. It is thus through our embodied encounters with material or sensible reality — encounters that inevitably threaten while at the same time they nourish the corporeal and conceptual logics of stable identity — that we gain access to this realm with its possibilities for creative transformation.

Deleuze and Guattari and the Constitution of the Subject

Lacanian psychoanalysis assumes that we can describe the unconscious and subjectivity through the categories of the symbolic, the imaginary, and the real; a subject initially emerges through imaginary identifications that relate to the desire for maternal contact, and becomes a full-fledged subject by taking up a position as a speaking subject in the symbolic meaning systems of a specific society. The 'real' is not reality (which is accessible to consciousness) but that which resists all articulation — that "which may be approached, but never grasped."[5] It is what makes any economy of subjectivity an open-ended process. Irigaray, as we saw, agrees with this view although she allows for more radical transformations of a culture's symbolic and imaginary structures than Lacanian psychoanalysis would permit. In *Negotiations*, Deleuze says that the Lacanian categories of the symbolic and the imaginary seem to Guattari and him to be false categories; the only element they know is that of the real. The Lacanian view assumes that the unconscious is a kind of theater where a self is staged and performed as the oedipal drama of mommy-daddy-child. Imaginary identifications can be traced back to the mother; symbolic positioning can be traced back to the law of the father. On this view, unconscious desire is always motivated by lack; it is always referred to the mother the subject cannot have, the father the subject cannot be. Deleuze and Guattari insist that the unconscious is not a theater but a factory, a production machine. To construe it as the theater of an oedipal drama is vastly to impoverish the possibilities it produces for us. When the unconscious unravels into delirium (for example, in schizophrenia), it is not through daddy/mommy but through races, tribes, and continents, history and geography — identifications drawn from the entire social field rather than merely the familial drama. Instead of referring unconscious desire to what is lacking to the subject in terms of the oedipal triangle, they posit an immanent notion of the unconscious, one that insists on its productive nature (N 144).

Deleuze and Guattari situate a theory of the production and producing of human beings as embodied subjects of desire with specific forms of consciousness in a broader process of production which includes nonhuman processes of production. The advantage of their perspective for a project of attending to both the corporeal and conceptual logics of human existence is that it insists on attending to material aspects of existence that defy linguistic articulation. The model of subjectivity that Deleuze and Guattari present in *Anti-Oedipus* insists on viewing human beings as formed by and participating in molecular processes of material production of which our perceptions and conceptions of the world are only symptoms.

They hold that life itself is a process of production which takes one thing and changes it into something else in cyclical transformations that are recorded in various ways, and which has no need of any transcendent principles in order to motivate its movement, but which instead operates through immanent principles of desire. The primary production of organisms at the organic level, for example, includes processes such as those that replicate genetic coding and the molecular structure of cells of the body. The social production of human subjects involves, in addition to the primary production of life processes, consumption and a recording process that ensures the reproduction of social structures. For example, goods are consumed both by workers as they work and by the work process itself, and these processes are recorded in order to ensure that they are efficiently replicated along with any innovations that may be introduced. The actions and passions of embodied individuals, social recordings in the form of coordinates that serve as points of reference for the social significance of actions and passions (the codes of conventional behavior and expectations), and consumptions in the form of sensual pleasures, anxieties, and pain are produced in the various human processes of production in concert with nonhuman processes of production.

The Body without Organs

Although we typically view phenomena as composed of distinct objects arranged in space, Deleuze and Guattari take a dynamic view of life that emphasizes becoming and the fluxes and flows of which all things are made. According to them, "everything is production" (A-O 4). That is, everything that exists is involved in the dynamic flow of life which is always in movement. Since all the forces of life are ultimately connected, the way we separate out particular things in order to distinguish them from other things presupposes a level of organization that chooses certain connections over others. At the molecular level of primary production, everything is connected, and connections continually metamorphose into new formations.[6] We might compare this conception to Irigaray's notion of the feminine sea where elements are in free-floating play. This sea is not an undifferentiated abyss but a differentiated, differentiating movement where any forms that emerge quickly change into something else. For Deleuze and Guattari, the web of life is made up of molecular forces, no one of which can be separated from the web except through abstraction. These forces have determinate relationships even though they are in constant flux. Deleuze and Guattari describe these forces-in-relationship at the molecular level logically prior to (and yet contemporaneous with) substances with determinate identities as desiring-machines. Not only are molecular desiring-machines analogous to Kleinian part-objects, which belong to the flow of the primary processes of the unconscious of a specific individual; they also constitute the flow of nonhuman as well as human life. The distinction between human individual and world is marked out not by the fluid, differentiating movement of desiring-machines but by the molar aggregates, which stabilize determinate configurations of that movement.

In *Anti-Oedipus*, Deleuze and Guattari describe desiring-machines as binary machines coupled together: "Desire constantly couples continuous flows and partial objects that are by nature fragmentary and fragmented. Desire causes the current to flow, itself flows in turn, and breaks the flows" (A-O 5). The binary series is linear in every direction because each flow-machine is connected to an interrupt-machine and vice versa. That is, each flow-producing machine is always connected to another whose flow is interrupted or partially drained off and vice versa in connective linear series where there is always "and . . ." "and then . . ." The breast and mouth make one such binary machine. The breast milk is a flow-machine and the mouth that sucks on the breast drains off this flow. The mouth is also a cavity filled with milk and so is a flow-machine which is drained by the throat machine which pulls down the milk. "Every 'object' presupposes the continuity of a flow; every flow, the fragmentation of the object" (6).

Desiring-machines make us an organism by grafting the production of various elements through the linear series of binary machines onto the organism as product. No one desiring-machine can determine the workings of the whole organism; every machine is connected to other machines. The identity of producing and the product of production constitutes a third term — an enormous, undifferentiated object which Deleuze and Guattari call the full body without organs.[7] The linear series of binary machines that produce a connective synthesis could always have been produced in another way. Other possible organizations of the body would have involved other kinds of connective syntheses. The production of one form of organization thus involves articulating unorganized masses that could have articulated alternative linear series of binary machines. It is only because certain series rather than others have been produced that any series can be produced at all. The body without organs belongs to the realm of antiproduction and resists linked, connected, and interrupted flows by setting up a "counterflow of amorphous, undifferentiated fluid" (A-O 9); it is the nonproductive stasis of production that resists any specific organization of desiring-machines.

Desire desires death in that the full body without organs brings a particular organization of the working machine to a halt and thus sets free the unorganized mass that was not articulated into working parts. Desiring-machines "work only when they break down, and by continually breaking down" (A-O 8). It is only because there are other possible configurations of desiring-machines that specific working machines can be produced at all. For movement and change to occur, there has to be fluidity in the machines, which means the series are always changing. Any production entails "an element of antiproduction" (8) in the sense that there is an apparent conflict between desiring-machines and the body without organs: "Every coupling of machines, every production of a machine, every sound of a machine running, becomes unbearable to the body without organs. Beneath its organs it senses there are larvae and loathsome worms, and a God at work messing it all up or strangling it by organizing it" (9). Only the halt to the production of a determinate configuration of desiring-machines could release desire from the constraints of specific forms of desiring-production that necessitate repressing other forms of desiring-production. Death is thus desired by desire as much as the working machines are.

> Desiring-machines make us an organism; but at the very heart of this production, within the very production of this production, the body suffers from being organized in this way, from not having some other sort of organization, or no organization at all. . . . The automata stop dead and set free the unorganized mass they once served to articulate. The full body without organs is the unproductive, the sterile, the unengendered, the unconsumable. . . . The death instinct: that is its name, and death is not without a model. For desire desires death also, because the full body of death is its motor, just as it desires life, because the organs of life are the *working machine*. (8)

According to Freud's conception of the death instinct, tension is unpleasurable and seeks release and ultimately the complete release of all tension which is death itself. Deleuze and Guattari are careful to distinguish the body without organs from a retroactive fantasy of a pre-oedipal, non-lacking body associated with the oceanic bliss of symbiotic union with the mother — a body that one might project but could never actually have lived. The full body without organs is imageless and organless because any image of the body and any configuration of the body into organs presupposes a specific configuration of desiring-machines, and the body without organs defies any and all such organization (A-O 8). The organism is the product — at a specific time and place — of a determinate configuration of desiring-machines. That the organism is made up of working desiring-machines — that is, that it is always in process rather than a finished product — is so because it craves complete release from any determinate organization of its working machines. The organism's resistance to any given pattern of its working machines leads to the formation of new patterns. The body without organs is Deleuze and Guattari's name for this resistance or struggle between production and its product. Like Freud's notion of the death instinct, this resistance can have both constructive and destructive effects; it is the motor force of innovative change as well as dissipative breakdown.[8]

Molar and Molecular and Oedipus

The unconscious is unaware of persons as such since desiring-machines operate at a molecular level of production where partial objects emerge from a nonpersonal flow by establishing breaks and flows with other partial objects (A-O 46). Deleuze and Guattari call molecular elements that group themselves into relatively stable configurations molar aggregates. It is only at the level of molar organization that persons appear. And it is only at the level of molar organization that lack is introduced into desiring. Desiring-machines constitute macroscopic social formations by forming patterns that are identifiable according to social systems of meaning. Social production produces stabilized formations of desiring-machines by grouping them according to replicable disjuncts. For example, language as a social system of meaning provides words with which to identify various aspects of personhood according to either/or disjuncts. Insofar as molar aggregates (for example, the body) are represented with one word, objects are referred to a totality that they in fact lack (the partial objects of the body cannot constitute a definitive whole since they are always in flux, do not operate in accordance with one master plan, are engaged in a self-mutating process in which the product affects the process, and extend out into the world). The molar aggregate of the individual is lacking only insofar as its molecular elements are referred to a representational totality which they can never in fact achieve.

The unconscious is productive in the sense that the desiring-machines that constitute it create flows and breaks in flows among molecular elements. Oedipalization is a secondary step in secondary repression in which the social investments of social repression are further narrowed down to the familial investments in which personal identity becomes stabilized. Referring molar aggregates to the totalizing representations made available in the familial context of social significance reduces what Deleuze and Guattari call the social 'aggregate of departure' to a familial 'aggregate of destination'. The structural unity imposed by the various identifications of a social subject made available by the social field (for example, American or European, black or Hispanic, Christian or Muslim) is personalized through oedipal identifications that distribute social identifications; some social totalities are taken to be personal totalities, that is, one's personal identity, while others are not. Thus, the familial relation is taken to be the paradigm for all social relations (A-O 307), and molecular productive elements are hindered from following lines of escape not contained within oedipal dramas.[9] Oedipal desire is not produced by the desiring-machines of the unconscious, according to Deleuze and Guattari, but is rather constituted in the exclusion of specific formations of desiring-machines in keeping with the social machines which impose an oedipal organization on the formation of molar aggregates. Whereas Freud and Lacan insist that unconscious desire conforms to an oedipal drama, Deleuze and Guattari insist that unconscious desire produces an infinitely variable range of syntheses which are organized and reduced through the work of social machines. Tapping the productive power of the unconscious, for Deleuze and Guattari, entails not simply challenging oedipal taboos but also tapping a creative potential for producing desires that have nothing whatever to do with oedipal dramas. De-oedipalizing the subject can rlease new formations of desiring-machines. For Deleuze and Guattari, the structure of the symbolic and the imaginary as delineated by Lacanian psychoanalysis indicates a determinate social production. Insofar as one assumes that this structure is necessary for human subjectivity, one closes off alternative forms of social production (83).

The schizo is a subject who has been able to de-oedipalize at least partially. Deleuze and Guattari's description of the schizo is very similar in some ways to Irigaray's description of the feminine other who has not attained full subjecthood in the masculine economy and yet represents a potential alternative form of subjectivity.

The schizo has his own system of co-ordinates for situating himself at his disposal, because, first of all, he has at his disposal his very own recording code, which does not coincide with the social code, or coincides with it only in order to parody it. The code of delirium or of desire proves to have an extraordinary fluidity. It might be said that the schizophrenic passes from one code to the other, that he deliberately *scrambles all the codes*, by quickly shifting from one to another, according to the questions asked him, never giving the same explanation from one day to the next, never invoking the same genealogy, never recording the same event in the same way. (A-O 15)

Irigaray also emphasizes the fluidity of the feminine subject.[10] And just as it may be a stretch to call such a subject a "subject," given conventional notions about identity and agency, so may it be a stretch to call the schizo a "subject." Just as Irigaray does not advocate femininity as a viable form of subjectivity, Deleuze and Guattari do not advocate schizophrenia. Instead they attempt to model a form of subjectivity that would continually incorporate fluidity without succumbing to the loss of subjectivity that actual schizophrenia and the position of feminine other entails.

Schizoanalysis

Schizoanalysis as a true politics of antipsychiatry involves liberating schizoid movements of deterritorialization so that these movements are not reterritorialized into mental illness, but instead affect "the flows of labor and desire, of production, knowledge, and creation in their most profound tendency" (A-O 321). Such deterritorialized flows liberate other flows which extend deterritorialization beyond the individual across the social field. Schizoanalysis must proceed quickly in its destructive task of "successively undoing the representative territorialities and reterritorializations through which a subject passes in his individual history" (318), but this task must nevertheless be carried out with "great patience, great care." In carrying out this task of what Deleuze and Guattari will call 'destratification' in *A Thousand Plateaus*, schizoanalysis assumes that libidinal investments ranging over the entire social field take precedence over familial investments (356). An important component of schizoanalysis thus turns out to be the "liberation" of 'prepersonal singularities' from the constraints of personal identities: "The task of schizoanalysis is that of tirelessly taking apart egos and their presuppositions; liberating the prepersonal singularities they enclose and repress; mobilizing the flows they would be capable of transmitting, receiving, or intercepting; establishing always further and more sharply the schizzes and the breaks well below conditions of identity; and assembling the desiring-machines that countersect everyone and group everyone with others" (362).

Capitalism is particularly wedded to oedipalization as the aggregate of destination of social production because capitalism is inherently deterritorializing. That is, unlike the social formations of territorialism and despotism, capitalism fosters the deterritorialization of social identities.[11] Owing to the unstable nature of capitalist enterprise, social identities mutate over time rather than remain stable. To replicate itself, capitalism needs to manage this deterritorialization. The decoded flows it produces must be doubly exorcised by the reproduction of an ever-expanding immanent limit (as capitalism continues to take over new territory), and by the "marking out of an interior limit that reduces this social reproduction to restricted familial reproduction" (A-O 304). Any genealogy of desire assumes a form in terms of disjunctions — the binary machines that form linear series of desire. Capitalism, insofar as it attempts to domesticate a specific genealogical form, requires oedipal triangulation. Deleuze and Guattari suggest, however, not just that this is not the only genealogical form that desire can or should take, but that oedipal triangulation of the disjuncts of productive desire constitutes an oppressive form (14–15).

Writing as Becoming-Imperceptible

Deleuze is especially attentive to writing as a practice that would enact the model of subjectivity he develops. Both Irigaray and Deleuze believe that theory, by introducing symbolization of alternative models of subjectivity into the social field, can foster actual manifestations of such alternatives. They believe that social identity is contingent upon, although by no means completely determined by, systems of significance that present a range of conceivable social identities. This means that the creation of new possibilities through discursive models could have practical effects at the level of lived experience. In reading Irigaray one gets the impression that she is trying to articulate something that she already lives; as a woman who has lived the position of mute feminine other, she struggles for the words to integrate what has been lived at the level of corporeal logic into conceptual thought. Deleuze, by contrast, deliberately attempts to deterritorialize his subject positioning through a practice of writing and philosophizing that shakes loose the molecular becomings of corporeal logic and integrates it into thinking. Perhaps this is why Irigaray tends toward images of

touching, breathing, and listening to what is here-right-now, while Deleuze tends toward nomadic images of deserts, wandering, and lines of
flight. Whereas one could say that Deleuze is motivated by the fear of stag-
nancy and the death of desire of the overly molarized subject (or, as Irigaray might put it, the entombed masculine subject who has lost his body),
Irigaray is motivated by the need to become a nomadic subject rather than
a schizophrenic (or, as Irigaray might put it, the need to integrate the corporeally loaded effects of femininity into a fully formed feminine subjectivity).

The project of schizoanalysis when put in the context of *A Thousand
Plateaus* becomes a project of destratification that involves mapping lines
of flight that release new possibilities from strata. Deleuze's notions of the
'between', a deterritorializing line of flight, and becoming-imperceptible
all map possibilities in destratifying determinate molar structures. In *Anti-
Oedipus*, Deleuze and Guattari present a kind of cartography of human
subjectivity in its implication with the background processes out of which
human subjects emerge. Such cartographies can highlight those points at
which contemporary formations of human subjectivity are unstable and
could transform into unprecedented formations. Schizoanalysis deliberately attempts to exploit such opportunities. Destratification is Deleuze
and Guattari's later term for a project of transforming subjectivity by noting and exploiting those points at which contemporary forms of subjectivity destabilize. The notions of deterritorialization and destratification suggest a model of subjectivity that minimizes the gap between embodied
subject and world and instead configures subjectivity as a kind of geographical terrain. A self, a conversation, a book, on this model, can be seen
as a configuration of random and aleatory elements converging to form
one location with its own peculiar topology, strata, and atmosphere. The
contours of this self suggest a rich sense of connectedness, inevitable and
mutually informing contact with surrounding terrain, and the arbitrari-
ness of any one way of staking out one's boundaries. Mapping such terrain
involves attentiveness to the intricate convergence of multiple singularities
that defy any imposition of a preconceived grid.

The writer who would map the terrain of subjectivity laid out by Deleuze must engage in a process of becoming-imperceptible; instead of locating herself vis-à-vis her subject matter, she must follow the lines of
flight that run through herself and the multiplicities of which she is a part.
This process entails betraying any recognizable positioning and ignoring
conventional boundaries in order to follow the moving lines of this terrain. The image of a nomadic subject evokes a multiply overdetermined

sense of a subject actively participating with rather than in or on the world. Nomadic subjectivity participates in a terrain that includes and engages processes other than itself as well rather than acting as a distinct entity upon objects. The interconnections of this subject and its world reach out in all directions and cannot be reduced to any one linear chain of cause and effect. Instead, this subject is a multiplicity among multiplicities, the various lines of which actualize movements of becoming. This model problematizes dichotomies of active/passive and agent/object and evokes an image of collaboration of embodied subject and world, a singular coming together of multiple lines in which the specific location and shape of the subject is impossible to pin down to any one point.

In *Dialogues*, Deleuze calls himself an empiricist and states that empiricism is linked to a logic of multiplicities. Empiricism starts with the phenomena presented to sense experience as data for philosophical investigation, but then investigates the conditions for those phenomena (D 86–87). Rather than posit a realm of the possible from which the conventional forms of reality can be derived, however, Deleuze investigates a transcendental field of the virtual. In his reading of Bergson, Deleuze affirms Bergson's critique of a traditional conception of the possible; the assumption that what is possible must conform to patterns abstracted from what has already happened obliterates the novelty of dynamic becoming. From the traditional perspective "it is not the real that resembles the possible, it is the possible that resembles the real, because it has been abstracted from the real once made, arbitrarily extracted from the real like a sterile double. Hence, we no longer understand anything either of the mechanism of difference or of the mechanism of creation" (B 98). Rather than abstracting intelligible structures from real experience in order to create the illusion that they are prior to and condition all experience, including experience still to come, Deleuze insists that the conditions of actual experience are concrete and empirical (see Baugh 1993, 21–22). It is the virtual, rather than the possible construed as an inversion of the real, which conditions experience. The virtual is unrepresentable. The singularities of life can form infinitely innumerable determinate relations, many of which are incompossible with other determinate relations. The formation of a determinate set of relations entails favoring certain relations and excluding others. Whereas the notion of the possible suggests a static set of conditions to which all of experience must conform, the notion of the virtual captures the dynamic quality of becoming. The transcendental field of the virtual "serves as the genetic or productive condtion of real experience" (Smith 1995, 1). Although what happens is conditioned, the conditions need not adhere to any one set of determinate forms. As Bruce Baugh explains, "the actuality of the empirical, instead of instantiating a rule or concept given by the understanding, is *empirically constituted* through a chance concatenation of forces . . . which together produce something new and unforseeable [sic]" (Baugh 1993, 23). It is only through a genealogical account that relates an empirical actuality to its causal history "in such a way that differences and singularities can be grasped in their uniqueness and positivity" (25) that we are engaged in a kind of thinking that does not subordinate difference to an identity logic.

The complete actualization of a virtual totality — for example, that of a set of social relationships — would be completely chaotic. The actualization of some of the virtual relations that could emerge among a group of people entails a differentiating process wherein some relationships would exclude other relationships and the relationships actualized would create further possibilities in relationships previously not possible. Many actualizations of this virtual totality would thus be incompossible with other actualizations. To assume that we can represent the possible through a kind of inversion of the real is to deny the novelty that emerges from the creative becoming of life. In order to grasp the conditions of an empirical phenomenon, we need to give a genealogical account of the differences and singularities specific to the unfolding movement of transformations resulting in that phenomenon in its present form. The formation of a friendship between two individuals, for example, is conditioned by the nexus of mutating relationships specific to each. It is through a genealogical account of the relationships of each of the two friends in the particular context from which those relationships emerge that we could come to know what relations condition the present friendship. It is unlikely that such an explanation would be equally applicable to another friendship; subjecting the conditions of empirical phenomena to a set of rules with broader application entails an inevitable loss of some of the specificity of a given passage of becoming. Analogously, conceiving of what is possible by projecting a future that is in conformity with such rules entails ignoring that the result of what is bound to be a unique configuration of conditions is unpredictable. The notion of the virtual allows us to take this inherent unpredictability of life into account.[12]

Unlike a positing of the possible which must conform to the conventional forms of the already-perceived and the already-thought, "transcendental" empiricism allows the theorization of what conditions real experience in all its peculiar unpredictability. This entails moving beyond representational thought in order to approach imperceptible happenings that give rise to the conceptions and perceptions of conscious awareness. Thus, although Deleuze calls himself an empiricist, his search for the conditions of the givens of sense experience and of conscious awareness leads him to a deconstructive reading of both that opens us up to new ways of living and new kinds of experiences.

In *Dialogues*, Deleuze characterizes *Dialogues* itself, his work, his work process, and his collaborative effort with Guattari in a way that reveals how his empiricism goes beyond a description of the phenomena of commonsense experience. *Dialogues* was meant to be an interview. Instead, it became a collaboration between Deleuze and Claire Parnet in which neither's contribution was clearly marked. In the English preface to *Dialogues*, Deleuze says about the book that emerged:

> What mattered was not the points — Félix, Claire Parnet, me and many others, who functioned simply as temporary, transitory and evanescent points of subjectivation — but the collection of bifurcating, divergent and muddled lines which constituted this book as a multiplicity and which passed between the points, carrying them along without ever going from the one to the other. Hence, the first plan for a conversation between two people, in which one asked questions and the other replied, no longer had any value. The divisions had to rest on the growing dimensions of the multiplicity, according to becomings which were unattributable to individuals, since they could not be immersed in it without changing qualitatively (D ix–x).

This description of the making of the book captures aspects of the writing process that are typically ignored. First, Deleuze chooses to emphasize the between of a collaborative process rather than label the origin and ownership of the ideas that make up the content of the book. Second, he emphasizes the aleatory nature of this coming together of a collection of lines rather than the mastery manifested by any individual vis-à-vis these lines. To say that *Dialogues* is a multiplicity is to say that the book emerged neither from Deleuze as author or interviewee, nor from Claire Parnet as interviewer, nor from Guattari or the various thinkers who affected Deleuze and Guattari's work. We could talk about Deleuze and Parnet as subjects of distinct histories and give an account of how they came together in the writing of this book. That is, we could give a narrative for each depicting their responses to their respective situations and the enactment of specific intentions in concrete action. But this would miss what for Deleuze is the crucial point: the book grew along lines that cannot be reduced to such a history. The becomings that make up the book are unattributable to individuals and cannot be accounted for by giving a history of its various factors construed as coherent unities with past and future effects. This does not, however, render the lines of the book any less real. Books, as well as subjects and other "things," can be thought of as unities with histories, or they can be thought of as multiplicities with lines of becoming that connect with the lines of other multiplicities in unpredictable ways. To think and write in terms of recognizable unities is to close off movement along lines of flight; it is to conform to a code of dominant utterances (74). Instead of responding to subtle shifts in terrain, such thinking conforms to an already established conceptual grid and so cannot introduce genuine novelty. To think and write in terms of becoming is "to release from becoming that which will not permit itself to be fixed in a term" (75). This kind of thinking challenges any preconceptions by bringing one up against that which forces a kind of thinking that is creative (and therefore, for Deleuze, "genuine") rather than constrained by a model of recognition (D&R 147).

Every "thing" is a multiplicity and is made up of a set of lines (D vii). One extracts concepts corresponding to multiplicities by mapping the lines (rather than the points) that make up a multiplicity. These lines are "true becomings." Becomings are not unities. They are not subjects of a history. They cannot be captured through a process of representation that would trace their origin to a specific moment in chronological time; instead, they happen behind one's back. Deleuze suggests that it is in such becomings that the real stuff of life occurs — the happenings that lead to encounters with others, novelty, creativity, and the singularity of existence when it just is rather than when it conforms to a preconceived schema: "Movement always happens behind the thinker's back, or in the moment when he blinks. . . . We think too much in terms of history, whether personal or universal. Becomings belong to geography, they are orientations, directions, entries and exits" (1–2). Mapping contextualizes the happenings of a terrain by providing the texture of the lay of the land; instead of tracing out a historical sequence with more or less linear sequences of cause and effect, it provides a cartography that can be pursued in any number of ways.

Deleuze thinks that traditional philosophy impedes and even prevents thinking. Emphasizing the centers of totalization and points of subjectivization of multiplicities, be they books, people, or thoughts, prevents the "transmutation of fluxes, through which life escapes from the resentment of persons, societies and reigns" (D 50). He deliberately contrasts his own approach to that of traditional philosophy (which he claims is "shot through with the project of becoming the official language of a Pure State" [13]). For Deleuze, the aim of writing is to follow out, rather than stop, the lines that make up multiplicities, even if this means running the risk of becoming unintelligible or unrecognizable: "Still way beyond a woman-becoming, a Negro-becoming, an animal-becoming, etc., beyond a minority-becoming, there is the final enterprise of the becoming-imperceptible. Oh no, a writer cannot wish to be 'known', recognized. . . . Writing has no other end than to lose one's face, to jump over or pierce through the wall, to plane down the wall very patiently" (45).

Perception involves resemblance and similarity. To be visible, a becoming must already be perceivable, and to be perceivable means that it will be perceived as being like something else. Becomings are imperceptible. In the third chapter of *Difference and Repetition*, Deleuze elaborates his claim that philosophy's image of thought is based on a model of recognition. This model assumes a coherence of both subject and object and a correspondence between the two. Subject and object are both taken to be unities, and these unities are determined through resemblance and analogy. Deleuze argues that the philosophical doctrine of faculties assumes this model of recognition and in so doing assumes the unity of a thinking subject and thus the convergence of various faculties upon a coherent object. Plato's theory of the forms created a representational image of thought which subordinated difference to identity and resemblance; the "truth" of thinking was measured against the originary ideals of the forms.[13] Kant continued in this tradition when he posited the 'I think' as the most general principle of representation; it is when each faculty "locates its given as identical to that of another" that the faculties are related in the 'I think' of the subjective unity of a consciousness with a recognizable object as its correlate.[14] For Deleuze, conceiving of thought in terms of recognition curtails its creative force. Harmonious accord of the faculties can be achieved only in terms of agreement on the identity of their respective objects. To assume that it is only such objects that are real is to subordinate difference to identity. What is thinkable or perceivable is that which is recognizable; what is recognizable is that which can be referred to what is the same.

Following lines of becomings might indicate a different story: "Something in the world forces us to think. This something is an object not of recognition but of a fundamental *encounter*. . . . It may be grasped in a range of affective tones: wonder, love, hatred, suffering. In whichever tone, its primary characteristic is that it can only be sensed. In this sense it is opposed to recognition" (D&R 139). Insofar as an object is unrecognizable, it is imperceptible. The object of an encounter cannot be recognized, Deleuze argues, because one's sensibility can recognize only that which can be apprehended by the other faculties as well, in the context of a coherent object upon which the faculties converge (140). The assumption that the various faculties of a self will converge in recognizing an object suggests that "the form of identity in objects relies upon a ground in the unity of a thinking subject, of which all the other faculties must be modalities" (133). In a discussion of Platonic reminiscence, Deleuze states that sensibility in the presence of the imperceptible "finds itself before its own limit . . . and raises itself to the level of a transcendental exercise" (140). Thinking that is forced to grasp "that which can only be thought" (141) unhinges the faculties and breaks with common sense: "Rather than all the faculties converging and contributing to a common project of recognising an object, we see divergent projects in which, with regard to what concerns it essentially, each faculty is in the presence of that which is its 'own'. Discord of the faculties, chain of force and fuse along which each confronts its limit, receiving from (or communicating to) the other only a violence which brings it face to face with its own element, as though with its disappearance or its perfection" (141). Kant's project delineates multiple forms that common sense can take. The faculty of understanding dominates logical common sense, reason dominates moral common sense, while "various faculties enter into an accord which is no longer determined by any one of them" (KCP xii) in the case of aesthetic common sense. That there can be more than one form of common sense suggests that there can be more than one way that one's faculties converge upon an object. Furthermore, Deleuze argues that Kant's notion of the sublime provides an example of faculties in a discordant harmony in which "there is . . . something which is communicated from one faculty to another" (D&R 146) without forming a common sense.

What Deleuze calls a "superior," "transcendental" empiricism would explore that which cannot be grasped from the point of view of common sense by exploring the point at which each faculty is brought to "the extreme point of its dissolution, at which it falls prey to triple violence: the violence of that which forces it to be exercised, of that which it is forced to grasp and which it alone is able to grasp, yet also that of the ungraspable (from the point of view of its empirical exercise)" (D&R 143). Objects apprehended according to the dictates of common sense may evoke nothing new — no creative thinking, for example. But life always eludes common sense. It is the violence of an aleatory encounter that brings a particular faculty to its own specific limit, thus rendering the communication among faculties necessary for achieving a harmonious convergence upon an object difficult or impossible. Without such a convergence, no empirical object can emerge, and yet, Deleuze suggests, it is precisely such violent encounters that make up the terrain of actual living.

A Deleuzian doctrine of the faculties would require determining what element carries the faculties to their respective limits: "This element is intensity, understood as pure difference in itself, as that which is at once both imperceptible for empirical sensibility which grasps intensity only already covered or mediated by the quality to which it gives rise, and at the same time that which can be perceived only from the point of view of a transcendental sensibility which apprehends it immediately in the encounter" (D&R 144). Deleuze's use of the term 'transcendental sensibility' approaches Irigaray's notion of the sensible transcendental. A sensibility that is transcendental is not a sensibility that accesses a realm removed from experience. Nor is it a sensibility we can construct as that which must be the case for the empirical sensibility we have to take the form it does. This sensibility is experienced when faculties are brought to their limit and the heterogeneity of faculties is revealed. That is, it is precisely when something in our experience eludes our familiar categories of perception and conception and so pushes us to create new ones that we are shocked into what Deleuze calls "genuine" thinking. Like Heidegger, who thought that one could follow the path of thinking only through openness to Being, Deleuze too advocates a thinking that is receptive to what is heterogeneous to thought. Like Irigaray, who advocates a practice of perception that entails a spiritualization of the flesh, Deleuze asks us to heighten our awareness of the becomings that are obscured by the organized forms of phenomena. For Deleuze, thought has to deal with pure difference rather than proffer the model of recognition as an image of thought because it is only due to "an original violence inflicted upon thought" that thought is awakened: "There is only involuntary thought, aroused but constrained within thought, and all the more absolutely necessary for being born, illegitimately, of fortuitousness in the world" (139).

For Deleuze, it would seem that we are brought to a thinking that goes beyond a dogmatic image of thought by something imperceptible about our experience — something that we encounter, that we experience, that we immediately apprehend and yet do not perceive. Such encounters, if pursued, challenge the unity of the self and the unity of an object presented to a self. Focusing on the element of difference involves both an intensity of experience as well as violence and the dissolution of one's faculties. One is precisely not a unified self attending to a unified object when one grasps this intensive element. This element is instead that which brings each faculty to its limit. Transcendental empiricism would explore the limits of each faculty in pursuit of the behind-the-scenes encounters that provoke vital living and thinking.

To write in a way that follows out this kind of thinking is to refuse a dogmatic image of thought — that is, to refuse an image of thought based on a model of recognition in which everything is referred to a self. To write, for Deleuze, should be a becoming-imperceptible wherein one allows lines of flight to release one from both the central reference of a personal self as well as the organizing focus of coherent objects. Instead, one follows intensities and flows without worrying where they come from or what their histories might be. "To write has no other function: to be a flux which combines with other fluxes — all the minority-becomings of the world. A flux is something intensive, instantaneous and mutant — between a creation and a destruction. It is only when a flux is deterritorialized that it succeeds in making its conjunction with other fluxes, which deterritorialize it in their turn, and vice versa" (D 50). Following out the lines of flight of a multiplicity involves delirium and betrayal. On such lines of flight one no longer has a past or future; one betrays the fixed and established powers of the earth which try to hold one back, and one turns one's face away from God who turns his face away from humanity. "It is in this double turning-away, in the divergence of faces, that the line of flight — that is, the deterritorialization of man — is traced." Thus, one "goes off the rails," betrays one's commonsense notions of oneself, one's place in society or history, one's relationship to people and things, and becomes demonic (40). A writer jumps across intervals and "makes one multiplicity pass into another" (52). She refuses traditional boundaries, and her utterance "is the product of an assemblage — which is always collective, which brings into play within us and outside us populations, multiplicities, territories, becomings, affects, events." Her proper name "does not designate a subject, but something which happens, at least between two terms which are not subjects, but agents, elements" (51). She is, in an important sense, impersonal. Although the lines that make her up form a singular multiplicity, none of these lines has a history. And each line presents the possibility of a line of flight that both escapes the limits of any commonsense understanding of personal boundedness and transmutates into other multiplicities.

Deleuze's conception of the self and of writing suggests that living and writing are inevitably collaborative processes that are reduced to the acts of individuals only by the discounting of living lines of flight among multiplicities. As writers who are becoming-imperceptible, we are not unified subjects with histories but nomads following lines of flight, traitors to established practices with neither past nor future. We map geographies of intensities in a desert bereft of traditional landmarks and yet full of becomings and encounters with the imperceptible. We are no one self with an interior and exterior, but are ourselves inventions of assemblages that in turn invent (D 51). Deleuze's overtly collaborative work with Guattari actively engages nomadic subjectivity in its free-flowing connection with the world. His way of presenting the collaborative process between them suggests the obvious parallels to be made between one self as a multiplicity and the multiplicity formed through the collaboration of two selves.

> We were only two, but what was important for us was less our working together than this strange fact of working between the two of us. We stopped being 'author'. And these 'between-the-twos' referred back to other people, who were different on one side from on the other. The desert expanded, but in so doing became more populous. This had nothing to do with a school, with processes of recognition, but much to do with encounters. And all these stories of becomings, of nuptials against nature, of a-parallel evolution, of bilingualism, of theft of thoughts, were what I had with Félix. (17)

Deleuze neither denies nor denigrates his part in this process of collaboration, and yet the place that he finds for himself in it is not predicated on having to claim or own any particular part of the work. He may present himself as becoming-imperceptible in his writing, but his writing maps this process by attending to the terrain of its occurrence. The encounters of this becoming-imperceptible are part of this terrain. The writing produced from this mapping results in a collaborative effort in which two selves become one multiplicity with neither self losing its specificity in the process.

By suggesting models of subjectivity that subvert and undermine traditional subject/object distinctions, Deleuze gives us a way to acknowledge and valorize the unspoken subtext of our interactions. His work suggests a way of characterizing a more "feminine" mode of being which does not assume that the only activity worth talking about is activity that originates in an agent with the intention of achieving a specific effect.[15] Clearly, on this model, such intended effects can be only one small part of the overall terrain of a location. I have interpreted Deleuze and Guattari's notions of destratification and mapping in terms of a geographical metaphor of the embodied self as terrain extending out onto the surrounding terrain of the world because it suggests the ways in which these notions can be relevant to the elaboration of corporeal logics. Like Irigaray's description of intrauterine experience, the geographical metaphor of self as terrain suggests an all-encompassing contact with a world in which life processes problematize conventional notions of personal boundedness. Although Deleuze, unlike Irigaray, avoids a vocabulary that evokes the body in a personal sense, I use the notion of the body in the geographical metaphor of the self for that range of elusive experiences — or sub-experiences — beyond the reach of conventional language which, it seems to me, Deleuze's work evokes.

If we consider the processes described in *Anti-Oedipus* as processes that organize various strata of the geographical terrain of subjectivity, we have an account of subjectivity that does not necessarily entail the oedipal drama of psychoanalytic theory. This alternative model evokes an open-ended and embodied involvement with the world which is never completely articulable and which is always moving in uncanny directions. Rather than suggesting the insertion of a subject into a world that is other to it, this model suggests that living is a collaborative encounter and that the most interesting encounters are those that occur beyond the reach of any kind of mastery.[16] Writing that is a becoming-imperceptible articulates a process of transformative encounters. This cartography refuses a deterministic account of the origins of subjectivity and instead lays out its terrain in the context of surrounding territory, thus suggesting new ways of understanding the interconnections of subject and world while retaining the specificity of the subject's local terrain.

This model has the added advantage of giving us a new way of understanding self-assertiveness. A feminist might wonder how a model of subjectivity that encourages becoming-imperceptible could be of political use for women. Irigaray, as we saw, is very interested in the project of symbolizing femininity precisely so that feminine creativity can no longer be appropriated by masculine subjects. Although Deleuze urges a kind of betrayal of any form of perceptible identity one might achieve in order to follow out lines of flight prompted by molecular becomings, one does not get the impression from reading his work that he really intends to disappear. Like Irigaray, he is more interested in developing an economy of subjectivity premised on becoming and difference than in obliterating subjectivity entirely. Perceptibility, on the geographical model developed here, is predicated not on maintaining a gap between the self and the world, but rather on attentiveness to shifts in terrain. A becoming-imperceptible that is mapped challenges traditional demarcations between self and other without sacrificing the distinctive features of specific encounters. Mapping refuses reductionistic categories of subjectivity as well as the failure of subjectivity. A subject whose vitality emerges from behind-the-scenes encounters is a subject immersed in a world of which it is an integral part. It is a subject who both affects and is affected by a vast range of heterogeneous multiplicities, who is formed and informing, and who is a collaborative result involved in further collaboration.

Irigaray attempts to get beyond the dynamic of domination implicit in specular subjectivity by suggesting that reciprocity is both possible and preferable. This is why her dialogue with Nietzsche is so important: she needs to shatter the mirror and get him to hear her so that both may achieve together a new way of living. This is not something that she can do alone. So long as the masculine subject denies the feminine other recognition, and so long as she gets no support for her own subjectivity, she is doomed to be his echo. But what a transformation could occur — Irigaray suggests — if only he were willing to relinquish his blindness in order to attempt a transformation of consciousness, subjectivity, and relationship to others. The touching of two lips, of two hands in prayer, the all-encompassing yet nourishing contact of a fetus in the womb — incomplete on its own and yet supported by the world in which it lives — provide provocative hints of collaborative encounters between two subjects. Providing symbolic support for contemporary femininity would enable women as women to resist the role of feminine other and demand masculine subjects to acknowledge the constitutive aspect of the role played by feminine others. This would bring about an acknowledgment of corporeality and a shift from a self-image as an intelligent entity with a body and a mind to a process of becoming with multiple points of convergence on an infinite world of sensation-feeling out of which selves need to be not only initially formed but continually reworked as well. Symbolizing femininity is one way in which the cultural imaginary and symbolic could be reworked in order to bring about new ways of living. For Irigaray this may be the only way, or perhaps simply our best hope at this historical juncture for this kind of change.

Mapping the strata of subjectivity in terms of destratifying lines of flight, however, could open up other creative possibilities in symbolization. Although, as I have argued, Irigaray's notion of symbolizing the feminine seems to me ultimately to insist on developing a logic of multiplicity that would overturn all dualisms, the notion of mapping could be more congenial to those who have their own binarisms to work against. Although Irigaray's work may be more readily accessible to women (and I am not at all sure whether or not this is the case), it is certainly not accessible to all of them, and for many different reasons — reasons that relate to the specific woman at issue. Since mapping proffers a limitless range of differences with which to work, it could provide a more congenial way of developing a line of flight. If one engages in the kind of rigorous and active thinking prompted by reading Deleuze, one engages in a form of active meditation that, I have suggested, entails a practice of thinking which integrates corporeal logics into conceptual thought.[17] Deleuze's experimentations call for bodily deterritorialization as well as conceptual deterritorialization. Like Irigaray's notion of opening to the sensible transcendental, Deleuze's notion of becoming-imperceptible calls for a transformation in our embodied experience rather than a preconceived program of social change. It allows us to go beyond the perceptions and conceptions of conventional life in order to touch upon the imperceptible reality from which innovative solutions to life's problems can emerge. Mapping lines of flight in keeping with a map of the social field that connects individual lines of flight with those of others could allow us to explore the open-ended possibilities that move us in concert with the others who form an integral part of our own terrain.

Deleuze's Reading of Philosophy

Deleuze and Guattari's last book together, *What Is Philosophy?*, presents an extended description of philosophy and what distinguishes it from science and art. I give a preliminary account of this characterization here in order to demonstrate how the project of thinking and writing philosophically turns out to be one form that the project of schizoanalysis or destratification can take. Like Irigaray's project of creating another language that can speak for a subject radically different from the contemporary norm, Deleuze's philosophical project will turn out to foster the becoming-imperceptible of a nomadic subject. Insofar as one thinks and writes philosophically, one can begin to chart the realm of imperceptible becomings that lies behind the scene of representational thinking. The new image of thinking for which Deleuze calls would require a new kind of subject. Enacting a new image of thought in one's thinking thus requires destratification from the representative territorializations and reterritorializations of a subject's individual history.

Whereas Irigaray develops a positive characterization of feminine subjectivity as an alternative that could break us out of a way of thinking, speaking, and living which privileges the masculine to the detriment of the feminine, Deleuze, in collaboration with Guattari, develops a positive characterization of philosophy which could transform contemporary forms of thinking, speaking, and living. Deleuze and Guattari focus on philosophy rather than the philosopher because their line of flight involves destratifying from the personal identity of oedipalization in order to release prepersonal possibilities. To write philosophically involves inventing conceptual personae — characters or perspectives like Nietzsche's Zarathustra which are distinguishable from the personal identity of the author. Like schizoanalysis, philosophy can release prepersonal singularities by approaching chaos through the alternative subjectivity of conceptual personae. That is, conceptual personae can enable the embodied philosopher to engage in thinking that goes beyond the thinking of a molar subject. It can thus be understood as a practice that deconstructs molar identities in order to release new possibilities at the level of molecular becoming. This in turn could be construed as an integrative practice that attempts to incorporate more of the realm of imperceptible becomings that both nourishes and threatens the ordinary scene of representation. In the context of the project of this book, this would amount to a practice of integrating and harmonizing corporeal and conceptual logics in order to bring about a transformation in conscious awareness that transcends traditional mind/body dualisms. I give here a preliminary sketch of this notion of philosophy in order to provide a point of comparison between Deleuze's and Irigaray's approach to philosophy. In Chapter 8 I will give a more complete account of the notion of philosophy that comes out in *What Is Philosophy?* and investigate more fully philosophy as a form of schizoanalysis.

In *What Is Philosophy?* Deleuze and Guattari describe philosophy as "the art of forming, inventing, and fabricating concepts" (WP 2). They claim that science, art, and philosophy are equally creative, but that only philosophy "creates concepts in the strict sense" (5), and they deliberately distinguish contemplation and communication from the act of creating a concept (6). Deleuze and Guattari indicate a way of doing philosophy that has immanent criteria for its production. That is, insofar as one philosophizes, one follows out movements of thought rather than representing phenomena. The philosophical problem with which one is concerned of course applies to the real world in which the philosopher lives, but in following out thought movements, one must be true only to the intensities that push thought forward.

Philosophical thought-movements adhere to the immanent principle of consistency; the creation of concepts pursues the internal consistency of concepts as well as the consistency of concepts with other concepts.[18] Every concept is related to other concepts, and each concept renders the components of which it is made inseparable. The latter components define the consistency of the concept. They are distinct and heterogeneous and yet not separable. For example, Deleuze and Guattari's concept of 'production' in *Anti-Oedipus* includes the components of the social production of human beings and the primary production of nonhuman life processes. Each component partially overlaps and "has a zone of neighborhood, or a threshold of indiscernability, with another one" (WP 19); certain phases of social production are indiscernable from certain phases of nonhuman forms of production, and yet in other phases the two components diverge.[19]

Concepts are not bound to the embodied awareness of a coherent person. Since they are bound by rules of consistency rather than of common-sense awareness, they break with personal consciousness and introduce extradiscursive elements into thinking. Concepts are related to human problems, but they are closer to becomings than to history. Rigorously pursuing consistency involves attentive pursuit of zones of intensity. In order to discern zones of neighborhood, the philosopher must betray personal identity in order to focus on subtle shifts in intensity. This kind of attention goes beyond the deductions of rational thought and involves heightened attunement to corporeal logic typically below the level of awareness.[20] The shock of genuine thinking is a corporeal as well as conceptual encounter that breaks one out of sterile formations of molar thought. Concepts could always have been created otherwise, just as organisms could always have produced an alternative arrangement of desiring-machines. If concepts set up certain zones of neighborhoods rather than others, it is because they unfold according to an immanent desire (or image of thought) which constitutes itself in the process of creating concepts. When one criticizes a concept, one may be able to establish that "a concept vanishes when it is thrust into a new milieu, losing some of its components, or acquiring others that transform it." But "those who criticize without creating, those who are content to defend the vanished concept without being able to give it the forces it needs to return to life, are the plague of philosophy" (WP 28). For Deleuze, writing a straightforward critique of a philosopher can only be inspired by *ressentiment*; like Irigaray, Deleuze feels compelled to invent a new style of reading and writing. Whereas Irigaray engages in subversive mimicry (see Chapter 2) when reading philosophical texts, Deleuze implements concepts and varies them in keeping with the immanent movements of his thinking. Both in his reading of other philsophers — in particular his book on Nietzsche, which I address in the next chapter — and in the work commencing with *Difference and Repetition*, Deleuze engages in a philosophical form of becoming-imperceptible by pursuing an immanent movement of consistency in the becomings of the concepts that he implements or creates.

In the next chapter I lay out Deleuze's appropriative relationship to Nietzsche. Deleuze has none of Irigaray's problems in taking what works for him from Nietzsche's conceptual armory and using it for experiments of his own. I then explore his rendering of Nietzsche's notions of forces and the will to power in order to develop the Nietzschean influence on Deleuze's conception of the dissolution of perceptions, subjects, things, and ideas into the forces that make them up. In *Nietzsche and Philosophy*, Deleuze develops the concepts of active and reactive forces, affirming and denying will to power, the dice-throw, and the eternal return in order to indicate a subjectivity and a practice that would acknowledge active forces in a practice that would ultimately lead to a transformation of consciousness. Active forces, like molecular processes, are imperceptible. Nietzsche claims that only reactive forces are perceptible; we perceive the effects of forces rather than forces in their dynamic becoming.[21] Insofar as we remain at the level of perceptible forces we miss the active forces that actually generate life. Deleuze's quest after the imperceptible could be read in the context of his book on Nietzsche as a quest after active forces and an affirming will to power that would actively affirm the being of becoming rather than the more stable forms (for example, of representational thought) that emerge from that becoming. Like Irigaray, Deleuze is inspired by Nietzsche's break with representational thought and his insistence on the forces and becomings of which we are unaware. Nietzsche's conception of phenomena as symptoms of the forces of becoming gives Deleuze an alternative vocabulary to the psychoanalytic account of the unconscious.

I also examine Deleuze's conception of the eternal return. Here Deleuze goes further than Nietzsche himself to articulate what he thought Nietzsche must have meant. The resulting interpretation is quite different from Irigaray's. By emphasizing the logic of multiplicity that Deleuze sees emerging in Nietzsche's work, he turns the eternal return into a double selection in which all becoming-reactive must become-active, thereby canceling out anything that is not affirming. Thus, instead of the return of the same, we have only the return of difference, or the being of becoming. Whereas Irigaray insists that Nietzsche ultimately withdraws from the body he would embrace owing to his inability to acknowledge sexual difference, Deleuze pursues Nietzsche's concepts down a liberating line of flight. This line of flight insists on the dissolution of self and perceptions into the prepersonal singularities of Deleuze's reading of Nietzsche's concepts of force and will to power. Since all forces are connected, since the lines of flight can run in all directions, to insist on sexual difference could be simply another trap. I will explore this conundrum through Deleuze and Irigaray's differing conceptions of the eternal return, and present some conclusions in the final section on sexual difference.

6

Deleuze's Nietzsche

Speaking in One's Own Name

It is perhaps because Deleuze feels so comfortable attaching proper names to his exercises in depersonalization that he is able to carry out Nietzschean experiments rather than worry about his position vis-à-vis Nietzsche. As someone who considers himself a philosopher and has even — in *What Is Philosophy?*, his last book with Guattari — delineated philosophy with respect to science and the arts, Deleuze is clearly not above mapping out his geography in a way that will stabilize his own identity despite his project of becoming-imperceptible. If Irigaray asks to be let in, it is because — as she insists — there is something about femininity that makes this kind of geographical placement problematic. For Irigaray to follow a line of flight, she needs to overcome an aspect of the social field that renders her creativity invisible and that regularly steals her creative capacities in order to appropriate them for its own. A line of flight must have orienting marks to follow even if those marks are no more than symptomatic indications of background processes which can be neither perceived nor articulated. In this chapter and the next two I further explore what goes into a Deleuzian line of flight. In the final chapter I return to Irigaray in order to investigate how Deleuze's notion of mapping might be related to Irigaray's notion of acknowledging the feminine other, and what kinds of effects this process of acknowledgment might have for the lines of flight that we map.

In a letter to Michele Cressole published in 1973 (N 6–7), Deleuze says that his book on Nietzsche broke him out of a certain style of writing commentaries more properly located in the history of philosophy. It was impossible to write such a commentary on Nietzsche. Instead, Nietzsche gave him a perverse taste for speaking in his own name. But speaking in one's own name turns out not to be about positing a self, a person, or a subject that speaks in his own name. Instead, a genuine proper name is acquired by the individual through a radical exercise in depersonalization in which that individual opens herself to the multiplicities that traverse her. Nietzsche set Deleuze in the direction of attempting to write as a flux rather than as a code. In *Anti-Oedipus*, Deleuze describes Nietzsche's own flux through the names of history.

There is no Nietzsche-the-self, professor of philology, who suddenly loses his mind and supposedly identifies with all sorts of strange people; rather, there is the Nietzschean subject who passes through a series of states, and who identifies these states with the names of history: "*every name in history is I . . .*" The subject spreads itself out along the entire circumference of the circle, the center of which has been abandoned by the ego. At the center is the desiring-machine, the celibate machine of the Eternal Return. A residual subject of the machine, Nietzsche-as-subject garners a euphoric reward (Voluptas) from everything that this machine turns out, a product that the reader had thought to be no more than the fragmented *oeuvre* by Nietzsche. . . . It is not a matter of identifying with various historical personages, but rather identifying the names of history with zones of intensity on the body without organs; and each time Nietzsche-as-subject exclaims: "They're *me*! So it's *me*!" (A-O 21)

According to Deleuze and Guattari, social systems of production vary from culture to culture. It is capitalism (as we saw in Chapter 5), as a specific form a social formation can take, which insists on the oedipalization of social subjects. Oedipalization is a further refinement of social repression; while the larger social field provides a wide range of social identities to choose from, oedipalization requires personalizing these identities in keeping with the oedipal scenario. Desire which could have ranged freely through a plethora of socially significant possibilities is thus restricted to a much narrower range of possibilities. Whereas the Nietzschean subject alluded to in the quoted passage can expand his identity to include all the names of history, a properly oedipalized subject can have only the desires of a subject with the limited perspective pertaining to her own familial drama.

Nietzsche as residual subject of the celibate machine of the eternal return is non-egoic in the sense that his identity is not limited to the personal identity of the oedipal triangle. This releases Nietzsche from the constricting repression of ego-identity and permits libidinal investment in an expanded range of identifications. These investments have no meaning on an unconscious level. They are productive rather than right or wrong and create flows and breaks that lead to other breaks and flows. The residual subject can attach various labels from the social field of language to the states through which he passes as an embodied subject. He names the states through which he passes not according to an oedipal scenario, but according to what satisfies a kind of equilibrium of the desiring-machines of his physical and psychic selves in tension with the body without organs which repulses any determinate form of organization and the possibilities in identification presented by the social formation in which he finds himself. The more loosely organized social identities of an anoedipal subject provide more possibilities in such equilibriums. For example, Nietzsche attaches the name of Zarathustra to the production of the thought of the eternal return, and the name of Dionysus to the production of the affirmation of dismemberment in the unity of becoming.

Nietzsche as the residual subject of the celibate machine of the eternal return "garners a euphoric reward from everything that this machine turns out," which is presumably more than could be turned out by Nietzsche as personal machine. Rather than suffering from repression so severe that there is nothing left to want, this subject flows from point to point; rather than experiencing emptiness and crippling inadequacy, he lives in the fullness of a movement that knows no lack. Through the thought of the eternal return, this subject affirms himself as a multiplicity of intensities which can pursue hitherto unexperienced forms of desire. Giving priority to the desires about which one can be most passionate leads to risking conventional formations of the self with its familiar desires. In the affirmation of these multiple experiments, this subject self-destructs; the pursuit

of desires that defy conventional identities demands the continual mutua-
tion of the self into unprecedented forms. These forms can be stabilized
through social identifications that go beyond those available within an
oedipal scenario.

Deleuze's book on Nietzsche reads less like a scholarly treatise on Nietzsche than a Nietzschean experiment.[1] In this book Deleuze develops some
of the concepts that he would continue to work on throughout his life. The
notions of force, will to power, the dice-throw, and the eternal return are
all concepts that Deleuze carries forward into his own lines of flight. The
subject that emerges from his reading of Nietzsche is not a personal self but
an assemblage of singularities, affects, intensities, experiences, and experiments. Such a self (if one could call it a self) has no lack because it is not
predicated on some ideal notion of its unity or completeness. Instead, it is a
process or movement that dynamically becomes in the space of the "between" without reference to any end result or ideal totalization. It is prepersonal or impersonal because it has no personal biography. It moves in the
immediacy of fluxes and flows that are only minimally referred to that
which transcends the immanent production of desiring-machines.[2]

The image of Nietzsche as residual subject of the desiring-machine of
the eternal return presents an audacious experiment in subjectivity. Although this image does not emerge until *Anti-Oedipus*, Deleuze's book
Nietzsche and Philosophy already lays out the concepts that are crucial to this
experiment. As the Nietzschean genealogist who interprets and evaluates
the phenomena of the world in terms of the dynamic forces and will to
power that make them up, Deleuze embraces a Nietzschean empiricism
that refuses to take phenomena at face value. As the residual subject of the
eternal return, he pursues connections that defy "common sense" and put
his own self into doubt. We can compare these experiments to those of
schizoanalysis, destratification, and becoming-imperceptible, discussed in
Chapter 5. The development of an attitude and perspective toward life
which is both attentively aware of even the painful and disorienting aspects of life and yet affirmatively creative is a crucial feature of all these experiments. The residual subject puts personal identity at risk in order to
experience the fluxes of a life in process. To write as a flux rather than a
code is to attempt to map some part of this process. Nietzsche's concepts
of force and will, the overman and the eternal return, provide some orienting markers for engaging in such a project.

We have seen that Irigaray reads Nietzsche's notion of the eternal return as a displacement of masculine specularity from an individual subject
to the individual as cosmos. If the Nietzschean subject can embrace dy-

namic becoming, it is because he excludes the feminine other who threatens his masculine self-sufficiency by centering all becoming around himself through the notion of the eternal return. That is, if all becoming is dynamically linked, then the continual return or repetition of this becoming can still be referred to the Nietzschean subject's own becoming (as a necessary link in the cycle), thus precluding recognition of what is truly other to his own creative power. Deleuze insists, as we will see, that what returns is becoming and not the same. And yet the notion of Nietzsche as residual subject of the desiring-machine of the eternal return entails what might be construed to be appropriative identifications with "all the names of history." I return to this issue and its implications in the final section of this chapter. Although Deleuze and Irigaray part ways in their readings of the eternal return, we will find striking resonance between some of the concepts Deleuze develops in his reading of Nietzsche and those of Irigaray. Like Irigaray, Deleuze is drawn to Nietzsche's attempts to speak the unspeakable: the dynamic flux of life which defies the conventional categories of perception and conception and invites us to a thinking that could radically transform the way we experience ourselves, our world, and our relationships to others.

Active/Reactive Forces and Will to Power

Deleuze, one might argue, wants to be the "philosopher of the future" that Nietzsche wanted; he is the philosopher-physician who interprets symptoms, the philosopher-artist who molds types, and the philosopher-legislator who determines rank and genealogy. He is a cultural diagnostician who tries to put his finger on the pulse of cultural degeneracy in order to determine a cure. In reading Deleuze, one is encouraged not simply to interpret and evaluate passively (reactively) what Deleuze is saying; one is encouraged to experiment, to actually try on the meaning of the words by interpreting and evaluating those words from one's own perspective according to one's own forces and quality of will. Some might say, despite Deleuze's obviously careful readings, that he leaves out important aspects of Nietzsche's thought. But by interpreting and evaluating Nietzsche's words in keeping with his own will to power, Deleuze is following the path he believes Nietzsche invites us to travel.

Traditional philosophical prose reflects conventional subject/object dichotomies through grammatically correct formulation of sentences with subjects and predicates. The authorial 'I' of such prose implies a clearly defined subject taking up a position vis-à-vis an object of thought. Nietzsche transforms the conventional image of thought which privileges questions about truth and falsity and creates a thought-movement concerned with the interpretation of forces and the evaluation of power. That to think is to create is, according to Deleuze, Nietzsche's greatest lesson (N xiv). Thought-movements do not represent a reality that we can then verify with reference to the world; they are participants in a world in which they make things happen. They thus instigate becomings that may not be apparent at the level of representational thought: "It is a question of producing within the work a movement capable of affecting the mind outside of all representation; it is a question of making movement itself a work, without interposition; of substituting direct signs for mediate representations; of inventing vibrations, rotations, whirlings, gravitations, dances or leaps which directly touch the mind" (D&R 8). Deleuze claims that this approach involves a transmutation of the principle on which thought depends and so entails thinking in a new way. This new way of thinking will be a thinking that affirms life and the will to life, "a thought which finally expels the whole of the negative; to believe in the innocence of the future and the past, to believe in the eternal return" (NP 35).

Nietzsche casts interpretations and evaluations of multiplicities in terms of dynamic movement. Rather than asking about the properties of a thing, he asks about what is happening. This question leads him to examine the relationships of the forces that constitute a proposition or a phenomenon along with "the genetic relationship which determines these forces" — the will to power manifest in the forces (NP xi). Will to power is the differential and genetic element internal to the production of force.

The Nietzschean genealogist is a physician who diagnoses values and provides a cure. A Nietzschean genealogical account traces the relations of forces that make up the history of a value and evaluates whether the will to power manifested through these changing relations is affirmative or negative. Her interpretation specifies the meaning of a phenomenon by indicating whether and how the relationships among the forces making it up are dominating or dominated, active or reactive. Her evaluation gives a value to the phenomenon by indicating whether and how it manifests an affirmative or negative will to power. Reactive force, according to Deleuze, is adaptive and partially limited; it separates active force from what it can do and it is separated from what it can do. Active force is plastic and dominating, goes to its limit, and affirms its difference. This means that it continually mutates in a self-transforming process whose effects are an additional influence in further transformations. That is, a reactive force produces effects without affecting itself in the process, while an active force preserves no part of itself that could be identified as the same in its mutating passage of becoming-other. It is only through interpretation subtle enough to take these nuances of forces and their relations into account in the context of their affinity to an affirmative or negative will to power that the genealogist is able to discover "what sort of baseness can find its expression in one value, what sort of nobility in another" (NP 55); it is an affirmative will to power which produces what for both Nietzsche and Deleuze is the "noble" becoming-active of forces.

Mediocre thought reflects a "mania for interpreting or evaluating phenomena in terms of reactive forces" (NP 56). It understands things through the inverted image; it takes what is and shows why it had to be that way, and it assumes that whatever exists is right or noble because it dominated other ways of being. This reactive perspective analyzes only what is already apparent. All-too-human philosophers typically attempt to analyze concepts, feelings, and actions from the "disinterested" perspective of one whose will is not involved in the analysis, and in terms of an object that is also attached to no will. The genealogist refuses to detach phenomena in this way from their differential element. It is the will to power that makes phenomena what they are.

In Nietzsche's terms, we must say that every phenomenon not only reflects a type which constitutes its sense and value, but also the will to power as the element from which the signification of its sense and the value of its value derive. *In this way the will to power is essentially creative and giving:* it does not aspire, it does not seek, it does not desire, above all it does not desire power. It *gives:* power is something inexpressible in the will (something mobile, variable, plastic); power is in the will as "the bestowing virtue," through power the will itself bestows sense and value. (NP 85)

It is the will to power that by estimating a determinate relationship of forces from a specific perspective endows a phenomenon with meaning (which includes a value — for example, the wonderful Wagnerian opera *Parsifal*), and it is also the will to power — as affirmative or negative — from which the value of that meaning derives (from Nietzsche's genealogical perspective, the will to power estimating *Parsifal* as wonderful must be a negative, life-denying one, and thus the value of its valuing is "base" rather than "noble"). To abstract phenomena from the will to power can only lead to a falsification of phenomena that is ultimately, according to Nietzsche, life-denying. To get beyond symptoms to essences, one must give a genealogical account of the nuance of the quality of the will to power. This means to interpret and evaluate how and in what way a phenomenon manifests itself as the symptom of a set of related forces informed by an affirmative or negative will to power. Rather than referring phenomena to a totalized ideal abstracted from becoming, Nietzsche's philosophy attempts to account for phenomena in terms of the active forces — or what the later Deleuze might call the imperceptible becomings — from which they emerge.

In the act of interpreting and evaluating, the genealogist is, of course, participating in the play of forces. She is herself a multiplicity of forces affecting and affected by the forces with which she interacts. Each interpretation and evaluation she makes can be, in turn, interpreted and evaluated. The thinker who can think with a new image of thought allows life to make thought active, and thought to make life affirmative: "Life would be the active force of thought, but thought would be the affirmative power of life. Both would go in the same direction, carrying each other along, smashing restrictions, matching each other step for step, in a burst of unparalleled creativity. Thinking would then mean *discovering, inventing, new possibilities of life*" (NP 101). Thoughts are neither true nor false but noble or base, high or low, "depending on the nature of the forces that take hold of thought itself" (104). Philosophy should expose base forms of thought and turn thought into "something aggressive, active and affirmative" (106). "Insofar as our thinking is controlled by reactive forces, insofar as it finds its sense in reactive forces, we must admit that we are not yet thinking" (108). Being, truth, and reality are evaluations that actualize the will and that have, up to now, served the power or quality of a negative will to power. Deleuze says that all three function in the same way as does the divine afterworld, which is figured in Nietzsche's work as a life-denying counterworld to this one. The will to power in its affirming quality "through which willing is adequate to the whole of life" (185) affirms life in all its particularity and renders it active.

To affirm is still to evaluate, but to evaluate from the perspective of a will which enjoys its own difference in life instead of suffering the pains of the opposition to this life that it has itself inspired. *To affirm is not to take responsibility for, to take on the burden of what is, but to release, to set free what lives.* To affirm is to unburden: not to load life with the weight of higher values, but *to create* new values which are those of life, which make life light and active. There is creation, properly speaking, only insofar as we make use of excess in order to invent new forms of life rather than separating life from what it can do. (NP 185)

To realize a Nietzschean critique, one must give a genealogical account of the permutations of the will to power as a plastic and creative element that qualifies forces. If we accept a culture's values as they are presented, without interpreting or evaluating them as symptoms of the culture, then we cannot effectively criticize them. It is by giving a genealogical account of those values that we can evaluate the will to power manifest in them as denying or affirming and thus prepare the way for a transmutation to an affirming culture. Deleuze is careful to distinguish Nietzsche's notion of an affirming will to power from an acquiescent attitude toward all that "is." First, given that Nietzsche reads the true and the real as symptoms of forces, and given that such an interpretation involves evaluation as well, one's relationship to "reality" is one not of acceptance but of creation — the creation of evaluations carried out in terms of an affirmative will to power. Second, genuine affirmation is so far beyond the capacity of reactive humanity that it is only the overman — an entirely new form of life beyond the human — who will be capable of it. By trying to articulate an alternative image of thought, Deleuze attempts to articulate another way of knowing and another concept of truth which presupposes a will completely different from that of humanity: "The aim of critique is not the ends of man or of reason but in the end the Overman, the overcome, overtaken man. The point of critique is not justification but a different way of feeling: another sensibility" (NP 94).

In the *Genealogy of Morals*, Nietzsche characterizes human history as nihilistic and analyzes the principal forms of nihilism as the *ressentiment* of Semitic thought, the bad conscience of Christianity, and the ascetic ideal of metaphysics. Nihilism in all its forms depreciates life, creates the fiction of something to be valued more than life (God, essence, the good, truth), and entails a negative will to power (a will to nothingness). Deleuze delineates three forms of nihilism: negative nihilism subordinates life to God; reactive nihilism supplants God with man and the ideals of truth and the good; passive nihilism puts even these ideals into doubt, creating "last men" too cynical to value anything above their own comfort and for whom life is so depreciated as to be stripped of all meaning and purpose (NP 151, 148). According to Deleuze, "nihilism reaches its completion by passing through the last man, but going beyond him to the man who wants to perish" (175). It is only when nihilism is completed that the negative will to power of humanity can transmute into an affirmative will to power and the overman can emerge out of the destruction of the all-too-human.

Although Nietzsche gives no positive characterization of the overman who is genuinely capable of affirming life, he does characterize the human types who manifest nihilism in its various forms. Deleuze's characterization of Nietzsche's man of *ressentiment* is of particular interest since it describes the reactive nature of consciousness which is foundational for the other nihilistic types. The creature who will be able to overcome nihilism and live actively — the overman — will not act according to the dictates of reactive consciousness, but will allow action to emerge from an affirmative will to power. We will see that the man of *ressentiment* becomes rigidified into familiar patterns of perception and conception. The forms of conventional experience become painfully constraining. The overman, instead of resenting life owing to the constraints of a painfully binding structuring of subjectivity, is able to affirm life actively as it is lived. In the vocabulary of the model of subjectivity I am developing here, we might say that the overman is highly capable of harmonizing corporeal and conceptual logics owing to a very rich and ongoing contact with the imperceptible becomings which make possible new formations of both. Exploring Deleuze's characterization of Nietzsche's man of *ressentiment* provides some clues as to what might be involved in such a radically affirming perspective.

According to Deleuze's reading of Nietzsche, an embodied subject is a multiple phenomenon composed of a plurality of irreducible forces. The dominant forces are active and the dominated forces are reactive (NP 40). Consciousness is the expression of certain reactive forces of the subject to the active forces which dominate (41). Conscious perception and conception require relatively stable forms; active forces mutate too quickly to come into conscious awareness. It is only by separating active forces from their true nature and power that consciousness can produce perceptible representations of them (cf. Goodchild 1996a, 30). "What makes the body superior to all reactions, particularly that reaction of the ego that is called consciousness, is the activity of necessarily unconscious forces" (NP 41–42). Deleuze claims that Nietzsche, like Freud, albeit with reservations, distinguishes the conscious and the unconscious as two systems within the reactive psychical apparatus.[3] Although Nietzsche includes a much wider range of forces in his conception of the unconscious than that of the unconscious memory system of consciousness, the latter system as well as the conscious system are both necessary for conscious awareness. The conscious system is supple enough to receive new excitations; the unconscious system traces the memories of past perceptions: "The reactive unconscious is defined by mnemonic traces, by lasting imprints. It is a digestive, vegetative and ruminative system, which expresses 'the purely passive impossibility of escaping from the impression once it is received'" (112). For the subject also to be receptive to present stimuli, another system is required "in which reaction is not reaction to traces but becomes a reaction to the present excitation or to the direct image of the object" (112–13). These reactive forces constitute a second system inseparable from consciousness which enables the latter to act as a "constantly renewed skin surrounding an ever fresh receptivity, a milieu 'where there is always room for new things' " (113).

For Nietzsche, the faculty of forgetting is an active force that separates the two systems of reactive forces so that mnemonic traces do not invade consciousness. Once mnemonic traces do invade consciousness, consciousness rigidifies, becoming inflexible and unable to adapt to the contemporary situation. When the faculty of forgetting is doing its job, reaction becomes something acted "because it takes conscious excitation as its object and reaction to traces remains in the unconscious, imperceptible": the faculty of forgetting "serves as 'guard' or 'supervisor,' preventing the two systems of the reactive apparatus from becoming confused. Although it is an active force its only activity is functional. It comes from activity but is abstracted from it. And in order to renew consciousness it constantly has to borrow the energy of the second kind of reactive forces, making this energy its own in order to give it to consciousness" (NP 113). When mnemonic traces take the place of present stimuli in the reactive apparatus, reactive forces prevail over active forces. That is, energy is invested in the reactive apparatus rather than the faculty of forgetting, the force of received excitations is invested in traces rather than in excitations as objects of perception, and the man of *ressentiment* becomes unable to act out his reaction to either traces or excitations: "Let us suppose that there is a lapse in the faculty of forgetting: it is as if the wax of consciousness were hardened, excitation tends to get confused with its trace in the unconscious and conversely, reaction to traces rises into consciousness and overruns it. *Thus at the same time as reaction to traces becomes perceptible, reaction ceases to be acted*" (114). Deleuze characterizes the consciousness of the man of *ressentiment* as being invaded by the traces of reactive memory. Reactive forces, unlike active forces, separate force from what it can do. Because reactive forces prevail in the man of *ressentiment*'s psychical apparatus, he becomes unable to bring his reactions to their limit. Instead of his spontaneously acting out his responses, his reactions become perceptible and turned into feelings without appropriate outlet: "As a result of his type the man of *ressentiment* does not 'react': his reaction is endless, it is felt instead of being acted. This reaction therefore blames its object, whatever it is, as an object on which revenge must be taken, which must be made to pay for this infinite delay" (115).

The man of *ressentiment* is in a lot of pain owing to the sclerosis or hardening of his consciousness. Instead of being able to receive and respond to fresh excitations, he finds himself trapped in the mnemonic traces of experiences that he has already had. Excitations freeze rapidly within him, and mnemonic traces invade him in a cruelly constraining way. The memory of traces itself is full of hatred. The memory of the man of *ressentiment* blames its objects for "its own inability to escape from the traces of the corresponding excitation" (NP 116). Instead of acting out his responses, the man of *ressentiment*, in his search for something on which to blame his pain, projects an inverted image through which reactive forces can represent themselves as superior to active ones. "It is this reactive projection that Nietzsche calls a fiction; the fiction of a super-sensible world in opposition to this world, the fiction of a God in contradiction to life" (125). Reactive forces thus triumph by pointing an accusing finger at the active forces of life.

Although in the case of the man of *ressentiment* mnemonic traces "invade" consciousness, some relationship between the fresh excitations of the present and memory of the past is clearly necessary for social life to take on the familiar forms of ordinary living. Deleuze, however, distinguishes two forms of memory in Nietzsche's thought: the reactive memory of unconscious mnemonic traces and the memory of the future which allows subjects to pledge themselves to shared projects of cultural becoming. Consciousness which is based on the faculty of forgetting needs something to give it consistency and firmness. According to Deleuze's reading of Nietzsche, it is culture that trains consciousness by endowing it with a memory of words in the form of a faculty of promising. While mnemonic traces of the unconscious relate to the individual subject's past, cultural memory is the memory not of sensibility but of the will and relates to a commitment to a future: "Justice is the generic activity that trains man's reactive forces, that makes them suitable for being acted and holds man responsible for this suitability itself. To justice we can oppose the way in which *ressentiment* and then bad conscience are formed: by the triumph of reactive forces, through their unsuitability for being acted, through their hatred for everything that is active, through their resistance, through their fundamental injustice" (NP 135–36).

Deleuze claims that Nietzsche believes culture has failed in its job of training faculties of forgetting and faculties of promising which can prevail against the reactive forces of nihilism: "Instead of justice and its process of self-destruction, history presents us with societies which have no wish to perish and which cannot imagine anything superior to their own laws"

(NP 138). Although nihilism has prevailed in human history, there is yet hope in the Zarathustras and philosophers of the future (among other free spirits) who could provide a cure for cultural degeneracy by transmuting a negative will to power into an affirmative one: "But there is a 'relatively superhuman type': the critical type, man *insofar as he wants to be gone beyond, overcome*" (94). If one takes phenomena at face value, for example, by returning to "the things themselves" in terms of a "purified" sense experience rather than as a symptom of forces not immediately perceptible to common sense, one misinterprets sense. If one defines the essence of phenomena with reference to the object of sense or to a reified ideal rather than in terms of the will to power which relates and qualifies forces, then one misinterprets essence. If one deals only with abstractions and phenomena as products rather than investigating the concrete relations of forces with respect to the differential element of the will to power, then one misinterprets change and transformation. Affirmative philosophy involves actively interpreting forces and evaluating will to power. This means actively forgetting the conventions of commonsense experience, thus preventing mnemonic traces from invading consciousness and allowing consciousness to make room for new things. Reactive interpreting and evaluating (for example, through analogical comparison with past perceptions and conceptions) invites resentment toward the objects of analysis; the incapacity to escape repetition of the past traps the philosopher in an uncomfortably constrained present. The separation of actve forces constituting her from what they can do (in the failure of active forgetting and the invasion of mnemonic traces) cuts such a philosopher off from a sense of herself as active. She resentfully posits a self by negating her objects (as not her) and so reactively establishing an "active" subject. The affirming philosopher would interpret forces in relation to dynamic will to power. This would lead her to the imperceptible becomings of active forces. This philosopher could be compared to the nomadic subject who engages in a process of destratification in order to pursue active lines of flight; she interprets and evaluates dynamic points of becoming, thus opening up a path toward an unprecedented future. Her self is a multiplicity of forces that emerge and mutate in constant interaction with other forces.

We might compare Deleuze's man of *ressentiment* to Irigaray's masculine subject and Deleuze's affirming philosopher or nomadic subject to Irigaray's feminine subject. The man of *ressentiment* posits himself through a double negation (projecting a fictional image of what he is not to which he opposes himself in order to establish what he is) and is invaded by mnemonic traces just as the masculine subject posits himself in opposition to a feminine other and is entombed in a body no longer able to respond to the present. The affirming philosopher actively forgets past forms of organization in order to attend to imperceptible becomings just as the feminine subject opens up to the sensible transcendental rather than forcing her experience to conform to familiar perceptions and conceptions. The notion of a genealogical reading of phenomena provides further clues as to how to create a line of flight or move toward a divine horizon of becoming within a specific social field; genealogical critique opens up new possibilities for the future through careful attention to the moving lines of contemporary terrain rather than the static points of reactive memory. According to Deleuze, it is only through the eternal return that nihilism can finally be completed, Zarathustra's transmutation from negative to affirmative will to power performed, and Dionysus' dance affirmed as the being of becoming. We will see why in the next section and compare this reading of the eternal return to that of Irigaray.

Deleuze's Reading of the Eternal Return

Deleuze interprets Nietzsche's doctrine of the eternal return as a process of double selection. First, "there is the selection of willing or of thought which constitutes Nietzsche's ethics," and then there is "the selection of being which constitutes Nietzsche's ontology" (NP xi). The first (ethical) selection is initiated by those who act in accordance with the thought of the eternal return in the form of the principle "Whatever you will, will it in such a way that you also will its eternal return" (68).[4] As an ethical doctrine, the eternal return presents an image of thinking with an implicit model of subjectivity that could lead to a transformation in human consciousness and life. The thought of the eternal return selects by making willing something whole; it "makes possible the elimination of all the half-desires and hesitant yearnings, the qualified excesses and provisional indulgences, of a cautious and calculating will" (Bogue 1989, 31). It confronts one with an image of forces and their relations that refuses to abstract particular forces out of the web of life. To play the game of life well, the player must affirm the roll of the dice that happens to fall. Affirming chance means not to hope for the outcome one is looking for, whether likely or not, but to embrace any outcome with all its implications. To affirm any one part of the whole entangled web of life, one has to take the dice-throw of chance as a single shot that brings everything else with it. It is this kind of affirmation that Zarathustra is able to carry out. Although inevitably still reactive and acting from a negative will to power, Zarathustra is able to set into motion the transmutation of the will. With the throw of the dice, he affirms whatever chance will bring.[5] Through such affirmation, all actions entailing resentment against life and any ambivalence about the consequences are eliminated. This turns willing into a creation, because it forces a stance of creative embracement. Instead of holding onto one's probabilities, one's "wish that it had been this way," one embraces whatever outcome falls as the outcome one wills. This is not the passive acceptance of someone resigned to "reality" as it is presented, but the creative affirmation of someone who interprets and evaluates forces from her or his own perspective.

The thought of the eternal return alone cannot transmute a negative will to power into an affirmative one or the becoming-reactive of human history into becoming-active. The thought of the eternal return may foster carrying out reactive forces to the limit of what they can do, but these reactive forces resist the first selection. It is in the second (ontological) selection that the will completes its transmutation and the eternal return makes "something come into being which cannot do so without changing nature" (NP 71). An affirming ethics is inherently dynamic. It entails the self-destruction of the reactive which in the context of reactive humanity entails the self-destruction of the human. Insofar as human beings enact the ethical principle of the eternal return, they foster the ontological selection of active subjects. Zarathustra's transmutation entails "downgoing" or the active destruction of "strong spirits which destroy the reactive in themselves, submitting it to the test of the eternal return and submitting themselves to this test even if it entails willing their own decline" (NP 70).[6] The strong spirit who wants to perish and to be overcome breaks alliance with reactive forces by negating her own reactive forces. Negation is completed when it "*sacrifices* all reactive forces, becoming 'relentless destruction of everything that was degenerating and parasitical,' " and passes "into the service of an *excess* of life" (175, citing "Birth of Tragedy"). Negation in the form of the strong spirit's no to her own reactive forces and the totalization of this no expel the reactive forces from the circle of the eternal return and transmute negation into a power of affirming.

As a physical doctrine, the eternal return affirms the being of becoming. As "selective ontology, it affirms this being of becoming as the 'self-affirming' of becoming-active" (NP 72). Active forces go to the limit of their power. Instead of separating force from what it can do, active forces manifest all of which they are capable without holding anything back. They affect other forces, but they are also themselves affected. As Ronald

Bogue helpfully puts it in his book *Deleuze and Guattari*: "Active forces impose forms on other forces, but they also change form themselves; they are forces of metamorphosis and transformation which shape other forces and simultaneously 'become other' themselves. In this sense, active forces alone affirm becoming, and since the world is a world of becoming, active forces alone have true being" (Bogue 1989, 32). In going to their limit, active forces play themselves out, changing other forces and themselves in the process.

To affirm life is to affirm becoming, which is to affirm multiplicity, but what is thus affirmed is unified and whole since the becomings of all space and time are so intermeshed and interconnected as ultimately to be one. Deleuze says that Nietzsche proposes affirmation as a new conception of being. Whatever is, whatever phenomena, things, or events are in the world, are the signs or results of forces that are related and qualified by the differential element of the will to power. In the synthetic moment of the second selection, multiple becomings are brought together; the dice fall back onto the table, and all the fragments cast in the throw of the dice are affirmed at once. The affirmation of chance and becoming in all its multiplicity turns into the affirmation of necessity, the being of becoming, and the unity of multiplicity. Whatever was negative is turned into affirmation through the double movement. Zarathustra's image of the entangled web of forces becomes Dionysus' "synthetic relation of the moment to itself, as past, present and to come" (NP 193). Becoming-reactive falls away from this understanding because it turns out to be a perspective that attempts to deny or be blind to parts of this whole. The god's-eye view implies an understanding of all space and time as it is laid out in linear events, but the perspective that the second selection evokes is from and of the world (rather than transcendent to it), and yet, despite the limitations of this inevitably partial perspective, able to affirm the whole as a synthetic unity of dynamic becoming.[7] Deleuze suggests that, rather than being the repetition of the same that becomes self-referential (as Irigaray might have it), the eternal return is about a process of becoming that, given its own terms, is ultimately affirmation itself.

In *Difference and Repetition*, Deleuze explains that the eternal return presupposes a world of the will to power in which all identities have been dissolved. It thus cannot mean the return of the same. Instead, the only identity involved is that of returning itself. The identity of returning is an identity produced by difference determined as 'repetition'. The conception of repetition at issue is not a theoretical representation but a "practical selection among differences according to their capacity to produce —

that is, to return or to pass the test of the eternal return" (D&R 41). The eternal return is the simultaneous being of a dynamic becoming which continuously repeats the production of difference. Conventional conceptions of difference and repetition fall under a schema of representation which orders space and time according to grid-like coordinates, but the notions of difference and repetition Deleuze is after defy representational thought. Deleuze insists that Nietzsche's notion of eternal return must be understood as a synthesis. What returns is not things that are identical to earlier things but "the fact of returning for that which differs. . . . This is why the eternal return must be thought of as a synthesis; a synthesis of time and its dimensions, a synthesis of diversity and its reproduction, a synthesis of becoming and the being which is affirmed in becoming, a synthesis of double affirmation" (NP 48).

In *Difference and Repetition*, Deleuze connects the eternal return with the third of three syntheses of time which indicate three different conceptions of memory and relationships with time. Correlating these three syntheses of time with different moments in the Nietzschean trajectory of the reactive man of *ressentiment* to Dionysian willing provides a useful framework for considering the kind of change in subjectivity the shift to an affirmative will to power demands.[8] The first synthesis is the synthesis of habit and can be correlated with the reactive memory of the man of *ressentiment*, the second synthesis is the synthesis of memory and can be correlated with Zarathustra's affirmation of becoming and creative willing, and the third synthesis is the empty form of time and can be correlated with Dionysus' affirmation of the affirmation of becoming.

The reactive memory Deleuze ascribes to the man of *ressentiment* is very similar to the notion of memory as bodily habit in the form of a sensory-motor apparatus Deleuze derives from Bergson.[9] According to Bergson, we screen our perceptions in keeping with what is of concern to us in the world. Perception provokes usefully adaptive movements, even if only in the form of subtle tendencies toward movement. "These movements, as they recur, contrive a mechanism for themselves [the sensory-motor apparatus], grow into a habit, and determine in us attitudes which automatically follow our perception of things" (Bergson 1991, 84). What distinguishes human beings from other creatures is that they have "the power to value the useless" and the "will to dream" necessary to achieve a form of memory different from the memory of bodily habit (83). What Bergson calls "true memory" entails imaging the past drawn from a virtual totality that presents possibilities for creative action in light of a hoped-for future. Nietzsche's "active forgetting" creates the same suspension of automatic sensory-motor response Bergson suggests is necessary for the creative approach to living of the subject who would exercise human freedom.

Bergson's "true memory" is the inspiration for Deleuze's second synthesis of time. Subjects like Zarathustra who manifest this kind of memory in addition to habitual memory are able to access their past in the form of recollection-images drawn from the virtual totality of all their past present moments. Because the past always informs the present, the present, from this perspective, can be thought of as a more or less contracted duration which includes a more or less detailed imaging of past presents. For example, when Deleuze decides to write a book on Nietzsche, he may be imaging a recollection of a specific reading of some passage of *Thus Spoke Zarathustra* and perhaps a particularly exciting discussion about that passage with a friend. According to Bergson, this process entails actualizing two possible images out of the virtual totality of a past replete with countless other possibilities for recollection. The virtual totality of the past consists of different levels we can access in any number of ways. Freedom "lies in choosing the levels." "All levels and degrees coexist and present themselves for our choice on the basis of a past which was never present" (D&R 83). Zarathustra is able to actualize recollection-images in affirmative acts of creative willing; this constitutes the all-too-human movement toward the third (and strangest) synthesis of time of the Dionysian subject.

The third synthesis of time is that of a time out of joint, a "demented time . . . freed from the events which make up its content, its relation to movement overturned" (D&R 88). The eternal return "is by itself the third time in the series, the future as such" (90). The Dionysian subject abandons the illusion of any form of identity and instead affirms Zarathustra's affirmation of becoming; instead of subordinating the future to a representation of the past, this subject actualizes relations drawn from the virtual totality of the pure past in a differentiating movement of metamorphosis. Despite Zarathustra's creative affirmation of present becoming, he still reifies many of his recollection-images into representational forms of past moments to which he expects the future will conform. For the Dionysian subject, "the ground has been superseded by a groundlessness, a universal ungrounding which turns upon itself and causes only the yet-to-come to return" (91). In this synthesis the Dionysian subject may lose his coherence, his habits, and even his life. The Dionysian subject is "the man without name, without family, without qualities, without self or I" (90). The time out of joint is the empty form of time where "time is the most radical form of change, but the form of change does not change" (89).[10]

Bergson's characterization of bodily habit is useful for conceptualizing the development of a corporeal logic. Bergson's contrast between habitual and pure memory provides rich detail for the process of integrating corporeal and conceptual logics suggested by Irigaray's notions of the sensible transcendental and spiritualizing the flesh. In Deleuze's trajectory of the three syntheses of time, we can see how the movement toward an affirming will to power requires the release of the body from reactive patterns in order to foster creative sensual response to a future that never repeats. For Deleuze, as for Irigaray, this response requires the integration of corporeal and conceptual logics in a metamorphosis that affects the subject at the experiential level of perception as well as at the conceptual level of thought.

Reading Nietzsche and Sexual Difference

Despite Irigaray's disagreement with Deleuze's reading of the eternal return, there are interesting resonances between what Deleuze takes up in his Nietzschean line of flight and Irigaray's own work. The faculty of forgetting can be compared to Irigaray's notion of spiritualizing the flesh. Just as active forgetting entails response to fresh excitations without reference to past perceptions, so does spiritualizing the flesh entail opening the body to experiences it has never had. The faculty of forgetting allows one to embrace each moment equally with a creatively interpreting and evaluating will to power rather than to deny or depreciate any one moment at the expense of another. The faculty of promising can be compared to Irigaray's notion of training perception. Just as cultural training can bring about an active pledge to future forms of life made in concert with others, so does training perception entail a pledge to open response to the other through whom one takes on form. The thought of the eternal return as ethical selection prompts the development of such faculties.

To be able to affirm the being of becoming, one must be able to experience the synthesis of becoming in a simultaneous whole. The Dionysian subject is a creature who has a different sensibility as well as a different (i.e., affirmative) will and therefore experiences life differently. This difference entails a radical shift in our experience of time and space not unlike the one that Irigaray attributes to the feminine subject. Just as at each moment the Dionysian subject can affirm the being of becoming as the unity of multiplicity, so can the feminine subject experience each moment as a whole with nothing lacking. Irigaray's description of the feminine sea is remarkably similar to the differentiating synthesis of the groundless form of time.

But to complete nihilism and to bring about an affirmative will to power for which negation is no more than a mode, humanity must perish. The perishing of the human in the ontological selection brings about the arrival of the truly affirmative creature, the overman. Implicit in Deleuze's descriptions of the being of becoming and a cultural training that promotes becoming-active rather than becoming-reactive is the conception of a creature who is forever in transformation. In the becoming-active of the being of becoming, only that returns which is actively moving toward a future rather than clinging to the formations of what is already in the past. Although it is hard to know how the radical reconception of time of the third synthesis would affect this process for the all-too-human women and men looking toward a more affirming future, some relationship with the past must still be established. And although the thought of the eternal return may prompt a more affirmative living, it is not clear what it could mean to live as Dionysian "subjects."

Irigaray's sea, like the being of becoming, is not a fusional abyss but an elemental differentiating movement which flows according to cosmic rhythms rather than adhering to any logic of the same. Although this feminine sea is powerfully creative and affirming, we also saw that it is problematic from the perspective of feminine subjectivity. At the same time that appealing to its differentiating movement presents hints of an alternative model of subjectivity, it also reveals some of the problems with playing the affirming role of feminine other. The model Irigaray evokes from these hints (as we saw in Chapters 3 and 4), insists on the creative contact of two subjects who, through affirmation of each other's difference, engender further active differentiating within each and through each other. Like Deleuze, Irigaray believes that active becoming is crucial to vital living. We saw in Chapter 2 that Irigaray critiques Nietzsche for appropriating rather than acknowledging feminine creativity. Such appropriation not only makes it impossible for the feminine other to speak in her own voice, but also deprives the Nietzschean subject of the creative engenderment that Irigaray insists can occur only when difference among subjects is acknowledged.

The celibate machine of the eternal return ascribed to Nietzsche as residual subject (discussed at the beginning of this chapter) presents a non-egoic conception of subjectivity which still relates intensities to social identities, but without oedipalization. This machine is that of the creator who wills the overcoming of reactive forces, the creator on his way from the subjectivity of a Zarathustra to Dionysian metamorphosis. The residual subject of the celibate machine wills the destruction of his personal, all-too-human self in order to affirm the being of becoming. He thus becomes, in effect, the residual subject of the being of becoming, a subject with difficulties analogous, perhaps, to the other inhabiting Irigaray's feminine sea. Unlike Irigaray, however, Nietzsche works toward rather than from this position. If it is through selection that becoming-active destroys becoming-reactive, and if affirmation is what will ultimately return, then an individual can turn her life into an attempt to live that kind of affirmation, achieving an ever more active becoming-active as she destroys reactiveness through repetition that affirms difference rather than the same. Insofar as one develops active faculties of forgetting and promising, one renders consciousness and memory more active than reactive. But, as we have seen, this entails active destruction of the all-too-human — including oneself. Only those who are willing to perish in self-overcoming can bring about the transmutation to an affirmative will to power.

According to Deleuze's reading of Nietzsche, it takes a second affirmation to raise becoming to the synthetic unity of the third synthesis in the being of becoming. Deleuze says that Nietzsche symbolizes this double affirmation with Zarathustra's eagle and serpent, the divine couple of Dionysus and Ariadne, and the labyrinth or ears. The symbolism of Dionysus coupled with Ariadne is of particular interest given its explicit connection of sexual difference to the notion of the eternal return. Dionysus represents the being of becoming, but, it turns out, only when affirmed by Ariadne. "Dionysus is the labyrinth and the bull, becoming and being, but becoming is only being insofar as its affirmation is itself affirmed" (NP 188). It is in Dionysus' dance that the fragmented limbs of Dionysus' multiple becomings come together into an affirmation of the unity of multiplicity. It is only when Dionysian willing is developed and reflected that it is raised to its highest power as the eternal return in which becoming is being, multiplicity is unity, and chance is necessity. The first affirmation can be raised to its second power as the eternal return or the being of becoming only through a second affirmation that affirms the first. One symbol of this second affirmation is "the loving feminine power" (188), Ariadne, "the mirror, the fiancée, reflection" (189) of Dionysus (186).

Dionysus, taken as an example for humanity rather than as a symbol for the being of becoming, may provide some clues for a becoming-active that would not end, as Nietzsche's own attempt did, in the isolation of madness. Deleuze's anti-Hegelianism may lead him to diminish the importance of recognition for human subjectivity, and yet in the Dionysus/Ariadne dyad we see that for the truly affirming subject to emerge — the beyond-human life-form that is the overman — the feminine moment of supportive other is necessary, both because this transmutation *is* "the feminine power emancipated" and because Dionysus needs his affirming to be affirmed in order to become truly Dionysian. One could conclude from this — even if Nietzsche himself did not — that the ontological transformation of reactive humanity into fully affirmative creatures requires active affirmation among subjects of their attempts to enact Nietzschean ethics: "But Ariadne has Dionysus' ears: affirmation must itself be affirmed so that it can be the affirmation of being. Araidne puts a *shrewd word* into Dionysus' ear. That is to say: having herself heard Dionysian affirmation, she makes it the object of a second affirmation heard by Dionysus" (NP 188). Ariadne is the second affirmation who reflects Dionysus' affirming will to power and thus affirms affirmation. At the same time that Deleuze's notion of becoming-imperceptible has revolutionary potential for those trapped in molar selves, the emphasis on the prepersonal forces running through individuals renders it difficult to acknowledge the constitutive power of personal others. Irigaray also wants to open up the subject to such becomings. But she is equally interested in establishing a new foundation for identity — one more adequate to contemporary times. If for Deleuze the problem is how to map out lines of flight from the molar identities we currently have, the problem for Irigaray is how to stabilize a molar identity that will allow us to live more ethically. For Deleuze, the notion of the dice-throw indicates the heterogeneous unity of a multiplicity that comes all at once owing to the interaction of forces that cannot be separated from their environment. Establishing identity models can only block flows by impoverishing possible lines of flight.

In Deleuzian terms one might say that Irigaray's project involves a deterritorialization from traditional molar identity, only to reterritorialize onto the oedipalized counterpart of traditional molar identity. If, however, we read Irigaray's notion of the feminine as analogous to Deleuze's notion of molecular becomings, then both become notions that indicate a conception of the unconscious that breaks out of the oedipal frame and suggests viable alternatives to the psychoanalytic model of subjectivity. Deleuze's images of a line of flight and the highly populated desert are oddly solipsistic. They suggest that it is through nomadic movement that one can retain one's individuality; it is by leaving the molar identities of one's self and others behind that one can preserve one's own creative power.[11] Irigaray wants to incorporate the participatory communion of mutually constitutive creativity into her model of subjectivity. Her model posits becoming-subject as a becoming in which two or more subjects emerge from encounter with the others transformed, a becoming in which a subject not only pursues her own line of flight but also attends to how her line of flight implicates and forms a web with the lines of flight of others. It may be that Deleuze takes such mutual implication of lines of flight for granted. There is nothing in his work that is incompatible with this, and much in his work that supports it. Organized forms — for example, those supporting personal identity — will always emerge just as they will dissolve. But challenging contemporary formations of oedipal selfhood requires some kind of supportive attentiveness to the other unless or until we are prepared to abandon the recognizable subjectivity of personal identity.

In the next two chapters I explore Deleuze and Guattari's notions of becoming-minoritarian, constructing a body without organs, and philosophy, as well as Deleuze's notion of Foucauldian cartography in order to develop further a model of subjectivity that is resonant with Irigaray's. In the final chapter I suggest a synthesis of the two that compensates for the weaknesses and brings out the strengths of each.

7
Deleuze's Becoming-Imperceptible

From the perspective of the Nietzschean philosophy of difference developed in *Nietzsche and Philosophy* and *Difference and Repetition*, human subjects are an inextricable part of a web of dynamic forces engaged in a continuous process of differentiation that is manifested to our conscious awareness as the phenomena of perception and conception. Insofar as this web is understood through the notion of the eternal return, it is a synthesis of the becoming-active of all forces which defies linear conceptions of space and time. The world conceived in terms of the interplay of forces determined by the differential element of the will to power is the Nietzschean counterpart to what Deleuze and Guattari later describe in terms of molecular becomings and an immanent principle of desire.[1] Nietzsche challenges traditional conceptions of the self and subjectivity and engages in a writing practice of becoming-active that could be viewed as the Nietzschean precursor of schizoanalysis.

Schizoanalysis, as we saw in Chapter 5, is a practice by which an individual or group of individuals can rework their participation in social processes of subjectification. Like psychoanalysis, schizoanalysis reads aspects of conscious experience as symptoms of unconscious (molecular) processes and attempts to alleviate alienation from oneself, others, and life itself by symbolizing manifest indications of the unconscious that allow for greater integration of these processes into conscious awareness. Unlike psychoanalysis, schizoanalysis draws on a wide range of disparate vocabularies to symbolize presently imperceptible processes. It also assumes that all life processes have molecular elements mostly imperceptible to us, whose configurations into larger aggregates are constantly changing. Human existence is but a part of this larger process. Rather than investigating the unconscious for secrets waiting to be revealed according to an oedipal plane of interpretation, schizoanalysis assumes that the unconscious is productive. The symbolization of unconscious processes in keeping with an immanent process of experimentation creates new possibilities in living rather than revealing ones that are already there. Deleuze and Guattari believe that psychoanalysis constitutes an interpretive framework with normative effects. Revolutionary change requires connecting the singularities of life processes in ways that will allow new patterns of living to emerge.

In *Anti-Oedipus*, Deleuze and Guattari describe the body without organs as the nonproductive stasis of production that resists any specific organization of desiring-machines. It is the imageless, organless body, an undifferentiated object, produced in the primary production of desiring-machines, and it brings production of determinate forms of organization to a halt (cf. Chapter 5). In *A Thousand Plateaus* they further develop the notions of the body without organs (which here they refer to as the 'BwO') and assemblages (their new term for desiring-machines) and advocate the construction of BwOs in the pursuit of lines of flight. Such construction allows for what they call 'destratification' and is closely aligned to the task of schizoanalysis as they describe it in *Anti-Oedipus*. They also develop an alternative vocabulary to that of *Anti-Oedipus*; constructing a BwO entails releasing molecular elements from stabilized patterns of organized breaks and flows in order to create what Deleuze and Guattari call a 'plane of consistency'. Planes of consistency, in contrast to planes of organization which transcend the formations they organize, are laid out according to immanent principles of organization which defy any specific pattern of replication. Construction of what Deleuze and Guattari call an 'abstract machine', like construction of a BwO, entails defying familiar patterns of organization in order to allow molecular elements to flow according to immanent principles of desire.

Just as Irigaray makes use of an "elemental" vocabulary full of references to air, fire, water, and earth in order to evoke the dynamic becoming of life, so do Deleuze and Guattari develop vocabularies attuned to process and flux rather than to substances with properties. A human individual is a set of molecular processes stabilized into an organism with a sense of corporeal boundedness, an ability to speak language and manipulate symbols, and a sense of personal continuity and the ability to experience pleasure and pain. Concrete assemblages — for example, the assemblage of eyes scanning the letters on a page — replicate stabilized patterns of molecular process. Since molecular processes can always stabilize into other patterns, the molecular elements making them up could always form new connections. The plane of consistency refers to a state in which the molecular elements of a given organization of flows connect with one another according to immanent principles rather than continuing to replicate the pattern dictated by a plane of organization that transcends those flows. This connection brings the elements into a state of comparative disorganization from which new organizations of breaks and flows can emerge — for example, scanning eyes can blur and then pursue the vivid colors of a landscape that had previously been barely noticed. Whereas the BwO tends to be the more appropriate term for speaking of the destratification of an individual subject, the abstract machine connects heterogeneous elements of the larger social field.[2]

In the first section of this chapter I explore the construction of BwOs as a form of destratification which allows new assemblages to emerge. In the next section I turn to Deleuze and Guattari's book on Kafka in order to offer further insight into how writing can provide a structure for the delicate process of destratification. The distinction Deleuze and Guattari make in *Kafka* between memory and blocks of becoming and the notion of becoming-minoritarian will be particularly useful. In the next-to-last section I return to *A Thousand Plateaus* in order to investigate Deleuze and Guattari's comments on becoming-animal and becoming-woman, and in the final section I further elaborate on the notion of becoming-imperceptible and connect this notion with that of constructing an abstract machine.

Constructing the Body without Organs

In the third plateau of *A Thousand Plateaus*, Deleuze and Guattari characterize strata as layers or belts that imprison intensities or lock singularities into systems of resonance and redundancy and produce large and small molecules which are organized into molar aggregates (ATP 40). Human beings, like other things, are stratified.[3] That is, they are made up of molecular elements whose fluxes and flows have been stabilized into organized patterns that privilege a determinate set of connections among the elements and exclude others. Human life is stratified into the larger strata of the physiochemical, the organic, and the anthropomorphic; the stratification of human life is an integral part of the stratification of life processes, including nonhuman ones. Deleuze and Guattari's characterizations of the strata of the organism, of significance, and of subjectification are particularly important for understanding this conception of human subjectivity; human assemblages regulate the relations among the human body as a biological organism, the individual in relation to social systems of meaning, and the consolidation of personal or social identity in a conscious subject (134).[4] Like psychoanalysis, schizoanalysis and destratification do not take the conscious subject we think of as fully human for granted. A sentient, language-speaking individual with self-conscious awareness is the effect of a complicated process. Deleuze and Guattari's descriptions of this process emphasize the continuity of human processes of production with other processes of production. On their view, all of life (which includes "inanimate" as well as animate objects) is a ceaseless flux of singularities that become organized into various forms which could always have been otherwise. Since human life is always implicated with "larger" productive processes, understanding human subjectivity requires theorizing human life in its ongoing implication with all of life. Just as desiring-machines are created in myriad ways contingent on the concrete processes and practices that constitute human beings and in which they participate (e.g., the flow of blood in the veins, the sucking of milk from the breast, the hammering of steel on an anvil), so are assemblages the working machines that connect different strata in determinate ways (e.g., an assemblage of writing hand and pen). Outside the strata is chaos. This chaos renders the movement of destratification possible at the same time that it renders it risky.

> For outside the strata or in the absence of strata we no longer have forms or substances, organization or development, content or expression. We are disarticulated; we no longer even seem to be sustained by rhythms. How could unformed matter, anorganic life, nonhuman becoming be anything but chaos pure and simple? Every undertaking of destratification (for example, going beyond the organism, plunging into a becoming) must therefore observe concrete rules of extreme caution: a too-

sudden destratification may be suicidal, or turn cancerous. In other words, it will sometimes end in chaos, the void and destruction, and sometimes lock us back into the strata, which become more rigid still, losing their degrees of diversity, differentiation, and mobility. (503)

Constructing a BwO involves dismantling the self with its specific organization of assemblages. This means deterritorializing fluxes and flows until the production of a particular assemblage comes to a halt. Recalling the description of the body without organs presented in *Anti-Oedipus*, we can say that desiring-production comes to a halt when the flows and breaks of the current configurations of an assemblage are equally resisted by the full body without organs (which resists any determinate organization of desiring-machines), thus bringing intensities into a nondeterminate continuum: "The body without organs is not a dead body but a living body all the more alive and teeming once it has blown apart the organism and its organization. Lice hopping on the beach. Skin colonies. The full body without organs is a body populated by multiplicities" (ATP 30). It is at this point that a new configuration of assemblages becomes possible; disruption of the previous configuration releases new possibilities from the multiplicities brought into a continuum of intensity. For example, I might decide to retire to a cave and meditate. Having abandoned my social identities as professor, housekeeper, and runner, and taken on the psychic identity and corporeal practices of a meditator, I construct a body without organs. That is, I become highly attuned to my body in an open context in which old forms of organization can become superseded by new possibilities. An embodied individual clearly can never (and should never) construct a BwO that would bring all her working machines to a halt: I will continue to eat and sleep, I hope, even if I no longer vacuum the living room floor. Construction of a BwO entails bringing a significant enough portion of the individual's working assemblages to a halt to allow new ones to form. Construction of such bodies involves "taking apart egos and their presuppositions" and "liberating the prepersonal singularities they enclose and repress" (A-O 362). These prepersonal singularities canthen mobilize flows that establish schizzes and breaks "well below the condition of identity" that can feed into and thus affect configurations of social production.[5]

It is a question of making a body without organs upon which intensities pass, self and other — not in the name of a higher level of generality or a broader extension, but by virtue of singularities that can no longer be said to be personal, and intensities that can no longer be said to be extensive. The field of immanence is not internal to the self, but neither does it come from an external self or a nonself. Rather, it is like the absolute Outside that knows no Selves because interior and exterior are equally a part of the immanence in which they have fused. (ATP 156)

The BwO of an individual could be conceived as a plateau communicating as a sort of passage with other BwOs. Deleuze and Guattari take the term 'plateau' from Gregory Bateson; it designates "a continuous, self-vibrating region of intensities whose development avoids any orientation toward a culmination point or external end" (ATP 22). Since the intensity of the BwO is zero, its intensities or multiplicities are not drawn into any determinate configuration. There is still movement, but it is the movement of singularities as they vibrate rather than the movement of a working assemblage relating segments of organized aggregates. Deleuze and Guattari claim that plateaus are always in the middle. They contrast arborescent connections with rhizomatic connections. The former stem from a tree trunk that provides the point of origin for a hierarchical series of paths branching off from it. The latter run from point to point following no hierarchical order and springing up at will.[6] Instead of beginning or culminating the nodal points of an arborescent system, plateaus are multiplicities "connected to other multiplicities by superficial underground stems in such a way as to form or extend a rhizome" (22). That is, connections among singularities flow from point to point according to an immanent principle of desire rather than adhering to the order imposed by a plane of organization transcendent to its own movement. "Every BwO is itself a plateau in communication with other plateaus on the plane of consistency. The BwO is a component of passage." The plane of consistency is reached by "conjugating the intensities produced on each BwO, by producing a continuum of all intensive continuities" (158). The BwO is never a contained body; it cannot be conceived as an organism with an inside and an outside, a skin that separates it from what it is not. Instead, it is an open system and as such is part of the world's plane of consistency. The plane of consistency is the totality of these BwOs constructed by "a great abstract machine" from the assemblages necessary to the fabrication of each BwO. Constructing a BwO opens one out onto the world in a way that encourages immanently produced connections with other BwOs, thus giving rise to unprecedented aggregates and working assemblages. Extending the geographical metaphor developed in Chapter 5, we can say that constructing a BwO allows the individual to situate herself as a plateau whose singularities can be brought into a continuum with the singularities of surrounding territories.

Brian Massumi suggests conceiving of one's BwO as a region of the Milky Way; one can thereby get a sense of how one is both part of a plane of consistency and yet not fused with the rest. That is, although one's region has determination, its boundaries can be construed in different ways. How we perceive these distinctions are colored by the social field that we are in. If the glare of city lights which render all but the brightest stars of a constellation invisible are the molar forms imposed upon the BwO, then the forms actually lived and the possibilities one perceives as meaningful are those left after the glare of city lights obscures other virtual possibilities. To construct a BwO may mean to evade some of these lights in order to come back to a degree o of the body that could then open up configurations of molecular process other than that dictated by the conventional norms of the social field.[7]

Constructing a BwO constitutes an experiment in destratifying from conventional formations of the strata of organism, significance, and subjectification (the strata related to organic forms, social systems of meaning, and the subjective experience of a conscious subject). This process entails bringing faculties to their limits and shocking conscious awareness into new modes of perception and conception. The resulting influx of previously unconscious material cannot be referred back to an oedipal scenario; instead it must remain depersonalized. If the unconscious is not the unconscious of an oedipalized subject but rather the prepersonal singularities that make up the molecular elements of conscious awareness, then opening up awareness to those singularities would mean challenging one's sense of corporeal boundedness and one's social identity as well as one's perceptions and conceptions of everyday life. According to Deleuze and Guattari, one can do this without risking the self-annihilation of schizophrenia or psychosis if one is careful: "You have to keep enough of the organism for it to reform each dawn; and you have to keep small supplies of signifiance and subjectification, if only to turn them against their own systems when the circumstances demand it, when things, persons, even situations, force you to; and you have to keep small rations of subjectivity in sufficient quantity to enable you to respond to the dominant reality. Mimic the strata. You don't reach the BwO, and its plane of consistency, by wildly destratifying" (ATP 160).

One can botch the BwO by either failing to produce it or producing it in such a way that nothing is produced on it — "intensities do not pass or are blocked." Then, like the hypochondriac, the paranoid, the schizo, or the drug addict, one has constructed an empty BwO.[8] The empty BwO fails to mobilize deterritorialization at the level of social production. To create the full BwO with implications for deterritorialization of the social field as well as of the individual, one should patiently look for the point at which one can dismantle and create new connections: "We are in a social formation; first see how it is stratified for us and in us and at the place where we are; then descend from the strata to the deeper assemblage within which we are held; gently tip the assemblage, making it pass over to the side of the plane of consistency. It is only there that the BwO reveals itself for what it is: connection of desires, conjunction of flows, continuum of intensities" (ATP 161). By delineating various aspects of human existence in terms of strata and assemblages, Deleuze and Guattari depict a subject with vastly expanded possibilities and connections to the world. Psychoanalytic self-understanding returns subjects to familial dramas; schizoanalysis and destratification comprehend the subject as a vast complex of structures operating on myriad levels, all of which could be reworked by connecting heterogeneous aspects of self and world in unprecedented ways.

In *A Thousand Plateaus*, Deleuze and Guattari present various examples of how one might construct a BwO. Masochism, whatever one may think of it, is one such example. The masochist, rather than striving to attain conventional objects of desire, "uses suffering as a way of constituting a body without organs and bringing forth a plane of consistency of desire." Deleuze and Guattari give the example of a masochist who partakes in a scenario of becoming like a horse. The training axiom of the masochist who partakes in horse-oriented scenarios is to destroy instincts "normal" to a socialized human being and replace them with forces transmitted from a horse. Deleuze and Guattari contend that this is less a destruction than "an exchange and circulation" (ATP 155). In this becoming-animal of the masochist, "one series explodes into the other, forms a circuit with it: an increase in power or a circuit of intensities" (156). The masochist inverts signs so that "the horse transmits its transmitted forces to him, so that the masochist's innate forces will in turn be tamed" (155–56). Whereas in living a "normal" life with conventional desires (as described, for example, by psychoanalysis) this individual would assume that she could only desire something lacking to her, she now satisfies desire in a horse-scenario. By bringing a heterogeneous series into the field of her desire, she creates a new set of connections that brings about an intensification of embodied experience. By pursuing the desire to become-horse without referring that desire to a plane of interpretation (for example, that of psychoanalysis) transcendent to the unfolding of that desire, this individual constructs a BwO; she pursues a desire that brings her to a threshold state (of suffering) from which new forms of life can emerge.[9]

Courtly love provides another example of the making of a BwO. According to Deleuze and Guattari, renunciation of the external pleasure of actually obtaining the woman who is the object of one's love leads to a state in which "desire no longer lacks anything but fills itself and constructs its own field of immanence" (ATP 156). The individual who engages in the rituals of courtly love is intensely engaged in them in a way that makes possible a flow of intensities. These intensities are not directed toward the transcendent goal of obtaining the object of one's desire; that is, satisfaction is not deferred until completion of a set of tasks that are prescribed by a different plane. Instead, since satisfaction is not part of the game, desire becomes immanent to the plane one is already on, and the intensities of one's BwO flow no longer according to a plane of organization but rather by virtue of impersonal singularities. The singularities involved in such intensities are no longer personal because they are not referred to a totalized subject presently lacking — the subject who will only come into being once he successfully acquires his beloved. Instead, it is the pleasure of pursuing the rituals in and of themselves without reference to totalized subjects that becomes important. It is from the kind of threshold state experienced in such rituals that desire can be revitalized and assemblages different from one's past assemblages can emerge.

The Taoist sexual practice of withholding ejaculation is also cited as a way of constituting a BwO in a field of immanence in which desire lacks nothing. Since the goal of sexual intercourse is no longer male orgasm, all aspects of sexual intercourse constitute a field of immanence in which the orgasm is not lacking. Since the whole act is not referred to an external or transcendent criterion which has not yet happened, it is the circuit of intensities between the two partners that becomes an immanent field of desire. This permits the connection of molecular elements previously trapped in the habitual patterns of working assemblages and thus the creation of a threshold state from which new patterns can emerge.

By attending to one's present moment one can intensify lived experience in a way that not only enriches it but also gives one a kind of somatic knowledge that goes beyond the knowledge provided by what Deleuze would call representational thinking. Constructing BwOs entails attentiveness to the here and now in a way that brings the "body" into play and challenges the traditional mind/body dualism of Western thought. Deleuze and Guattari would have you use caution in your deterritorialization by mapping the process: Pay attention to where you are! Meticulously map your relation to the strata in which you find yourself and see where you might free a line of flight. Pay attention to your social formation, make a diagram of the strata and then see where you can go. Make your BwO — that is, find out where your degree o is and where your desires connect, your flows conjoin, your intensities continue.

Deleuze and Guattari's refusal to remain with a psychoanalytic account of desire prompts them to explore an exciting range of possibilities in destratification. Psychoanalysis can lead one to believe that the only route to destructuring overly constrictive forms of subjectivity in order to stimulate richer integrations of libidinal drive is through pursuing the secret of oedipalized desire. Although Irigaray works out of a psychoanalytic paradigm, I have tried to make clear how her account of embodied encounter between two subjects is not constrained by regression to the mother-child dyad. Instead it entails open receptivity in the present and an active practice of perception that destabilizes corporeal and conceptual logics in the same way that destratification does. Although there are important reasons for Irigaray's insistence on foregrounding sexual difference, however, Deleuze and Guattari's account has the advantage of expanding the creative spaces in which we could remake ourselves in rejuvenating ways. In the next section I turn to Deleuze and Guattari's book on Kafka because it provides an illuminating account of becoming-child, becoming-animal, and becoming-minoritarian which will be useful to a better understanding of their conception of the creative becomings of a destratifying line of flight.

Kafka and Becoming-Minoritarian

In their book on Kafka, Deleuze and Guattari contrast two motifs drawn from Kafka's novel *The Castle* and correlate these motifs with a reactive notion of memory and what they call a "block of becoming," which is their term for an active conception of memory. According to their reading of *The Castle*, Kafka connects the image of an inclined head with the image of a portrait photo, thus creating a motif that indicates "a blocked, oppressed or oppressing, neutralized desire, with a minimum of connection, childhood memory, territoriality or reterritorialization."[10] They associate this motif with reactive memory and compare it to Kafka's opposing motif which connects the image of a straightened head with that of a musical sound. They claim that the latter motif indicates "a desire that straightens up or moves forward, and opens up to new connections, childhood block or animal block, deterritorialization" (K 5). It is this motif which they correlate with their active conception of memory, a 'block of becoming'. Considering their characterizations of these two motifs in light of Deleuze's distinction between active and reactive forces and his discussion of the man of *ressentiment* in his book on Nietzsche (see Chapter 6) provides a useful way of distinguishing these two forms of memory. Reactive force, which separates force from what it can do, is the separation of an individual from what she can do through the blockage of flow. When memory is reactive, some aspect of the individual is disconnected from the rest — frozen like a snapshot into an old configuration of mnemonic traces. In the process desire is blocked, that is, separated from what it can do. A straightened head and a musical sound indicate a deterritorialization that opens up to new connections. Instead of confining the subject to the mnemonic traces of past experience disconnected from the fresh excitations of the present, one deterritorializes from habitual patterns and comes into fresh contact with present stimuli, thus reeasing new possibilities in the production of assemblages.

As we saw in Chapter 6, Bergson conceives of memory as the recollection of images drawn from the duration of one's past in the context of the present moment. The reactive memory of a blocked subject would recollect only those images that confirm the perceptions and conceptions of an already established sensory-motor apparatus with its familiar set of bodily habits. Memory in the form of oedipalized "snapshots" calcifies the mnemonic traces of past perceptions so that the subject ends up repetitiously reacting to those traces rather than actively responding to the present. Memory as a block of becoming (for example, a childhood block of becoming) is not the reactive contemplation of a self that one no longer is, but the release of molecular becomings from habitual configurations of corporeal and conceptual patterning which leads to revitalized action in the present.[11] In order to affirm such a memory, one must participate in it fully and bring that experience into living contact with a full range of connections in the present that will lead to further transformations beyond whatever happened in the past. The process of affirming such a memory can be compared to the active interpretation and evaluation of a Nietzschean subject free of *ressentiment*, which entails creatively embracing becoming rather than passively experiencing the present in keeping with forms of representation derived from the past. Such a subject would actualize recollection-images from the virtual totality of the past which allow for an unprecedented future. Rather than actualizing recollection-images that are representations of the past to which present perceptions and conceptions must conform, blocks of becoming actualize recollection-images in response to the novel requirements of an always unique situation. Blocks of becoming, unlike snapshot memories, require transformations at the corporeal level of bodily habit in creative response to the novelty of the present as well as transformations at the conceptual level of the psyhic self in creative reappropriations of one's past.

Deleuze and Guattari insist that despite the oedipal themes that pervade Kafka's work, to give it a psychoanalytic reading would be to subject it to a reactive interpretation. Reactive interpretation disconnects memory as a multiplicity of forces from surrounding forces. By referring Kafka's text to memories of his life interpreted according to the preconceived triangle of psychoanalytic theory, one stabilizes specific assemblages and closes off other assemblages that could have been created in the construction of an immanent field of desire. Deleuze and Guattari insist that from a libidinal point of view, Kafka was not reacting to his relationship with his father but instead experiencing "completely positive motivations" (K 9). They read Kafka as projecting a photo of the father onto the map of the world. Kafka takes the oedipal snapshot of the father, frozen from connection, rendered static in and by a fixed oedipal structure, and projects it onto the shifting terrain of a rich range of connections that opens out in all directions. Kafka unblocks the impasse of the oedipal snapshot and deterritorializes "Oedipus into the world instead of reterritorializing everything in Oedipus and the family" (10). Instead of either denying Oedipus or accepting the reduction of desire to the oedipal scenario, Kafka constructs an immanent field of desire which unfolds other forms of assemblages. These assemblages make use of the assemblages that are socially available — the identities and names of history of Kafka's social field. By constructing assemblages from Oedipus out onto the world, he releases new flows of desire. He does this not by ignoring Oedipus but by enlarging Oedipus to the point of comedy: "One discovers behind the familial triangle (father-mother-child) other infinitely more active triangles from which the family itself borrows its own power, its own drive to propagate submission, to lower the head and make heads lower. Because it's *that* that the libido of the child really invests itself in from the start: by means of the family photo, a whole map of the world" (11). The reactive memory of an oedipalized subject sets everything up according to familial dramas, freezing family life into snapshots subordinated to the oedipal scenario. Thus desires, fluxes, and flows are all reduced to the triangular scheme. But what Deleuze and Guattari call the childhood block is deterritorializing: "It shifts in time, with time, in order to reactivate desire and make its connections proliferate; it is intensive and, even in its lowest intensities, it launches a high intensity" (78–79). A child constructs intensities with all sorts of people and things, most of which are not his parents. The child may reterritorialize everything back onto his parents in order to lower intensities, "but in his activity, as in his passions, he is simultaneously the most deterritorialized and the most deterritorializing figure — the Orphan" (79). These blocks may shift with time and reanimate the adult by giving the adult an expanded range of living connections.

Nonfamilial libidinal investments are condensed into the family triangle rather than vice versa. Human beings as multiplicities of forces have available to them a much larger range of libidinally intense connections to their world and others than that dictated by the oedipal triangle of desire. Referring desire to the plane that organizes familial connections closes off these connections. Creating an immanent field of desire opens up the possibility of entering into assemblages on the basis of a non-lacking desire that actively pursues the intensity of corporeal and conceptual flow. Kafka's experiments with becoming-animal — the narrator's investigations from a dog's perspective, Gregor's metamorphosis from human to insect — like becoming-child, can open up new possibilities in assemblages by introducing novel formations into habitual configurations of molecular flow.[12] Destratification cannot be bound to any determinate linear order since the binary series of assemblages are multiply overdetermined and so are more akin to a Nietzschean web of forces than to a single unraveling chain. Kafka's animal descriptions foster the deterritorialization of both writer and readers and opens them up to new connections with the world: "There is no longer anything but movements, vibrations, thresholds in a deserted matter: animals, mice, dogs, apes, cockroaches are distinguished only by this or that threshold, this or that vibration, by the particular underground tunnel in the rhizome or the burrow. Because these tunnels are underground intensities" (K 13).

Deleuze and Guattari claim that Kafka makes arid language vibrate with a new intensity by opposing a "purely intensive usage of language to all symbolic or even significant or simply signifying usages of it" (K 19). They insist that there is no figurative sense for the metaphor of metamorphosis, "but only a distribution of states that is part of the range of the word." Man and animal do not resemble each other, and Kafka is not trying to say anything with conventional significance by writing about the transformations from one to the other. Instead "there is no longer man or animal, since each deterritorializes the other, in a conjunction of flux, in a continuum of reversible intensities" (22). In Kafka's writing, things become intensities from which deterritorialized sound and words make their escape.

To make the sequences vibrate, to open the word onto unexpected internal intensities — in short, an asignifying *intensive utilization* of language. Furthermore, there is no longer a subject of the enunciation, nor a subject of the statement. It is no longer the subject of the statement who is a dog, with the subject of the enunciation remaining "like" a man; it is no longer the subject of enunciation who is "like" a beetle, the subject of the statement remaining a man. Rather, there is a circuit of states that forms a mutual becoming, in the heart of a necessarily multiple or collective assemblage. (22)

In the crisscross of circuits opened up in Kafka's metamorphoses, animal and man form a mutual becoming. Destratification from conventional forms of organization is effected by deliberately crossing the circuits of socially significant identities, thus releasing new forms of life. Whereas Irigaray counts on the touch of an embodied other for creative engenderment of new possibilities in living and speaking, Kafka's writing cross-circuits already symbolized identities. His special use of language deterritorializes signifiers from the molar identities they represent and thereby sets into motion the extralinguistic intensities of corporeal logic. Insofar as this cross-circuiting intensifies sensation and thus revivifies one's desire and active participation in the world, it is guided by immanent desire. Kafka and his readers turn to the social field of language rather than to an embodied other for this transformative encounter. Corporeal as well as conceptual logic is transformed in such encounters, and attention to the (imperceptible) sensual is important in bringing such encounters about. But the emphasis on the (solitary) activities of writing and reading as the arena for playing out these encounters emphasizes symbolic mediation of corporeal logic.

To be a sort of stranger *within* his own language; this is the situation of Kafka's Great Swimmer. Even when it is unique, a language remains a mixture, a schizophrenic mélange, a Harlequin costume in which very different functions of language and distinct centers of power are played out, blurring what can be said and what can't be said; one function will be played off against the other, all the degrees of territoriality and relative deterritorialization will be played out. Even when major, a language is open to an intensive utilization that makes it take flight along creative lines of escape which, no matter how slowly, no matter how cautiously, can now form an absolute deterritorialization. (K 26)

Deleuze and Guattari advocate making use of the polylingualism of one's own language. By opposing the "oppressed quality of this language to its oppressive quality" one can create zones "by which a language can escape, an animal enters into things, an assemblage comes into play." One

can play even a major language against itself by making a minor or intensive use of it by finding "points of nonculture or underdevelopment"
within it (K 27). Kafka makes the world and its representation take flight.
He dismantles assemblages and thus "makes the social representation take
flight in a much more effective way than a critique would have done" (47).
Instead of laying out an understanding of society according to conventional norms of representation, Kafka makes things happen with his literature which opens up lines of escape toward new ways of perceiving and
speaking. His writing thus translates and dismantles assemblages. According to Deleuze and Guattari, the two are the same thing. These new ways
of perceiving and speaking do not happen only at the conceptual level —
for indeed, the conceptual level often cannot keep up with these happenings. They happen at the level of intensities and fluxes that are nonsignifi-
able. These intensities are not even necessarily experienceable, although
their effects may become known through the new actions, the new ways of
perceiving and speaking that come about through them.

Kafkian metamorphoses can be defeated. Photos functioning as an
oedipal reality or childhood memory can capture desire in an assemblage, thus reterritorializing it and cutting it off from new connections.
Like constructing empty BwOs, challenging oedipal taboos can lead to a
dead end if this challenge does not open subjectivity onto a larger social
field.

> Oedipal incest is connected to photos, to portraits, to childhood mem-
> ories, a false childhood that never existed but that catches desire in the
> trap of representation, cuts it off from all connections, fixes it onto the
> mother to render it all the more puerile or spoiled, in order to have it
> support all the other, stronger interdictions and to prevent it from
> identifying itself as part of the social and political field. Schizo-incest,
> in contrast, is connected to sound, to the manner in which sound takes
> flight and in which memory-less childhood blocks introduce themselves
> in full vitality into the present to activate it, to precipitate it, to multiply
> its connections. Schizo-incest with a maximum of connection, a poly-
> vocal extension, that uses as an intermediary maids and whores and the
> place that they occupy in the social series — in opposition to neurotic
> incest, defined by its suppression of connection, its single signifier, its
> holding of everything within the limits of the family, its neutralization
> of any sort of social or political field. (K 67)

Kafka's projection of oedipal dramas onto the map of the world can provide lines of flight from oedipalized desire, but it also carries the risk of

reterritorializing desire back onto the oedipal triangle. Deleuze and Guattari believe that the Kafkian works which construct a bachelor machine are most able to thwart this risk. Like Nietzsche's celibate machine of the eternal return, Kafka's bachelor agent, by freeing himself of familial desire, is able to proliferate lines of flight which extend across the social field.

> The highest desire desires both to be alone and to be connected to all the machines of desire. A machine that is all the more social and collective insofar as it is solitary, a bachelor, and that, tracing the line of escape, is equivalent in itself to a community whose conditions haven't yet been established. Such is the objective definition of the machine of expression, which, as we have seen, corresponds to the real state of a minor literature where there is no longer any "individual concern." Production of intensive quantities in the social body, proliferation and precipitation of series, polyvalent and collective connections brought about by the bachelor agent — there is no other definition possible for a minor literature. (71)

In their descriptions of Nietzsche's celibate machine and Kafka's bachelor agent, Deleuze and Guattari seem to be emphasizing that the social field holds myriad possibilities for (constructive) destratification which familial molar identities can only thwart. The implication is that destratification can and should leave personal (oedipalized) identity behind. "Man" as the ultimate paradigm of oedipal molar identity is too locked into the many strata of human existence to allow for molecular becoming. To set becomings into motion, one must deterritorialize from "man" and engage in becoming-minoritarian.

We have seen that Kafka's work, like the construction of planes of consistency, connects the molecular elements of heterogeneous aspects of words and things in ways that deterritorialize both, thus releasing lines of flight from conventional norms of social representation. This entails the becoming-minoritarian of Kafka's bachelor agent as well as of Kafka's language. Just as both Nietzsche's and Kafka's style connect minor elements of language in unprecedented ways, so do they both evoke subjects deterritorialized from oedipal manhood. The examples of Nietzsche and Kafka suggest that destratification from personal identity can, but need not, proceed directly to reterritorialization to "all the names of history" or "all the machines of desire" of the larger social field. Nietzsche only rarely evokes familial identities; Kafka creates bachelor agents and figures becoming-animal but also projects oedipal dramas onto the map of the world. Just what destratification from personal identity involves, however, is far from clear. Although Deleuze and Guattari imply that insofar as personal identity is oedipalized, it is oppressive, and they also seem to imply that personal identity *is* oedipal identity, the advantages as well as the risks of destratifying from either (or both at once) need to be more carefully delineated. In the next section I further explore destratification from "man-hood" in the forms of becoming-animal and becoming-woman and return to this issue.

Becoming-Animal, Becoming-Woman

According to the descriptions that Deleuze and Guattari give in *A Thousand Plateaus* of various forms of becoming, such as becoming-animal, becoming-molecular, and becoming-imperceptible, we live in a world surrounded by multiple types of becomings of which we are an integral part. We are thus continually engaged in destratifying from stable forms of organization whether we are aware of it or not. Since these becomings, for human beings, involve destabilizing recognizable patterns of organization at the level of organic structures as well as at the level of linguistic structures, they have unpredictable effects. Articulating these becomings not only demonstrates our ongoing participation with nonhuman as well as human processes but also indicates new possibilities in self- and world-transformation.

Deleuze and Guattari point to the work of Scherer and Hocquenghem on "wolf-children" to hint at possibilities for becoming that we may not typically contemplate. Human processes could have stabilized into strata quite different from that of the socialized human animal. Autistics as well have entered into a quite different kind of possibility. Deleuze and Guattari suggest that these possibilities are not just aberrations of peculiar cases but possibilities that are there for all children. Independent of the "normal" route toward adulthood are " 'other contemporaneous possibilities' that are not regressions but creative involutions bearing witness to '*an inhumanity immediately experienced in the body as such,*' unnatural nuptials 'outside the programmed body' " (ATP 273). Even fully stratified adults have opportunities for becoming-animal. And indeed, part of Deleuze and Guattari's point is that these opportunities are often the reality of our interactions with animals whether we are consciously aware of it or not.

Deleuze and Guattari deliberately distinguish becoming-animal from conscious imitation of an animal. Imitation sets up analogies between ourselves and what we imitate, and thus does no more than replicate models of thinking and being that already exist. True becoming-animal engages the subject at the limits of the corporeal and conceptual logics already formed and so brings on the destabilization of conscious awareness that forces the subject to a genuinely creative response. The process of imitation may set up analogies between ourselves and what we imitate but cannot engage us in creative becomings. Irigaray says something similar when she insists that our encounters with others — in particular the feminine other to whom we would like to relate — must involve mutual becoming rather than specular identifications that maintain the self-same identity of the masculine subject. Setting up analogies only replicates the models of thinking and being that already exist. For something new to happen, something more than one's intellectual or commonsense understanding must be involved. Becomings are encounters that engage the subject at the limits of the corporeal and conceptual logics already formed and so bring on the destabilization of conscious awareness that forces the subject to a genuinely creative response.

According to Deleuze and Guattari, to become-dog is to "make your organism enter into composition with *something else* in such a way that the particles emitted from the aggregate thus composed will be canine as a function of the relation of movement and rest, or of molecular proximity, into which they enter" (ATP 274). Entering into a composition with a dog entails bringing the molecular elements of one's own organism into relation with the molecular elements of a dog. Making a list of correspondences between oneself and a dog and correlating behaviors of corresponding parts can only impose a new plane of organization on an already stratified subject. This is unlikely to entail destratification; the analogy would be conceptualized and performed, leaving the human structures of organism, significance, and subjectification intact. To engage in a true becoming-dog is to "emit corpuscles that enter the relation of movement and rest of the animal particles, or what amounts to the same thing, that enter the zone of proximity of the animal molecule" (274–75). If one barks with enough feeling, "with enough necessity and composition" (275), one emits a molecular rather than a molar dog. That is, one constructs a BwO that allows human intensities to create a continuum with dog intensities. Or to put it another way, one allows oneself to be "contaminated" by dog particles in a way that sweeps human patterns of molecular flow into dog patterns of organization and behavior at the expense of human ones. This precipitates molecular becoming that breaks formation with the aggregates of one's molar self. One then breaks with old behavior patterns and starts acting in an unprecedented way — not through reference to some external image but through a kinetic series of actions that unfold of themselves with novel implications for how one moves as well as how one perceives and conceives one's surroundings.

Becoming-animal (or becoming-insect or becoming-plant) for a human being involves the cross-circuiting of two heterogenous series which constitutes a line of flight from the molar identities of each. Becoming-dog entails a becoming-human of the dog as well as a becoming-dog of the human. What is "human" becomes deterritorialized and reterritorialized onto what is "dog," and vice versa. The line of flight is a rhizome common to both dog and human. The human organization could be said to imitate a dog organization in the sense that the strata of each are parallel. Dogs, like humans, are organisms with sentience. But the rhizomatic line of flight of becoming-dog can no longer be attributed to "anything signifying" since it is contained by the molar identity of neither "dog" nor "human."[13] Since dog-strata are organized differently than human-strata, cross-circuiting the two series will connect heterogeneous singularities, producing novel configurations at the organic level as well as at the levels of linguistic meaning and conscious experience. Such destratification will thus entail deterritorialization (and reterritorialization) of corporeal as well as conceptual levels of organization. The strata of the organism, of significance, and of subjectification are all brought into play in such a becoming. The body no longer has the same contours, one's relationship to social meaning systems shift, and personal identity is challenged. "Dog" no longer means what it once did any more than "human" does.

In describing various forms of becoming, Deleuze and Guattari create a vocabulary for a range of phenomena which indicate that the unconscious is productive and thus far more encompassing than the oedipal unconscious of psychoanalysis. They develop this vocabulary by trying to capture the uncanniness of the subtle transformations that processes — including the processes we ourselves are — undergo in their ongoing participation with the larger flow of life-as-process from which they can never be completely extricated. Deleuze and Guattari's notions of becoming-other and becoming-imperceptible, which are akin to their notions of schizoanalysis and destratification, involve challenging conventional body boundaries, taking the risk of becoming indiscernable as a social subject, and unsettling a coherent sense of personal self. Becoming-other and becoming-imperceptible are worth these risks because such becomings put the elements of molecular processes into a continuum that could result in new forms of living. One thus makes the world and everybody and everything in it into a becoming; instead of excluding the world in order to maintain a determinate organization of self, one opens up the patternings of molar aggregates to the influx of molecular flow. One will inevitably transform the world as well as be transformed by the world in the process.

One can become human things as well as other kinds of things. And this kind of becoming is also not an imitation of a molar entity that has a definite form with organs and functions and a specific subject assignation. Becoming-woman, for example, is entering into the proximity zone of the "microfeminine." This involves "emitting particles that enter the relation of movement and rest" and that "produce in us a molecular woman" (ATP 275). Individuals who are women "as a molar entity" need to do this as much as men do. Although doing so does not eliminate the need for a "molar politics," it is as dangerous to confine oneself to the molar form of womanhood as it is to remain in any other molar configuration. The price: loss of creativity and an unnecessary narrowing of life's rich possibilities.

Deleuze and Guattari suggest that the masculine has been and is opposed to the feminine in the great dualism machines which are operative in human organisms, history, and subjects of enunciation. They advocate becoming-woman as a way of thwarting these dualism machines: "Writing should produce a becoming-woman as atoms of womanhood capable of crossing and impregnating an entire social field, and of contaminating men, of sweeping them up in that becoming. Very soft particles — but also very hard and obstinate, irreducible, indomitable" (ATP 276). Becoming-woman could thus constitute a "micropolitics" that would circulate deterritorializing molecules of becoming throughout the social field. In the process, molar manhood would unravel, thus also releasing other possibilities in becoming. This could, presumably, occur on an "unconscious" level. That is, many of the effects produced would not be consciously intended, and yet there would be a critical point at which the accumulation of effects beneath the level of awareness would result in a transformation of conscious awareness as well. Although Deleuze and Guattari do not go very far in mapping sexual difference, they do present several hints of what their mapping might look like. They claim that there is no becoming-man because "man is majoritarian par excellence." They also claim that "in a way, the subject in a becoming is always a 'man,' but only when he enters a becoming-minoritarian that rends him from his major identity." Man is majoritarian in the sense that the "man-standard" "assumes as pregiven the right and power of man" (291). In becoming, one is deterritorialized. Since man constitutes the molar identity par excellence, one cannot deterritorialize insofar as one engages in becoming-man. Any becoming-man cannot but reterritorialize onto strata as they are. It is perhaps in this sense that they mean that the subject of a becoming is always a "man." They say that "it is perhaps the special situation of women in relation to the man-standard that accounts for the fact that becomings, being minoritarian, always pass through a becoming-woman" (291). If they hold anything like the view that "woman" is the negative counterpart of "man" (that is, the Lacanian view that "woman" as a symbolic category is defined as "not-all" or the other of the masculine subject), then it would make sense that any deviation from the man-standard would "pass through" a becoming-woman.

Deleuze and Guattari claim that "the reconstruction of the body as a Body without Organs, the anorganism of the body, is inseparable from a becoming-woman, or the production of a molecular woman" (ATP 276). Apparently this is so because it is from the girl that our bodies are first stolen; the girl is told how she is and is not to behave, while the boy is allowed a greater freedom of movement. The girl is the first victim, as well as an example and a trap for the boy. She is "like the block of becoming that remains contemporaneous to each opposable term, man, woman, child, adult. It is not the girl who becomes a woman; it is becoming-woman that produces the universal girl" (277). "Girl" as a block of becoming rather than a memory of an actual girl (whether oneself or an other) echoes Deleuze and Guattari's distinction between reactive and active memory: one does not regress to a childhood memory in order to construct a BwO; one rather creates a childhood block of becoming that is always available to one in the present. This block reconfigures singularities that make up one's present molar configuration. It is thus not a matter of retrieving a memory — a family snapshot — that one can then imitate, but rather a matter of releasing one's singularities as they are now into a new pattern. Becoming-girl may entail deconstructing patterns of stabilized molecular flow to an earlier node of an unfolding series of molar aggregates. Thus, the girl represents an earlier node or branch in a series of disjuncts leading to the other molar entities opposed to her. If she is crucial in destratifying from contemporary forms of molar identities, it is because according to our social map or diagram, the girl is situated at a less differentiated node. It is in becoming-woman that one becomes the universal girl, because it is in breaking down molar blocks that one goes back to this earlier place with the expanded possibilities of an earlier node of branching possibilities. But Deleuze and Guattari are adamant in their conception of becoming as a rhizomatic line of flight that passes between two things in such a way that the "line frees itself from the point, and renders points indiscernable" (294). Thus, "to become is not to progress or regress along a series" (238). Becomings do not follow an arborescent line of development but rather pursue unpredictable, nonhierarchical lines of flight. Nevertheless, even if Deleuze and Guattari are not suggesting tracing one's levels of stratification by regressing back through one's development as construed through a psychoanalytic story of one's origins, they do seem to subscribe to the view that becoming-girl and becoming-woman have a privileged relationship to the unconscious realm of productive molecular becoming. More detailed mapping of this aspect of the social field could reveal an interesting resonance with Irigaray's notion of the feminine. Their assumption that destratification entails becoming-woman in the context of failing to map the terrain of sexual difference, however, carries the risk of the masculinist appropriation of feminine power which Irigaray is so concerned with circumventing. If sexual difference is anything like Irigaray describes it, then one thing that Deleuze and Guattari have overlooked, especially in their discussion of becoming-woman, is that this process is sexually differentiated — that is, the project of becoming-woman is going to be radically different for women and men.[14] A woman who becomes-woman without the benefit of the secure molar identity of a man may well experience more difficulty in following this line of flight. If one is to exercise the kind of caution Deleuze and Guattari recommend — which involves a careful survey of one's cartography — then becoming-woman may entail the risky dissolution of identity, leading to an empty BwO rather than the release of creative possibilities if no steps are taken to stabilize a new form of subjectivity. To ignore this possibility is to assume the kind of universalism for the masculine perspective (and the blind spot toward sexual difference this entails) that Irigaray is fighting against. In addition, the assumption of the man-standard for the major identity seems to assume the stability of such a standard and a failure to investigate other possible standards. Whereas Irigaray attempts to give a positive characterization of a feminine subject able continually to incorporate fluid transformation in concert with others, Deleuze and Guattari seem to assume a stable standard against which war machines must continually be launched.[15] The man-standard thus becomes a kind of point of origin, or worse, a point of reference required for orienting the direction of deterritorializing lines of flight.

It appears, then, that the kind of sexuality Deleuze and Guattari concern themselves with is a masculine one. The kind of becoming they describe is a masculine one with a masculine bias. How would a specifically woman's perspective open this up? And what other kinds of biases might be revealed by thinking about their failure to acknowledge sexual difference fully? These questions about becoming-woman are closely aligned to the issue raised at the end of the last section regarding destratification from personal and/or oedipal manhood. If "man" is the majoritarian molar identity par excellence, and if this excludes the possibility of becoming-man (as Deleuze and Guattari claim), then mapping lines of flight requires deterritorialization from manhood. But if the structures of personal or oedipal manhood are far from clear, the structures of "man" as the majoritarian molar identity par excellence are even less so. A great advantage of Deleuze and Guattari's notion of schizoanalysis and destratification as practices for fostering constructive change is that one does not need to pin down the content of one's identity in order to set becoming into motion. Unlike identity politics, which requires one to determine the specific features of one's molar identity, Deleuze and Guattari's micropolitics unfolds with the spontaneous flow of an individual or group entering into an assemblage created in keeping with immanent principles of desire. The assemblage created by such an individual or group may emerge from the cross-circuiting of two heterogeneous series. Atoms of womanhood, for example, may contaminate a group of men, sweeping them into an assemblage with other women working together to promote nonhierarchical styles of communication in a specific workplace. But labeling a becoming 'becoming-woman' is already to trade in stereotypes that the move from identity politics to micropolitics was meant to counter if the possibility of the becoming-man of woman as well as the becoming-woman of man is excluded.

If Deleuze and Guattari mean to escape the man-standard and oedipalization by launching an escape from personal identity, it seems to me that they fail. Rather than assuming that such an escape is either necessary, possible, or desirable (do we really want to destratify personal relationships?), we might be better off welcoming opportunities for stabilizing molecular flow in alternative ways. If, for example, we open personal identity to a broader range of stabilizing connections, oedipalization need no longer present overly normalizing constraints. Just as Kafka destratifies oedipalization by projecting oedipal dramas onto the map of the world, Irigaray destratifies oedipalization by mapping femininity onto the social field. Deleuze and Guattari's notion of becoming-woman is premised on destratification from the man-standard. Such a premise threatens to leave that man-standard intact. Irigaray's notion of feminine subjectivity attempts to symbolize a standard for personal identity that is an open-ended system without specific content. Just as Deleuze calls for a Nietzschean becoming-active that would bring about a subject with a "completely different will," a different way of feeling, and another sensibility, so does Irigaray's notion attempt to support a new kind of subjectivity at the same time that it recognizes a need and desire for personal identity. In addition, it provides a model that conceives of personal identity as mutually constitutive and continually transforming in interdependent relationship with others.

Deleuze's, and Deleuze and Guattari's, maps of alternative subjectivity (e.g., the Nietzschean celibate machine, the nomadic subject, the Kafkian bachelor agent) imply that personal subjectivity entails oedipalization; challenging the man-standard thus entails depersonalizing lines of flight. But until or unless we are prepared to abandon personal identity, depersonalizing lines of flight can only evade the man-standard, leaving the contemporary economy of subjectivity intact rather than transforming it. Mapping a new kind of personal identity — an identity that is an openended process rather than a molar entity — could be more effective.

I will return to this question in the final chapter after a closer look at social mapping in Chapter 8. In the next section I turn to the becoming that is closest to Irigaray's conception of the sensible transcendental — becoming-imperceptible — the becoming toward which, according to Deleuze and Guattari, all other becomings rush (ATP 279). Irigaray's notion of the sensible transcendental evokes an imperceptible beyond that touches upon conscious awareness to which a feminine subject is receptive. A practice of spiritualization of the flesh can tap into this beyond and render it perceptible. Deleuze and Guattari's notion of becoming-imperceptible also involves tapping into what is beyond conscious awareness in order to render it perceptible. The notion of a nomadic subject who engages in becoming-imperceptible can provide a mapping of an open-ended economy of personal subjectivity so long as we do not succumb to the romantic fallacy that we are whole subjects only insofar as we are unboundedly self-creating.

Becoming-Imperceptible

Becoming-imperceptible, as we saw in Chapter 5, involves bringing faculties to the limit of communication with one another, thus fragmenting the coherent subject and disabling the convergence of the faculties upon an object of commonsense experience. Irigaray's notion of the sensible transcendental also hints of a sensibility that goes beyond ordinary sense experience. In receptivity to the divine that is the horizon of one's becoming, the feminine subject touches upon that which is always beyond and yet contiguous to her experience. Receptivity to this immanent transcendental requires transformation of oneself as well as transformation of one's understanding of the world. Self and world (including the others within it) thus partake in a mutually engendering communion wherein no identity can remain fixed. Becoming-imperceptible also requires leaving behind not only the perceptible boundaries of the body but also one's conventional understandings of oneself, of others, and of one's world, in order to respond to the informing impact of imperceptible encounters.

In the context of the three strata of human subjectivity, becoming-imperceptible involves challenging conventional body boundaries, taking the risk of becoming indiscernable as a social subject, and unsettling a coherent sense of personal self. Becoming-imperceptible is worth these risks because it puts the pre-personal singularities of molecular processes into a continuum that could result in new forms of living. One thus makes the world and everybody and everything in it into a becoming; instead of excluding the world in order to maintain a determinate organization of self, one opens up the patternings of molar aggregates to the influx of molecular flow. One will inevitably transform the world as well as be transformed by the world in the process. Thus, the BwO as a plateau in communication with the territories around it will transmit its fluxes and flows, just as the fluxes and flows of surrounding territory will move through it. Molecular patterns travel swiftly, communicating their effects throughout the plane of consistency, coming into being and passing away too quickly to replicate themselves in perceptible molar aggregates. By constructing a plane of consistency, one releases the flows excluded on a given plane of organization and sets into motion a world of becoming: "For everybody/everything is the molar aggregate, but *becoming everybody/everything* is another affair, one that brings into play the cosmos with its molecular components. Becoming everybody/everything (*tout le monde*) is to world (*faire monde*), to make a world (*faire un monde*)" (ATP 279–80).

Deleuze and Guattari say that movements are by nature imperceptible. Becomings as pure relations of speed and slowness are pure affects that are "below and above the threshold of perception." An adequate threshold operates as a function of a perceptible form and a perceived subject, "so that movement in itself *continues* to occur elsewhere." Movement is imperceptible in relation to a given threshold of perception: "It is the plane of organization and development, the plane of transcendence, that renders perceptible without itself being perceived, without being capable of being perceived. But on the *other* plane, the plane of immanence or consistency, the principle of composition itself must be perceived, cannot but be perceived at the same time as that which it composes or renders" (ATP 281). The line of flight of an assemblage is an abstract line of creative causality that can be activated but not explained by "general causalities of another nature" (283). It is this kind of line of flight that a project of becoming-imperceptible produces. Whether this project is engaged in terms of constructing a BwO, cross-circuiting two series of becomings, creating an immanent plane of desire, or engaging in the practices of philosophy or art (as described in the next chapter), becoming-imperceptible accesses the chaos that is the outside of determinate strata and so creates new possibilities in living that can be rejuvenating although they can also be destructive. Through the creation of planes of consistency, heterogeneous, molecular becomings are put into continuity in new ways that go beyond any existing plane of organization and touch upon the infinite movements of what Deleuze and Guattari call virtual reality.

Deleuze and Guattari call writing that is a form of becoming-imperceptible a mapping rather than a tracing, and they prefer the former to the latter: "Write, form a rhizome, increase your territory by deterritorialization, extend the line of flight to the point where it becomes an abstract machine covering the entire plane of consistency" (ATP 11). Tracings organize, stabilize, and neutralize multiplicities "according to the axes of significance and subjectification belonging to it. . . . What the tracing reproduces of the map or rhizome are only the impasses, blockages, incipient taproots, or points of structuration" (13): "What distinguishes the map from the tracing is that it is entirely oriented toward an experimentation in contact with the real. The map does not reproduce an unconscious closed in upon itself; it constructs the unconscious. It fosters connections between fields, the removal of blockages on bodies without organs, the maximum opening of bodies without organs onto a plane of consistency. It is itself a part of the rhizome" (12). Desire moves and produces by way of the rhizome. Instead of interpreting the unconscious or making it "signify according to a tree model," we need to "*produce the unconscious*, and with it new statements, different desires" (18). By plugging tracings back into a map, we can open up blockages and impasses to a line of flight. The nomadic subject who becomes-imperceptible in the context of making maps can set a world of becoming into motion without succumbing to the fantasy of becoming everybody/everything if she is careful to acknowledge the blockages that enable her to exist. The diagrams or abstract machines thus created connect heterogeneous elements of the social field and by thus connecting the deterritorialization of concrete assemblages construct "a real that is yet to come" (142).

In the next chapter we will see that Foucault's distinction between the nondiscursive and discursive practices of a social field are described by Deleuze in terms of a historical stratum. There is a gap between nondiscursive and discursive practices which can be put on a plane of consistency through the diagram of an 'abstract machine'. This gap indicates what is "outside" to both aspects of the stratum — a "non-place" of mutability which can resist contemporary power formations and out of which creative change can emerge. Mapping the social field indicates the creative points of resistance from which nomadic subjects can launch lines of flight to a new future.

8
Mapping Lines of Flight

Foucauldian Cartography

In his book *Foucault*, Deleuze notes that in *The Archaeology of Knowledge*, Foucault distinguishes two formations with no correspondence or direct causality between them — the discursive and the nondiscursive. The "realm of statements" constitutes the "manifestly present," discursive realm of the articulable and the already formulated. This realm cannot produce possibility or potentiality: "No sense of possibility or potentiality exists in the realm of statements. Everything in them [statements] is real and all reality is manifestly present. All that counts is what has been formulated at a given moment, including any blanks and gaps" (F 3). Deleuze calls the nondiscursive realm a realm of "visibles" and characterizes it as analogous to and yet distinct from the realm of statements.[1] Although Foucault designates the nondiscursive realm negatively in *The Archaeology*, his descriptions of the workings of disciplinary power in *Discipline and Punish* give it positive form. The realm of visibles constitutes the manifestly present realm of the perceptible. This realm also cannot produce possibility. It is due to the lack of isomorphism between the two heterogeneous realms that both realms touch on an indeterminate outside from which new formations of the articulable and the perceptible can emerge.

The reading Deleuze gives of Foucault demonstrates how Foucault's methodology resonates with Deleuze's own. Deleuze characterizes the Foucault of *The Archaeology of Knowledge* and *Discipline and Punish* as a cartographer. In seeking to reveal the specificity of various discursive formations as practices obeying certain rules in their relationships to other discursive formations and to nondiscursive practices (Foucault 1972, 138, 157), Foucault diagrams an abstract machine that "acts as a non-unifying immanent cause that is coextensive with the whole social field" (F 37). The immanent cause of the disciplinary diagram of the social field of seventeenth- and eighteenth-century France, for example, diagrammed by Foucault in *Discipline and Punish*, is disciplinary power which is realized, integrated, and distinguished through the effects it produces in the concrete assemblages of schools, workshops, army, and prisons. The diagram of an abstract machine of a specific social field shows how various assemblages open onto other assemblages through the decoding edges of their territories. These assemblages are heterogeneous not only in the sense of constituting distinct territories but also in the sense that each assemblage is divided into nondiscursive and discursive practices.

Instead of deducing historical phenomena from a set of "facts," Foucault diagrams the abstract machine which puts statements and visibilities on the same plane of consistency. A plane of consistency "is a plane of continuous variation" (ATP 511).[2] Construction of such a plane involves linking heterogeneous, disparate elements rather than ordering them according to a plane of organization (for example, that of psychoanalysis or Marxism). The Foucauldian abstract machine "maps" the concrete assemblages of, for example, school, prison, and courthouse that indicate the various lines linking disparate elements of the social field; in particular, elements of nondiscursive practices are brought into continuity with elements of discursive practices. For example, disciplinary power is the immanent cause linking the rows of desks nailed to the floor of a classroom, the configuration of the cells of a prison, and the legal discourse delineating certain acts as criminal.

Although Foucault is interested in knowledge and power whereas Deleuze is interested in desire, Foucault is clearly an important influence in

Deleuze's work. Mapping discursive practices indicates specific historical formations of what I have been calling conceptual logic; mapping nondiscursive practices indicates corporeal logic. It is one of the great strengths of Deleuze's work that he insists on symbolizing or finding a vocabulary for the organizing structures of extralinguistic experience. Irigaray is engaged in a similar project in attempting to symbolize the feminine. Both maintain the heterogeneity of linguistic and extralinguistic realms of experience and insist on attending to that which destabilizes the logics of each and any binary division between the two: "Every diagram is intersocial and constantly evolving. It never functions in order to represent a persisting world but produces a new kind of reality, a new model of truth. It is neither the subject of history, nor does it survey history. It makes history by unmaking preceding realities and significations, constituting hundreds of points of emergence or creativity, unexpected conjuctions or improbable continuums. It doubles history with a sense of continual evolution" (F 35). Foucault's diagram of disciplinary power does not represent society but rather indicates points of instability where change can occur; school desks can be unnailed from the floor, the cells of a prison can be differently arranged, and what was once considered a criminal act can become the act of an individual in need of psychiatric help. Foucault's diagram challenges static conceptions of social reality by demonstrating the effects of disciplinary power on various aspects of the social field as well as showing how these effects in turn generate further effects in the continually mutating processes of living.

We could compare the process of diagramming an abstract machine to constructing a BwO (cf. Chapter 7). Just as the construction of a BwO at the level of an individual releases lines of flight through the construction of an immanent field of desire, so does mapping a diagram of an abstract machine demonstrate possible lines of flight with respect to the whole social field. Writing as cartography highlights creative nodes in contemporary culture. Such writing can foster a becoming on the part of writer and reader that can engage the subject's desire at the level of an individual in new ways. Deleuze and Guattari advocate forms of schizoanalysis whose effects produce change across the social field; empty bodies without organs are undesirable because they are unable to create the connections with other bodies without organs which are neccessary for proliferating new forms of desire. Foucauldian cartographies could provide the maps crucial to situating individual projects of schizoanalysis or becoming-imperceptible with respect to society as a whole.

Deleuze says that *The Archaeology of Knowledge* invokes a method whereby series of statements converge with other statements, thus forming a family, or else diverge, thus forming another family. Since there are various kinds of thresholds for the distinct discursive formations through which language circulates — for example, the threshold between the discourses used in educational and criminological settings or between legal and religious discourses — a statement can be a diagonal line in the sense that it may pick up various expressions relevant to various thresholds. This makes it more akin to music than to a signifying system because a signifying system establishes correspondences between signifers and signifieds, whereas, according to Deleuze, Foucault's notion of the statement suggests that statements are enunciated in refrains that may cross different thresholds, varying in meaning as they do so (F 52). The same is true for visibilities. The curves formed through these convergences regularize and align the relations of force. The statement-curve "integrates into language the intensity of the affects, the differential relations between forces, the particular features of power (potentialities)" (79). Visibilities must integrate the intensity of the affects, the differential relations between forces, and the particular features of power, in a different way.

This is so much so that light, as a receptive form of integration, must follow a comparable but non-corresponding path to that of language as a form of spontaneity. And the relation between the two forms at the heart of their 'non-relation' will be the two ways in which they fix the unstable relations between forces, localize and globalize diffusions, and regularize particular points. For visibilities, in the light of historical formations, form scenes which are to the visible element what a statement is to the sayable or readable. (79–80)

The practical assemblage of knowledge unique to a culture at a specific historical epoch is defined through a combination of statements and visibilities. Just as statements are part of a larger system irreducible to any one sentence, so are visibilities part of a larger system irreducible to a thing or object; statements are what allow sentences to exist, and visibilities are what allow things and objects to exist. We cannot perceive either statements or visibilities as such because they are forms of language and forms of luminosity that allow the articulable and the perceptible to emerge (F 33). An individual subject is aware neither of the conditions of articulability nor of the conditions of visibility since she is herself a function derived from articulability and visibility. When we open up things, objects, and qualities and discover the visibilities that make them possible, and words, phrases, and propositions and discover the statements that make them possible, we break the link that we assume automatically exists between things and words, "so that each reaches its own unique limit which separates it from the other, a visible element that can only be seen, an articulable element that can only be spoken." Articulable and visible elements are heterogenous: if we can talk about what we perceive and perceive what we talk about, there is obviously some connection between the two elements, and yet, Deleuze suggests, opening up words and things to the system of statements or visibilities which conditions each brings these two aspects to their limit, "the common limit that links one to the other, a limit with two irregular faces, a blind word and a mute vision" (65).

Foucault's diagram of disciplinary power shows concrete assemblages in their local specificity as well as the abstract machine that connects them up and diffuses them throughout the larger social field.

> It is as if the abstract and the concrete assemblages constituted two extremes, and we moved from one to the other imperceptibly. Sometimes the assemblages are distributed in hard, compact segments which are sharply separated by partitions, watertight barriers, formal discontinuities (such as school, army, workshop, and ultimately prison, and as soon as you're in the army, they tell you 'You're not at school any more'). Sometimes, on the other hand, they communicate within the abstract machine which confers on them a supple and diffuse microsegmentarity, so that they all resemble one another and prison extends throughout the rest, like the variables of the one continuous, formless function (school, barracks and the workshop are already prisons). (F 40)

Bringing words and things to their limit confronts us with what is "outside" both the discursive and nondiscursive realms of concrete assemblages. Foucault's diagram, instead of assuming an isomorphic relationship between discursive and nondiscursive practices, refers these practices to the abstract machine as immanent cause. Power relations "designate 'the other thing' to which statements (and also visibilities) refer" (83). Deleuze says that power relations are "merely virtual, potential, unstable, vanishing and molecular, and define only possibilities of interaction, so long as they do not enter into a macroscopic whole capable of giving form to their fluid matter and their diffuse function" (37). Although the abstract machine is taken to be the immanent cause of both perceptible matter and articulable functions, there is a gap between the two realms that renders the diagram unstable. For Deleuze, and Deleuze and Guattari, any form of organization entails an "outside" which resists it. The Foucauldian abstract machine of disciplinary power diagrams a specific configuration of power as an immanent cause of determinate relations of the social field in relation to the "outside" from which novel forms of power will emerge. The diagram thus constitutes a singular, creative plateau that brings elements of discursive and nondiscursive social practices into continuity thus indicating possibilities for lines of flight. The gap between statements and visibilities opens each onto an outside or "non-place" that renders the diagram unstable and suggests creative sites of change.

In his characterization of Foucault, Deleuze not only emphasizes the inherent instability of diagrams that integrate without assimilating the heterogeneous realms of discursive and nondiscursive practices, but also emphasizes Foucault's insight that just as one can do an archaeological analysis of rules governing discursive formations, one can also analyze the rules governing nondiscursive visibilities. This insight is in keeping with Deleuze's reading of Nietzsche as a genealogist who interprets phenomena as symptoms of forces of which we may not be aware. In his work after his book on Nietzsche, Deleuze advocates a form of genealogy of his own that involves performing experiments that allow him (and his readers) to encounter the becomings that occur at a different level from that of conscious experience. The notion of cartography developed in his book on Foucault provides a context for such experiments in becoming-imperceptible that could highlight their revolutionary potential.

Deleuze refers to specific social fields as strata — " 'sedimentary beds' . . . made from things and words, from seeing and speaking, from the visible and the sayable, from bands of visibility and fields of readability, from contents and expressions" (F 47).[3] Each stratum or historical formation "implies a distribution of the visible and the articulable which acts upon itself" (48). From one stratum to the next the distribution of the visible and the articulable varies as visibility changes in style and statements change their system. Deleuze says that Foucault presents "that determination of visible and articulable features unique to each age" (48–49) which makes any behavior, mentality, or set of ideas possible. Deleuze points out that on Foucault's conception of knowledge there is no object of knowledge prior to knowledge as a practical assemblage, "a 'mechanism' of statements and visibilities" (51).

Knowledge is the unity of stratum which is distributed throughout the different thresholds, the stratum itself existing only as the stacking-up of these thresholds beneath different orientations, of which science is only one. There are only practices, or positivities, which are constitutive of knowledge: the discursive practices of statements, or the nondiscursive practices of visibilities. But these practices still exist beneath archaeological thresholds whose shifting points of demarcation constitute the historical differences between strata. (51)

Instead of asking what power is or where it originates, we should ask how it is practiced. Once the third term of power is introduced, the spontaneity of statements and the receptivity of visibles take on the new meaning of affecting or being affected. Power relations are stabilized and stratified by operations that consist in "linking, aligning and homogenizing singularities, placing them in series and making them converge" (F 75; translation modified). These operations bring about a multiplicity of local and partial integrations, each of which has an affinity with other relations or points. Since, according to Foucault's notion of power, one can neither locate the origin of power in a privileged place nor confine it to a limited locale, one must analyze power by following the particular points through which it passes (27). A serial method allows one to "construct a series around a single point and to seek out other series which might prolong this point in different directions on the level of other points" (21). When series begin to diverge and become redistributed in a new space, a break takes place. A new formation never appears all at once but "emerges like a series of 'building blocks', with gaps, traces and reactivations of former elements that survive under the new rules" (21–22). Following phenomena and statements by moving along a transverse or mobile diagonal line allows one to pursue different series along different levels, across all thresholds, instead of remaining within the conventional constraints of dominant social reality. Although there is nothing of a determinate nature outside of the strata formed by various combinations of the visible and the articulable, mobile, diffuse relations between forces "form the outside of strata" (84). Whatever is not stratified does not lie in some primitive realm of pure experience but instead forms the outside of what it is that we actually experience.

In brief, forces are in a perpetual state of evolution; *there is an emergence of forces which doubles history,* or rather envelopes it, according to the Nietzschean conception. This means that the diagram, in so far as it exposes a set of relations between forces, is not a place but rather 'a non-place': it is the place only of mutation. Suddenly, things are no longer perceived or propositions articulated in the same way.

No doubt the diagram communicates with the stratified formation stabilizing or fixing it, but following another axis it also communicates with the other diagram, the other unstable diagrammatic states, through which forces pursue their mutant emergence. This is why the diagram always represents the outside of the strata. (85–86)

What is exterior has form, but the outside concerns force: "Forces necessarily refer to an irreducible outside which no longer even has any form" (F 86). Forces operate in a kind of "non-place" or space of the outside, from which history emerges. They constitute the unthought of the discursive and the imperceptible of the nondiscursive which instigate unprecedented forms of both.

Like transcendental empiricism (see Chapter 5) and Nietzschean empiricism (see Chapter 6), Foucauldian cartography maps the imperceptible relations that condition what appears to representational consciousness (F 36). Just as transcendental empiricism pursues the intensive element to the point of challenging the unity of selves and objects (see Chapter 5) and Nietzsche's affirmative philosophy pursues the differential element of the will to power (see Chapter 6), so does Foucauldian cartography pursue the microphysics of power relations. Foucault's elaboration of the schism between words and things allows for a more detailed account of the difference between what I have been calling corporeal and conceptual logics. Nondiscursive as well as discursive practices develop recognizable patterns of organization, but the two are neither isomorphic or conflatable. Mapping diagrams creates lines of flight by locating the limits of various discursive and nondiscursive formations, thus indicating the thresholds that could be crossed. Mapping (as opposed to tracing) entails creative thinking, which breaks with the forms of conventional perception and conception. Mapping lines of flight with respect to a diagram of a specific social field could help us choose the lines of flight we want to pursue to a new future: "If seeing and speaking are forms of exteriority, thinking addresses itself to an outside that has no form. To think is to reach the non-stratified. Seeing is thinking, and speaking is thinking, but thinking occurs in the interstice, or the disjunction between seeing and speaking" (87).

The determinate relations of a social field could always have been otherwise; power is a dynamic force of becoming which is always mutating. Power relations in their determinate form operate completely within the diagram, while resistances to specific formations of power relations operate in direct relation "with the outside from which the diagrams emerge" (F 89). A diagram not only maps a specific formation of power relations in terms of a non-unifying immanent cause but also marks the points at which that specific formation destabilizes. It is at such points that the possibility of alternative formations of power emerges. The outside from which these new possibilities emerge constitutes the limit to thinking. Conventional sentences and objects are formed within the realms of the sayable and perceivable. Real thought, however, comes from the outside. The thought of the outside is a thought of resistance, and Deleuze insists that the social field offers more resistance than strategies. Foucault as cartographer maps out a social field in terms of the lines of flight that break free from the realms of the perceivable and the sayable: "From this we can get the triple definition of writing: to write is to struggle and resist; to write is to become; to write is to draw a map: 'I am a cartographer' " (44).

Thinking is not the product of an interiorized consciousness, a mental substance or soul. It is also not something that deals with the already perceivable or articulable. Deleuze's reading of Foucault emphasizes the gap between nondiscursive and discursive practices — that is, the gap between the realm of the perceivable or the sensible and the realm of the articulable, which is the realm of statements. The mobile, fluid forces constituting the "outside" of the stabilized conventions of the perceivable and articulable are always intruding, forcing themselves upon us, forcing us to think, and yet this outside does not constitute a realm unto itself. Whatever determinate form of integration a concrete assemblage may achieve between the realms of the perceivable and articulable is dismembered by this outside which always touches upon both realms. Abstract machines, knowing "nothing of forms and substances" (ATP 511), constitute deterritorializing becomings that multiply creative connections among assemblages and so resist determinate formations of the perceivable and articulable. When molar structures break up, when "words and things are opened up by the environment without ever coinciding" (F 87), forces come in from the outside. Thought is shocked into thinking by the confrontation with what is the outside to already established forms brought on by emergent and mutating forces.

Deleuze's reading of Foucault emphasizes the heterogeneous realm of the perceivable and sayable and contests any conception of experience that would posit it as an organic whole. Comfortably familiar conceptions and perceptions are always no more than the symptoms of the processes that are their condition. No matter how the sayable and the perceivable may converge in the experiences of subjects living within specific epochs, they are no more than the symptom of forces that are imperceptible from the plane of social organization. Just as conceptual and corporeal logics at the level of the individual can diverge, so can discursive and nondiscursive practices at the level of the social field. Deleuze emphasizes the creative possibilities that the gap between the two kinds of practices creates; it is due to the instability created by this schism that new lines of flight can emerge. Irigaray is intent on harmonizing conceptual and corporeal logics (for example, through the spiritualization of the flesh — see Chapter 4) and overcoming mind/body dualisms at the cultural level (through symbolizing the feminine). Deleuze is more wary of integration; integration would seem to close down rather than open up lines of flight. But just as Irigaray's notion of the sensible transcendental entails contiguity with a divine which renders complete integration impossible, so does Deleuze's conception of the Foucauldian "outside" render impossible any attempt to completely integrate discursive and nondiscursive practices. For both, the insistence on delineating points of contact with a third term which forever problematizes any mind/body division allows them to account for dynamic flow in their models of culture and subjectivity.

Diagrams and Resistance

Deleuze's emphasis on the gap between the perceivable and the sayable and what is outside both of these realms invites the reader to conceive her corporeal body and her conceptual self as heterogeneous aspects implicated within a specific social field with an outside from which changes in that social field can emerge.[4] Deleuze's notion of the writer as a cartographer who creates lines of flight through experimentation suggests a practice with revolutionary potential for the individual subject as well as for the social field.

Deleuze claims that Foucault is haunted by the theme of the double. The unthought that forces us to think is not outside of thought in the sense of being external or transcendent to thought. Rather, the impossibility of thinking lies at the heart of thought and doubles the outside (F 97). "It is not the emanation of an 'I,' but something that places in immanence an always other or a Non-self." Representational thought finds this "outside" incomprehensible. From the perspective of a thought that can think difference, this "outside" is a kind of fold, "the invagination of a tissue in embryology, or the act of doubling in sensing: twist, fold, stop, and so on" (98). Irigaray suggests that masculine subjectivity tends to deny what is other to thought, pushing it off onto the feminine other in order to maintain a clear-cut repetition of sameness; Deleuze's reading of Foucault's notions of the outside and subjectification suggests that there is always an outside and that what is impossible to think is not something distant from us but an otherness that is the inside of our outside.[5] Irigaray would agree that the imperceptible and the inconceivable constitute a kind of otherness much closer to us than we might like to think, but she insists on attending to the mark of sexual difference on this otherness; if we tend to construe the other of thought differently, if we tend to place what is impossible to think at a clear-cut remove from ourselves in order to repeat our own identities rather than acknowledging the stranger within, it is because the feminine other allows us to do so. To change this regime would involve a reconfiguration of masculinity and femininity.

Although Deleuze does not engage in a Foucauldian project of mapping social fields with respect to assemblages of knowledge, the projects of schizoanalysis, destratification, and becoming-imperceptible have important points of convergence with Foucauldian cartography. Irigaray's project as well could be viewed from this perspective. Her "diagrams" map gender in a way that those of Deleuze and Foucault do not. They demonstrate the instability of gendered categories of "seeables" and "sayables" and indicate the feminine as an important site of creative resistance. Although other diagrams could indicate equally viable lines of flight, investigation of a binary opposition crucial to the contemporary social field at the level of personal identity has important implications for self-other relations which Deleuzean maps tend to overlook. Dualism machines of contemporary culture operating at the level of personal identity — like that of sexual difference, race, sexual preference, and so on — are particularly important sites of creative destabilization for unraveling oppressive active subject/supportive other divisions perpetuated by specular economies of subjectivity. Irigaray herself believes that sexual difference is the key to creative resistance and an ethical future. One lesson of Deleuze and Guattari's anti-psychoanalytic stance, however, is that destratification does not necessarily have to retrace the route of one's personal history; cross-circuiting other series of becomings — for example, becoming-animal or becoming-imperceptible — necessitates neither accessing retroactive memories of the maternal body nor sexually differentiated becomings.

In Deleuze and Guattari's last book together, they lay out a conception of philosophy that distinguishes it from science and art and demonstrates the affinity of philosophy to a project of becoming-imperceptible. Although their earlier work together, particularly *A Thousand Plateaus*, and their conceptions of science and art (both of which they respect) indicate their preference for proliferating strategies in destratification and becoming-imperceptible rather than trying to put any one strategy forward as the only, or even best, one, Deleuze clearly has a particular affinity for a philosophical strategy. Reading *What Is Philosophy?* in light of Deleuze's book on Foucault demonstrates how philosophy, like Foucauldian cartography, can engage a project of resistance in the spirit of destratification. What was the "outside" in Deleuze's account of Foucault becomes "chaos" or the "virtual" in the book on philosophy. Like the processes of constructing a BwO or abstract machine that composes planes of consistency from which new possibilities can emerge, philosophy creates concepts that render chaos consistent and provide new perspectives for living.

According to Deleuze and Guattari, art, science, and philosophy are the three 'chaoids' — forms of thought or creation which are realities produced on the "planes that cut through the chaos in different ways" (WP 208). They define chaos "by the infinite speed with which every form taking shape in it vanishes." The virtual forms of chaos constitute a void "containing all possible particles and drawing out all possible forms, which spring up only to disappear immediately, without consistency or reference, without consequence" (118).[6] The chaoids constitute three different approaches to this virtual chaos. All three chaoids can be viewed as forms of becoming-imperceptible in which the embodied artist, scientist, or philosopher breaks up the coherent convergence of a unified subject perceiving or understanding a familiar world in order to access pre-personal singularities and create new perceptions and conceptions. The artist does this by creating 'percepts' and 'affects' from the perspective of aesthetic figures. The scientist does this by determining functions from the perspective of partial observers. And the philosopher does this by creating concepts from the perspective of conceptual personae.

What defines thought in its three great forms — art, science, and philosophy — is always confronting chaos, laying out a plane, throwing a plane over chaos. But philosophy wants to save the infinite by giving it consistency: it lays out a plane of immanence that, through the action of conceptual personae, takes events or consistent concepts to infinity. Science, on the other hand, relinquishes the infinite in order to gain reference: it lays out a plane of simply undefined coordinates that each time, through the action of partial observers, defines states of affairs, functions, or referential propositions. Art wants to create the finite that restores the infinite: it lays out a plane of composition that, in turn, through the action of aesthetic figures, bears monuments or composite sensations. (197)

In the context of the project of theorizing a viable model of subjectivity, I consider Deleuze and Guattari's characterizations of philosophy and art in terms of destratifying from overly restrictive economies of subjectivity.[7] Philosophy, as Deleuze's own preferred strategy in becoming-imperceptible, provides a compelling example of one form that reconceiving oneself within and through the set of forces of which one is a part could take. Like Irigaray's notion of the sensible transcendental and becoming toward the horizon of a feminine divine, philosophy provides a horizon for a process of becoming that continually touches upon what is "outside" to lived experience. Whereas Irigaray prefers to access this "outside" through a practice of perception that entails a spiritualization of the flesh, especially in mutually constitutive encounters with embodied others, Deleuze lays out planes of immanence which through conceptual personae take consistent concepts to infinity. It may turn out that Irigaray's approach to what she calls the divine (and what Deleuze and Guattari call chaos or the virtual) is more akin to Deleuze and Guattari's conception of art than to their version of philosophy, despite Irigaray's situating of her work within philosophy. Comparing their differing conceptions of what for each constitutes a philosophical project may shed further light on the implications of sexual difference for a project of becoming.

Philosophy and the Virtual

Philosophy gives the virtual consistency by selecting "infinite movements of thought" and creating concepts "formed like consistent particles going as fast as thought" (WP 118). Mental things, like other things, are multiplicities. Since any determinate mental formation could always have been otherwise, it always touches upon the "outside" of thought from which novel mental formations emerge. This "outside' — the virtual forms of chaos — is infinite in the sense that there is no end to the various formations thoughts can take. Philosophy's distinctive approach to this "outside" is to adhere to the immanent principle of consistency: "A concept is a set of inseparable variations that is produced or constructed on a plane of immanence insofar as the latter crosscuts the chaotic variability and gives it consistency (reality). A concept is therefore a chaoid state par excellence; it refers back to a chaos rendered consistent, become Thought, mental chaosmos" (208). Concepts are mental things with multiple components. The Cartesian cogito, for example, entails the components of doubting, thinking, and being (29).[8] These heterogeneous components are inseparable in the concept of the cogito; they are "traversed by a point of absolute survey at infinite speed" (21). That is, a thought-movement creates a concept by linking various components according to a principle of variation that renders the components inseparable; doubting, thinking, and being are distinguishable, and yet all are crucial to Descartes's concept that "myself who doubts, I think, I am, I am a thinking thing" (or, in its more popular formation, "I think therefore I am"). Doubting, thinking, and being overlap in some of their phases of variation (for example, doubting is a phase of thinking, and a finite thinking being is a phase of being) and not in others (doubting is not imagining, a finite thinking being is not an infinite being). The phases of a component which approach overlapping the phases of other components constitute 'zones of neighborhood or indiscernability." These zones produce passages from one component to the other "and consitute their inseparability" (25). This concept condenses at the point "I" where all three components coincide ("I doubt," "I think," "I am"). This point constitutes a point of "absolute survey" on its components. The creation of a concept stabilizes mental multiplicities into a relatively consistent form.

Chaos is characterized by determinations which take shape and vanish at infinite speed (WP 42). The philosophical creation of concepts allows for the infinite speed of a thought that continually connects heterogeneous aspects of mental multiplicities. Because these connections are defined through a principle of consistency (rather than through a principle of reference or composition), the forms that philosophical thinking stabilizes out of the chaotic virtual can allow infinitely fast travel between various aspects of human existence. Thinking gives itself an image of what it means to think; this image of thought is a plane of consistency (or, as Deleuze and Guattari refer to this plane in *What Is Philosophy?*, a plane of immanence) and acts like a sieve which sections chaos (35). That is, thinking privileges certain thought-movements over others, and these thought-movements resonate on the plane of immanence in which they are related. The plane of immanence is pre-philosophical since it is presupposed in the creation of concepts; the particular form it takes could always have been otherwise (40).

Propositions, unlike concepts, are defined by their reference to a state of affairs or body. The conditions of the relationship between propositions and the states of affairs to which they refer are extensional. Since concepts are intensional, they are not discursive, "and philosophy is not a discursive formation, because it does not link propositions together" (WP 22). Each concept is "the point of coincidence, condensation, or accumulation of its own components" (20); it is incorporeal and has intensive ordinates rather than spatiotemporal coordinates. Although it is effectuated in bodies, it is not "mixed up with the state of affairs in which it is effectuated." Actualizations of the virtual relations of the components of a concept and of that concept with other concepts are not constrained by the determinate configuration of a specific state of affairs. The concept is "immediately co-present to all its components or variations, at no distance from them, passing back and forth through them" (21). Philosophical time is one of super-imposition; since concepts are not referred to the specific grid of space-time points of conventional experience, they allow a perspective on human existence which can survey various space-time points at infinite speed. A concept represents neither a state of affairs nor the lived experience of the philosopher; it is a creation that unfolds through the immanent principle of consistency, and it expresses what Deleuze and Guattari call an event.

The notion of the event is connected to Deleuze's notion of transcendental empiricism, which challenges traditional conceptions of the possible (cf. Chapter 5). Possibility is traditionally determined by abstracting intelligible structures from real experience in order to posit them as conditions of experience to which the future must conform. According to Deleuze, this renders the possible a kind of inversion of the real. Deleuze's notion of an event deliberately thwarts this conception of possibility; an event is not a universal or general rule which can be instantiated by a state of affairs, but refers to a virtual reality from which unprecedented actualities can emerge.

Events are actualized in states of affairs, in bodies, and in the lived — the event of the cogito was actualized by Descartes himself — but there is a "shadowy and secret part" of the event that is "continually subtracted from or added to its actualization" (WP 156). The event of the cogito is not Descartes's enactment of it, nor is it derived by representing Descartes's lived experience. Discerning the zones of neighborhood of the components of a concept and of that concept with other concepts requires breaking with the conventional norms of the already-lived in order to follow out the movements of conceptual becoming. The event is the incorporeal meaning which is the "pure reserve" of what is actually effectuated in states of affairs; it is always still to come and has always already happened (158). In *The Fold*, Deleuze characterizes the Stoics' conception of the event as the incorporeal predicate of the subject of a proposition that states the "manner of being" of a thing (Deleuze 1993, 53). Neither attribute nor quality, the incorporeal predicate is more akin to an infinitive verb than an adjective. For example, the proposition "the tree greens" in contrast to "the tree is green" states a manner of being of a tree rather than ascribing an attribute to a substance. "To green" is the incorporeal predicate hovering over specific instances of green trees as well as over other green things. The concept as a pure event is a virtual reality whose components are incorporeal predicates which are both more than and less than any given state of affairs. The concept can survey any number of its effectuations in states of affairs and yet retain its infinite movement; there are always virtual relations among its components and with other concepts which have not been actualized. Any number of people can actualize a specific configuration of the virtual relations of the components of the cogito in a thought-movement unique to them. Any number of states of affairs can effectuate a given event.

In *The Logic of Sense*, Deleuze claims that the pure event is "sense itself, insofar as it is disengaged or distinguished from the states of affairs which produce it and in which it is actualized" (LS 211). Events are actualized in states of affairs with a specific sense, but no state of affairs can exhaust the sense of an event; there is always a counteractualization of the state of affairs which extracts the extra-being or incorporeal effect of its sense: "With every event, there is indeed the present moment of its actualization. . . . But on the other hand, there is the future and the past of the event considered in itself, sidestepping each present, being free of the limitations of a state of affairs, impersonal and pre-individual, neutral, neither general nor particular" (151). The enactment of the cogito in a specific state of affairs, for example, a specific instance of Descartes's own thought-movement, can always be counteractualized; another enactment of a thought-movement can always actualize a novel configuration of the cogito's components drawn from the cogito's virtual relations.

Deleuze and Guattari refer to the various characters of philosophical writing as 'conceptual personae' (cf. Chapter 5). These may be explicitly named — Plato's Socrates or Nietzsche's Dionysus — or implicit in the form of an attitude of thought to be distinguished from the author herself. Conceptual personae are the intermediaries through which philosophical enunciations produce movement (WP 64–65). Just as the great aesthetic figures of novels, paintings, sculpture, and music "produce affects that surpass ordinary affections and perceptions," so do the concepts of conceptual personae "go beyond everyday opinions" (WP 65). "*The role of conceptual personae is to show thought's territories, its absolute deterritorializations and reterritorializations.* Conceptual personae are thinkers, solely thinkers, and their personalized features are closely linked to the diagrammatic features of thought and the intensive features of concepts. A particular conceptual persona, who perhaps did not exist before us, thinks in us" (WP 69).

The philosopher as biologically embodied subject cannot possibly live out all the variations of lived experience which a concept surveys. The Cartesian cogito as concept or event is not instantiated in the lived experience of someone who thinks its components; its infinite movement always exceeds any such effectuation. In attending to the variations of conceptual becomings, the philosopher creates an infinite speed in thought that moves beyond conventional thinking and beyond the bounds of commonsense experience to something that lies beyond both. The immanent principle of consistency unfolds a series of connections which constitutes a new perspective on human life. Since this immanent principle is not constrained by the space-time grid of an individual life lived in a "commonsense" experience shared with others, it can provide revolutionary perspectives. And since these perspectives are referred to conceptual personae rather than to the philosopher as an individual, they can provide impetus for experiments without shattering the individual's capacity to participate in dominant reality. Deleuze and Guattari are careful to distinguish the schizophrenic conceptual persona "who lives intensely within the thinker and forces him to think" from the schizophrenic as psychosocial type "who represses the living being and robs him of his thought" (WP 70). Philosophical thinking can allow one to approach chaos without succumbing to it.

As we saw in Chapter 5, although capitalism is inherently deterritorializing in the sense that the drive for profit entails the continual deterritorializations of persons and institutions so that new (more profitable) social identities and institutions can form, social identities are stabilized through oedipalization. Deleuze and Guattari claim that modern philosophy takes the relative deterritorialization of capitalism to an absolute deterritorialization. Because philosophy refers itself to conceptual personae rather than the personal perspective of oedipalized subjects, it can refuse oedipalization. Philosophy can then become political and take "the criticism of its own time to its highest point" (WP 99). "Possibilities of life or modes of existence can be invented only on a plane of immanence that develops the power of conceptual personae. The face and body of philosophers shelter these personae who often give them a strange appearance, especially in the glance, as if someone else was looking through their eyes" (73).

Philosophy thus provides opportunities for experiments in destratification from oedipal identity. Conceptual personae allow the breakdown of the personal subject and the emergence of new connections among prepersonal singularities. The events or becomings constituted by the infinite speed with which a philosopher can connect various conceptual components in an organized way stabilizes a new perspective on the lived out of the virtual forms of chaos. Since this perspective is that of a conceptual persona rather than that of an embodied reality of an individual, it opens a possible line of flight without necessitating its completion in the actions of a living person.[9]

Philosophy breaks with the rules of conventional experience and renders the chaotic virtual — that which constitutes the "outside" of conventional perception and conception — real by rendering it consistent. The heterogeneous components of a concept are simultaneous; the speed of the movement of thought that links the various components according to an immanent principle of consistency is infinite. The infinite speed of thought brings these components into the composite becoming of an event. Although events provide perspectives on lived experience, the event itself is not about an actual historical happening. Concrete happenings are phenomena subject to the rules of conventional experience. Events can be effectuated in the states of affairs of historical happenings, but extracting an event from a state of affairs always entails constructing a concept from "that part that does not let itself be actualized, the reality of the concept" (WP 160). That is, the creation of a concept always entails more than merely representing the lived; it entails rendering chaos or the "outside" of thought consistent. Although it can provide a perspective on the lived, it is always in excess of the lived; it is a becoming rather than a phenomenon.

Becoming is the concept itself. It is born in History, and falls back into it, but is not of it. In itself it has neither beginning nor end but only a milieu. It is thus more geographical than historical. Such are revolutions and societies of friends, societies of resistance, because to create is to resist: pure becomings, pure events on a plane of immanence. What History grasps of the event is its effectuation in states of affairs or in lived experience, but the event in its becoming, in its specific consistency, in its self-positing as concept, escapes History. Psychosocial types are historical, but conceptual personae are events. (110)

Philosophy, science, and art all confront a virtual chaos that eludes conventional forms of perception and convention. All three forms of thought reach deeply into the unthought of thought in order to generate their determinate forms, but the realm of the unthought which is contiguous to all three realms of thought is inexhaustible. An ethical philosophy affirms the event by becoming equal to it. Creating concepts entails countereffectuating a lived situation in order to determine virtual relations which were not actualized in that situation. A revolution may be effectuated in a state of affairs, but whether it is "successful" or not, we can still continue to engage in revolutionary struggle; the revolution, like the cogito, is an event that is always already past and yet to come. Philosophy does not simply affirm the status quo of conventional experience, but instead resists it by extracting from it the virtual relations that could be actualized in a new future. "The creation of concepts in itself calls for a future form, for a new earth and people that do not yet exist" (WP 108). According to Deleuze and Guattari, "there is no other ethic than the *amor fati* of philosophy" (159). Philosophy responds to the force of imperceptible becoming which is the differentiating movement of creative life by thinking. Thinking entails the creation of concepts that affirm lived experience by engaging the thinking subject in a metamorphosis of herself and her perspectives on life.

Chaos, Philosophy, and Art

Like philosophy, art exceeds lived experience by creating an approach to chaotic virtuality. While philosophy invents conceptual personae and creates concepts that can move thought at infinite speeds, art creates aesthetic figures and composes percepts and affects which define zones of indiscernability for sensory becomings. Percepts are "no longer" perceptions since they are independent of the state of those who experience them. And affects are no longer feelings or affections since they "go beyond the strength of those who undergo them" (WP 164). For Deleuze and Guattari, perceptions and affections refer to conventional experience or "opinion": "What *opinion* proposes is a particular relationship between an external perception as state of a subject and an internal affection as passage from one state to another. . . . We pick out a quality supposedly common to several objects that we perceive, and an affection supposedly common to several subjects who experience it and who, along with us, grasp that quality. Opinion is the rule of the correspondence of one to the other" (144). Opinion codifies affections and perceptions by turning them into the variables of a rule of perception. This entails selecting from passages of sensory becoming only what can be subjected to the rule. Art undoes "the triple organization of perceptions, affections, and opinions" (176) by composing monuments of percepts and affects which break with convention and render the imperceptible perceptible. Just as the perceptible and the articulable adhere to the recognizable forms of a specific social field, so do the perceptions and affections constituting conventional experience. Just as a Foucauldian diagram creates an abstract machine revealing creative points of destabilization, so does artistic vision create a plane of composition revealing creative points of destabilization in conventional experience. Composing percepts and affects entails approaching the "outside" of perceptions and affections. Creating a monument that peserves them as a block of sensations entails creating a universe that is the embodiment of an aesthetic possibility drawn from virtual chaos. It preserves a block of sensations that are compounds of percepts and affects able to stand on their own: "By means of the material, the aim of art is to wrest the percept from perceptions of objects and the states of a perceiving subject, to wrest the affect from affections as the transition from one state to another: to extract a bloc of sensations, a pure being of sensations" (167).

One writes not "with childhood memories but through blocs of childhood that are the becoming-child of the present" (WP 168). We saw in Chapter 7 that snapshot memories are disconnected from the becomings that condition the subject's present living. They are thus static objects of reflection with no dynamic impact on the present. Childhood blocks, by contrast, engage the subject in a process of destratification at the level of corporeal as well as conceptual logics. Representation of lived perceptions and affections which fails to bring them into contact with the dynamic flow of molecular processes has little impact on subjectivity. Style is needed — "the writer's syntax, the musician's modes and rhythms, the painter's lines and colors" (170) — to bring lived perceptions and affections to the level of percepts and affects. The lived reality of the artist, confined as it is within the forms of organization of conventional experience, is a shadow of that part of the virtual forms of chaos which the artist confronts. Just as the philosopher breaks with — or, in Deleuzian-Guattarian terms, deterritorializes from — conventional thought by pursuing the movement of conceptual becomings, the artist deterritorializes perceptions and affections by pursuing the movement of sensory becomings. Percepts and affects, like concepts, challenge the coherence of commonsense experience; percepts are "nonhuman landscapes of nature" and affects are "nonhuman becomings of man" (169). Instead of using the artistic medium to imitate or represent a familiar experience, the artist "is a seer, a becomer" (171). She renders a moment of the world durable enough to exist by itself. To create percepts, she saturates her medium and eliminates "everything that adheres to our current and lived perceptions" (172). For example, Melville's aesthetic figure Ahab enters into a relationship with Moby Dick of becoming-whale. Ahab's perceptions of the sea in this becoming form "a compound of sensations that no longer needs anyone" (169). This compound is the percept of the ocean created by Melville. The percept makes perceptible "the imperceptible forces that populate the world" affecting us and making us become (182). While conceptual becomings link the components of mental multiplicities, sensory becomings put the elements of physical multiplicities into "continuous variation."

Percepts and affects evoke the passage between heterogeneous sensations in the ceaseless becoming-other of life (188).

Deleuze, in his book on the painter Francis Bacon, and Deleuze and Guattari in *What Is Philosophy?*, characterize three elements of an artistic monument, citing the paintings of van Gogh, Gauguin, and Bacon as examples, which together render imperceptible sensory becomings perceptible. These elements are the flesh, the house, and the universe-cosmos. Deleuze says that the new problem of painting after Cézanne for all three painters was that of creating vast homogeneous fields "that carry toward infinity" as the ground for a figure/flesh which preserves the "specificity or singularity of a form in perpetual variation." One might say that the "flesh," as the element of the painting most closely associated with an embodied subject, represents a perspective on sensory becoming. Although flesh is involved in revealing sensation, however, Deleuze and Guattari say that it is no more than a thermometer of sensory becoming. The portraits of van Gogh, Gauguin, and Bacon depict flesh in unnatural colors and broken tones. This conveys some of the variability of a passage of sensory becoming in relationship to the universe-cosmos — the monochrome fields that ground the flesh. These fields are painted in "very subtle shifts of intensity or saturation determined by zones of proximity" indicating sensory passages to the imperceptible (FB 12).[10] The relationship between the first element of flesh and the third element of the field or universe-cosmos is mediated by the second element, the house, or what, in reference to Bacon's paintings, Deleuze calls the contour. In Bacon's paintings, Deleuze claims that the contour — the circle or oval, chair or bed, on which the flesh or figure is placed — acts as the membrane through which a double exchange between the figure and the background field flows (15, 21). It is in this second element of the house or contour that the body blossoms. It is the house or contour that gives sensation the power to stand on its own by acting as a kind of filter for cosmic forces (WP 182) The painting creates a being of sensation that stands on its own. The being of sensation is not located in the figure of the painting; that is, it is not the flesh but rather the relationships among figure, house or contour, and universe-cosmos or field. It is "the compound of nonhuman forces of the cosmos, of man's nonhuman becomings, and of the ambiguous house that exchanges and adjusts them, makes them whirl around like winds. Flesh is only the developer which disappears in what it develops: the compound of sensation" (183). The artistic monument renders perceptible the imperceptible forces which condition the conventional experience of an embodied subject. These forces defy the separation of personal self from a world of becoming. The monument not only deterrritorializes conventional perceptions and affections but also constitutes an approach to the chaotic virtual by embodying an alternative aesthetic possibility. Being drawn into the becoming-other of an artistic monument allows the spectator as well to approach the chaotic virtual from the finite perspective of an embodied world.

Just as concepts are created through the zones of indiscernability of their components, so are blocks of sensation compounding percepts and affects created through the zones of indiscernability of sensations. If we recall Deleuze and Guattari's various discussions of becoming-other in *A Thousand Plateaus* (discussed in Chapter 7), art would seem to be closer than either science or philosophy to the actual becoming-other of lived experience; art, like lived experience, involves the sensory becomings of determinate aggregates. Both conceptual and sensory becomings connect heterogeneous singularities, but conceptual becomings survey or express lived experience rather than embody it. That is, the sensory becomings of art connect the heterogeneous singularities of a specific (finite) space and time in the aesthetic possibility of a universe. This creation of a plane of composition indicates the chaotic virtual by hinting at the alternate formations the singularities of finite experience can take. Art challenges commonsense experience by composing sensations which are a composite of percepts and affects from the perspective of aesthetic figures. Like conceptual personae, aesthetic figures break with the convergence of faculties into a coherent subject and perceptible objects and make perceptible the becomings that are imperceptible to common sense. Whereas philosophy creates events that are "the reality of the virtual, forms of a thought-Nature that survey every possible universe" (WP 177–78), art composes chaos "that becomes sensory" (206). Philosophy saves the infinite by giving it consistency; art wants to create the finite that restores the infinite.

Both philosophy and art create perspectives on life which defy the unity of a coherent self with stable psychic and corporeal boundaries. The embodied philosopher and artist does this through conceptual personae and aesthetic figures. Deleuze and Guattari suggest that art may begin with the animal, for example, birds (WP 183). They suggest an analogy between the flesh, house, and universe of the artistic monument and the postures and colors of a bird, the territory marked out by its songs, and the relation of this territory to other territories. Thus, while philosophy and art provide approaches to the chaotic virtual, more ordinary life-forms also constitute an approach to chaos. The bird's territory encompasses or cuts across the territories of other birds and other species, as well as the trajectories of animals without territories, "forming interspecies junction points" (185). Territories are neither isolated areas nor simply joined onto other territories, but instead open onto cosmic forces "that arise from within or come from outside," perceptibly affecting the inhabitants of those territories (186). Just as the figure and house of a painting must open onto a cosmos-universe, so do these territories open onto an infinite symphonic plane of composition: "If nature is like art, this is always because it combines these two living elements in every way: House and Universe, *Heimlich* and *Unheimlich*, territory and deterritorialization, finite melodic compounds and the great infinite plane of composition, the small and large refrain" (WP 186).

The distinctions Deleuze and Guattari make between the flesh, the house, and the universe suggest a novel way of considering the relationship of an embodied subject to the world. The flesh is never separate from a world of imperceptible forces, but changes with it, registering the effects of these forces as developer registers the effects of light on a roll of film. The flesh derives some protection from the cosmic forces which could overwhelm it through the organization of a house. The notion of a territory drawn from ethology further elaborates how the territory separating and relating the flesh to other territories and to a much larger universe of process is marked out through a repeated series of expressive postures, movements, and speech. Whereas territorial behavior may become locked into repetitious patterns, an artistic practice would continually re-evoke the relationship of house or territory to a larger universe through a practice of rendering the imperceptible perceptible. In an art of living, the creation of percepts and affects would not be monumentalized, but would rather play out in the reworking of territorial marking which provides a livable realm for the flesh as well as connection to others; embodied subjects would continually reshape their postures, movements, and speech in a responsive becoming-other. Philosophy may provide the concepts that elicit new perspectives on what we should do next, and art may provide the monuments that elicit participatory becoming-other, but it is artful as well as philosophical living that could allow us to embody our philosophical perspectives in response to sensory as well as conceptual becomings.

If we consider Deleuze and Guattari's contrast between philosophy and art, we can see the distinctive advantages of both to a project of destratification that would foster nondualistic forms of subjectivity. Philosophy allows us to "save" the infinite. Conceptual personae travel lines of flight that unfold in adherence to the immanent principle of consistency. Conceptual becomings incorporate corporeal and conceptual logics because the immanent principle of consistency cuts across body/mind dualisms. There is no "right" or "wrong" way to determine a zone of indiscernability; the intensities traditionally associated with the body (fleeting sensations, twitches and flows, mood, emotions, half-thoughts) are as much of a factor as the rules of logic more traditionally associated with conceptual thought. Conceptual personae allow the embodied philosopher to release pre-personal singularities from the conventional formations of both conceptual and corporeal logics, allowing new forms to emerge. *A Thousand Plateaus* as an example of "philosophy" indicates just how heterogeneous conceptual becomings can be. Art also involves a process of incorporating corporeal and conceptual logics; creating the finite that restores the infinite involves composing sensory becomings in a way that demonstrates their affinity to the virtual; percepts and affects challenge conventional perception of phenomena and introduce unprecedented possibilities in perception and conception.

Irigaray, like Deleuze and Guattari, wants to evoke a future that goes beyond the possibilities derived from conventional experience. Like them, she challenges representational forms of thinking in order to provoke a thinking that is a creative response to the forces of life of which we are unaware. Also like them, she wants to call our attention to the passage between — the zones of indiscernability of conceptual and sensory becomings which defy the familiar categories of conception and perception. Unlike Deleuze and Guattari, however, who tend to think of personal identity as a trap that disables the creative encounter with pre-personal singularities that, for example, conceptual personae and aesthetic figures can provide, Irigaray continually evokes the possibility of creative engenderment in personal self-other relations. In Irigaray's work it is the personal identity of the masculine subject, who uses the feminine other for a mirror in which he can repeat himself as the same, that is the trap; it is specular forms of personal identity that freeze the creative passage that can occur between two embodied subjects.

The creation of conceptual personae and aesthetic figures need not disable the identity of the embodied philosopher or artist, although they are bound to affect it; Deleuze and Guattari do not display the same kind of concern as Irigaray for personal identity, and yet they are just as cautious as she in their deterritorializing experiments. Like Irigaray, however, they do not believe that deterritorialization will necessarily lead to the complete breakdown of identity that the normative insistence on dominant reality may suggest. All three thinkers believe that the willingness to engage in creative experimentation can result in rejuvenating self-transformation as well as ethical transformations of one's relations with others and with the world.

Irigaray's concern with the appropriative effects of certain forms of identity-formation, in particular that of masculine specularity, leads her to give special attention to self-other relations in which personal identity is recognized and confirmed. But on her account, it turns out that non-appropriative personal identity can no more remain within the constraints of conventional experience than can other approaches to the chaotic virtual. Like philosophy and art (as well as science), Irigaray's suggestions for an experiment in living relationship requires going beyond the conventional forms of conception and perception in order to actualize virtual relations into unprecedented forms. In order to smash the specular mirrors that separate us and freeze the becoming-other which could, and should according to Irigaray, generate a mutually constitutive process of transformation, we need to develop an art of perception. The art of perception for which Irigaray calls could be compared to the artistic practice of marking a territory in relation to a universe. The postures and gestures we enact as well as the words we speak could be conceived as compositions created in response to the imperceptible forces that condition our interpersonal relations as well as our relations to the world.

It is interesting to note that Irigaray, with her insistence on sexual difference and the traditional relegation of the feminine to the realm of matter-nature-body, combines more of the artistic approach in her version of philosophy. Her "elemental" vocabulary with its images of fire, air, earth, and sea, her rewriting of Greek myths, and her lyrical style continually return her readers to sense experience and the sexed body. For Irigaray, it is precisely the ceaseless becoming-other of the embodied subject that needs to be taken into account if we are to overcome the blind spot of masculine subjectivity. And yet, Deleuze and Guattari's distinction between philosophy and art still serves to mark Irigaray's work as philosophical. Despite her emphasis on sensual language, she too is interested in creating concepts that are the constellations of states of affairs yet to come. She too would like to "save" the infinite by creating concepts that can herald new ways of being. But since she is equally concerned with how these concepts can be applied by the living individual, she is also concerned with how concepts may (or may not) facilitate a creative, finite living that restores the infinite.

Deleuze and Guattari, of course, make clear that all three chaoids implicate one another; the distinctions they make between them are ultimately as bound to be blurred as other distinctions. And their own work, particularly *A Thousand Plateaus*, certainly does not shun sensual language. But because Irigaray launches her project from the perspective of the feminine other rendered mute at the level of embodied personal identity, she continually links her philosophical project to the more "artistic" problem of how to apply her concepts to embodied subjects in specific situations. If "philosophy" can open up new perspectives on actual happenings without being constrained by them, maybe it is to "art" that we need to turn for a model of how an embodied subject could go about finding creative solutions to the specific problems faced by those with physical as well as mental selves. Events may be able to survey the whole of life, but it is in opening up our own perceptions — as subjects with personal identities and histories — that we will be able to fill in the details of how such events are relevant to the happenings of our own lives. In the next chapter I further explore a comparison of the two projects and present a synthesis.

9
Corporeal Cartographies

Irigaray criticizes philosophers who take an interest in the "deconstruction of ontology" without concerning themselves with "the constitution of a new, rationally founded identity" (TD 32). Despite her interest in revealing and dismantling the economy that supports masculine subjectivity, she taunts deconstructive philosophies for providing modes of release for subjects according to a masculine model of sexuality. Such release puts contemporary subjectivity at risk without providing alternative forms of subjectivity.

This sort of cultural semi-release [an explosion or release of overly saturated or overly entropic theoretical models, with a considerable risk to human bodies and minds] is often accompanied by an acceleration of theoretical and practical contradictions, an ever-increasing estrangement from our corporeal matter and its properties, a search for self in abstraction or dream, an unthought-of gap between the technological environment, its influence upon us and ideological entropies that cannot be counter-balanced, in my opinion, except by cultivating our *sexual* bodies. (33–34)

According to Irigaray, despite the need to risk contemporary forms of subjectivity in order to find new ones, we need to consider the question of how "in all these disintegrations, explosions, splits, or multiplicities, these losses of corporeal identity" (TD 33), we are to find a new form of subjectivity. The question of how to break out of the forms that deaden us and impoverish life cannot be separated for Irigaray from the question of how to find life-sustaining forms of subjectivity that integrate the corporeal and conceptual logics contemporary society rends asunder through its structuring of sexual difference.

Irigaray's criticism of an "explosion or release" from entropic theoretical models resonates with her criticism of Nietzsche's Dionysian release from individuality. She accuses both of an ever-increasing estrangement from corporeal matter in the search for an autogenerating self. Dionysian release from individuality plunges the masculine subject into a primitive fusion in which he is as much out of touch with the singularity of sensible existence as is the man who refers himself and his being to a god set at a distance from corporeal life. Despite Nietzsche's attempt to leave behind the distinctions of a self-identical subject and incorporate more of the sensual and "natural" body, Irigaray accuses him of leaving behind a nuanced sensitivity to difference as it plays out in the realm of the corporeal. His blindness to the feminine other, and his tendency to center the whole world around himself through an appropriation of the creative energy of the feminine other, lead him to another kind of entombment — one in which the creative engenderment of two in a mutually transformative encounter cannot occur. Instead, he becomes the whole world, but he loses the world in the process. In refusing acknowledgment of the negative and that which limits him in his specificity in favor of the conjunctive synthesis of an and . . . and . . . that knows no limit, he satisfies the dream of self-creation by abstracting himself out of his corporeal limits and conceiving of himself as limitless.

One can see the possible applicability of such a criticism to Deleuze's project. From an Irigarayan perspective, insofar as Deleuze leaves behind vocabulary and concepts that evoke the specificity of a living body in space and time, he is prone to what Irigaray might term a masculinist fantasy of self-creation. Just as in Nietzsche, although he breaks down traditional masculine specularity and attempts to evoke the singularities unrecognized by specular subjectivity, his tendency to overlook the constitutive influence of nurturing others entails flight from his own corporeality. One could charge Deleuze's nomadic subject with flight from matter and human corporeality in order to perpetuate the illusion of masculine self-sufficiency in a self-creating whole. Clearly neither Nietzsche nor Deleuze intends to leave the realm of the corporeal behind. Indeed, an important feature of their philosophies is a kind of radical empiricism that insists on diagnosing corporeal as well as conceptual symptoms in their reading of the world. Irigaray, too, would reveal the behind-the-scenes workings of the representations that are manifest in conscious experience. But Irigaray mocks a release from such structures of representation if it is only going to lead to the "semi-release" of a buildup of tension for a specular subject. Finding outlets for release without considering the mechanisms of specularity will not lead to the new forms of subjectivity for which both Irigaray and Deleuze call.

For Irigaray, subjectivity must be premised on a felt encounter with our own corporeal limits and an acknowledgment of the difference of the other who allows us to experience our limits. Perhaps because Irigaray — as a woman — writes from the position of one who has allowed the structures of her experience to be dictated to her, she is insistent on the need for such structure in order to continue to engage in a creative process of transformation within a living world. Without some relationship with oneself, without a relationship to the horizon of one's gender, without something to which to refer one's own becomings, one is liable to be drawn into the becomings of another. At the same time that Irigaray agrees with Deleuze that the structures that organize our experience should be flexible enough to allow for continual change and creative growth, she insists that we need to consider the form those structures take. Speaking as one who is all too clear on what happens to those who are not able to protect themselves from the coercive appropriation of subjects who are more structured than herself, she considers the positive characterization of alternative subjectivities to be as important as paths of release from the structures in which we currently find ourselves. If she believes that these structures must be found in the context of an exploration and elaboration of our sexual bodies, it is because she believes that we must start from where we find ourselves, and because she believes that sexual difference provides a crucial key to how we deny our own corporeal limits (for masculine subjects) as well as how we fail to elaborate our own possibilities for structured subjectivity (for feminine others).

Representing Origins and Becoming-Intrauterine

Irigaray returns to the maternal body in order to investigate what comes prior to the phallus and the desire to be desired by the mother with reference to the third term of the father. Irigaray, like Deleuze and Guattari, believes that oedipal subjectivity is too reductive. If it succeeds in rendering a coherent subject, it is only through the effacement of a broader range of forces which present other possibilities that are thus cut off. Deleuze and Guattari refer to this broader range of life processes with the notions of desiring-machines (*Anti-Oedipus*), assemblages (*A Thousand Plateaus*), and pre-personal singularities; Irigaray refers to this broader range with the notions of the sensible transcendental, mucous and passage, and the origin of a coherent body from the material breaks with the mother as original nature-body (S 40–41).

Irigaray is concerned with the morphology of a personal body. Although she is as interested as Deleuze and Guattari in breaking free from a reductionistic economy of subjectivity that she believes to be impoverishing, she wants to maintain human subjects as subjects with bodily integrity and personal selves. For Irigaray, this means maintaining some kind of relationship to familial figures and gender. Although the familial figures of the oedipal drama in their contemporary form are overly constricting, Irigaray's concern with empowering women makes it impossible simply to evade, rather than rework, the family arena. Since stratification is endemic to living, one could argue that the more stable formations of personal identity would be an inevitable epiphenomenon of the pursuit of nomadic lines of flight; de-oedipalization could not dissolve a life-narrative even if one wanted it to. But even if identity — including the personal identity of a coherent subject with a life-narrative — is as much the effect of nomadic lines of flight as of oedipal dramas (and I am not convinced that this is the case), for Irigaray some forms of identity are more empowering than others.

Deleuze and Guattari bypass the question of the relations to one's origins that Irigaray uses to interrogate the psychoanalytic paradigm; nomadic subjects, conceptual personae, and aesthetic figures need not relate themselves to their origins. Deleuze and Guattari's emphasis on geographical experiments initiated from where one finds oneself may open a larger range of creative possibilities than Irigaray's emphasis on origins. Nevertheless, they lose some part of the mapping of interdependent subject constitution that Irigaray makes available. Owing to her emphasis on sexual difference, she throws into relief a whole series of questions and possibilities that relate to the way that subjectivity interlocks with the subjectivity of others. In this section I explore Irigaray's evocation of intrauterine experience and suggest that it could be read as a construction of a BwO with important implications for the specific configuration of the contemporary social field in which we live.

Irigaray claims that the oedipal triangle of Freudian theory is based on matricide. The phallus is a displaced symbol of desire veiling the lost umbilical cord, the lost place of wholeness of intrauterine experience in which the whole child was sheltered in the womb of a whole mother. If contemporary culture is obsessed with the phallus, it is because this is a displaced symbol of the umbilical cord. For Irigaray, the intrauterine space is an anoedipal space, a space of plenitude rather than lack, singularity rather than universality, and the interactive attunement of singularities rather than the grid of social positioning that pertains to all. The umbilical cord represents desire for this anoedipal space. Privileging the phallus as symbol of desire veils this desire for one's own origin in the mother.

One might object that from a Deleuzean perspective, Irigaray's use of the intrauterine metaphor, especially since it evokes a pre-oedipal experience, works only to bring disparate experience back under the rubric of oedipalizing discourse.[1] To appeal to an intrauterine metaphor to make sense of present experience would be to evoke the strange myth of origins that psychoanalysis invents. Appealing to a retroactive and fantastical memory of a time and place prior to the emergence of ourselves as subjects does no more than commit us to snapshot pictures of our pasts which are maintained in a space that is more or less isolated from the multiple encounters of our current becomings. Such a metaphor puts experience in a safe past that can no longer touch us. If one reads her metaphor in terms of a Deleuzean-Guattarian block of becoming, however, such a metaphor can enable one to take on the patterns of intrauterine becoming. Thus the intrauterine metaphor for one's origins becomes the construction of a BwO — a particularly important one in a social field marked by the oedipalization of subjects.

According to Deleuze, the body is not a thing but a process that retains some degree of coherence by maintaining a fairly constant pattern. Massumi suggests conceiving of the body without organs as a virtual body (1992, 68–80). The pre-personal singularities of bodily processes have innumerable virtual relations, only some of which are actualized in the determinate configurations of actual assemblages; the body without organs is the virtual totality of those relations from which determinate bodily processes emerge. Although certain things may be possible or impossible for the body I currently am, my virtual body constitutes a ground zero or release from at least some of the many patterns organizing bodily processes. The formation of a particular configuration of bodily process patterns renders the actualization of certain other patterns impossible; the virtual body includes incompossible forms of bodily organization. In evoking intrauterine experience in terms of a block of becoming, one is accessing one's virtual body in ways that will open up patternings of experience that are impossible for contemporary corporeal patternings. Accessing intrauterine experience as a block could therefore open up a wide range of experiencing by cross-circuiting one's present organization with becoming-intrauterine.

Constructing a BwO does not necessarily entail accessing childhood blocks of becoming in order to open up new ways of seeing and thinking in one's current life. Although psychoanalysis seems to imply that the only way to rejuvenate one's present life is through unraveling the knots of one's past and reordering them according to an oedipal scheme, Deleuze and Guattari's notions of desire and the BwO suggest that any number of strategies could work for constructing BwOs and thus opening up a creative space for unanticipated becomings. Deleuze and Guattari strongly object to reducing material fluxes and flows of corporeal life to the oedipal triangle by assuming that they relate to unconscious oedipal fantasies, and conjuring up snapshot memories of one's past in order to explain one's present (cf. Chapter 7). Irigaray's description of intrauterine experience, however, evokes a block of becoming we can now enter into that can permit the construction of a BwO in the present with enlivening possibilities.

Both Irigaray and Deleuze want to affect people with their writing on multiple levels, and they want these affects to be intellectual, passional, and physical in nature. I have contended throughout this book that both Irigaray and Deleuze are interested in overcoming mind/body dualisms. Irigaray's use of a more traditional vocabulary of the body in carrying out her project is indicative of an important difference between her project and that of Deleuze. Irigaray refuses to let us forget that the symbolic and the imaginary of contemporary culture in which we are situated entail a sexual division of labor that implicates self/other dualisms on all levels of identity formation and sustenance. Irigaray's use of the intrauterine metaphor, in addition to being able to affect a block of becoming in the present, also underlines the cultural significance of motherhood in the process. Thus, if we make a becoming-block out of Irigaray's metaphor, we cannot help but break open our conception of motherhood as well in the process. If we read the metaphor this way, it is not just as a pregnant woman or as a fetus that we have the amorphous contact and interchange with the world of intrauterine experience; it is an experience that is still right now available to us, an experience that is retained in the virtual body open to new connections to the world in which it is always encompassed.

At times it seems that Deleuze and Guattari do not heed their own advice to destratify from where one is; their counter to the oedipal structure is to ignore it: cross-circuit molar organization and release lines of flight that will take you beyond the oedipal frame. Irigaray is much more suspicious of such lines of flight. If they entail a denial of the mother, she fears that they are as oedipal as any more conservative structuring of the unconscious. Desiring-machines (or assemblages) will not release us from the oedipal structure which she also believes to be impoverishing if they do not take note of what has been covered over in the process of oedipalization. What has been covered over on her view is the umbilical cord and our fascination with our own origins in the body of another. On the one hand, denying this fascination can only perpetuate fantasies of omnipotence and self-creation that have serious ethical consequences vis-à-vis other people. On the other hand, unveiling this fascination could have rich potential for reconceiving identity and constructing an ethical subjectivity more in keeping with our lived reality and hence more adequate to who we feel ourselves to be. Part of Irigaray's strategy, then, is to insist on unveiling the fascination with the father as a displacement of our fascination with the "original matrix" — our origins in the maternal womb — and to find another, more honest means for representing our relationship to "that first body, that first home, that first love" (S&G 14). It is important to represent the relationship to the original matrix of our existence because the contemporary lack of an honest representation of this relationship leaves us feeling destitute, lost, and vulnerable to other less satisfying representations based on the exploitation of feminine and marginal others.

Irigaray suggests representing our origins with an image of difference. We could, for example, refer our origins to a woman and man come together in a process of mutual engenderment in which both were active subjects and each manifested both creative becoming and the material limits of corporeality (S 35). Unlike the maternal body of a woman reduced to the maternal-feminine, such a point of origin would entail a differentiating principle of process. Representing our origins in this way, rather than as a maternal body, could allow our life-narratives to take more dynamic forms. Instead of either opposing ourselves to or substituting ourselves for the maternal body, we could see ourselves as emerging from differentiating forces. Instead of needing to replicate a relationship to a stable place to reaffirm our identities, our identities could incorporate an ongoing relationship to dynamic becoming. In every repetition of mutual engenderment we could once more be confirming participatory communion with the differentiating power of becoming with which we would be most deeply identified. It would then be through further differentiation rather than repetition of a specular relationship that we could confirm our identities.

Deleuze and Guattari claim that we are invested in the social field of history before we are invested in the familial field of the oedipal. That is, we name various zones of intensity in terms of cultural, economic, and political structures before we reduce them to the oedipalized names of a personal history. This claim contests the impression that psychoanalysis can give that one is made in a social vacuum and opens familial identities out onto the social field by emphasizing the role that social positioning plays in identity from the very start. The broader patterns of identity constitution are to be found not in familial patterns but in the pattern of social functioning that occupies the whole social field. According to Irigaray, contemporary culture represents our origins as a nondifferentiated place. Reconceiving our origins as a differentiating process engendered between two characters of the oedipal drama ("mother" and "father") is one step in transforming a specular economy of subjectivity. Conceiving the familial characters of the oedipal drama as molar aggregates drawn from more fluid formations of identities that range the entire social field suggests another step. If "mother" and "father" are conceived as milieus or territories emerging from a social field, they can no longer be reduced to the positions of an oedipal triangle. That is, in addition to reconceiving the womb as a place of dynamic corporeal becoming, we could reconceive familial identity in terms of larger social processes. Just as the fetus is in a nonsymmetrical relationship entailing dynamic participation in a process extending beyond it, so does a familial identity emerge from larger social processes that extend beyond it. Familial dramas would then have to be read as being precipitated by these larger social processes; a psychoanalytic story about an individual life could be no more than an abbreviated account of a more complicated story about social forces.

Although it is obvious that a specific individual has parents with specific social identities and histories, Deleuze and Guattari's account allows us to posit sexual difference as an important component of personal identity without making it foundational. Sexual difference is a site of creative destabilization not because it founds any social identity whatsoever but because it stabilizes a fluid range of possible identities. The maternal-feminine stripped of the specificity of an individual could be compared to the reduction of a complicated series of social identifications to a familial identity of which Deleuze and Guattari speak. Unlike Deleuze and Guattari, however, Irigaray would have us recognize that the contemporary structure of the cultural imaginary represents our origins as feminine and that this has specific effects in the contemporary social field. In particular, it disables a different kind of approach toward subjectivity, one that could begin to think of social identity as being mutually informing rather than a solitary flight, and mutually implicating rather than specular.

The scar where the umbilical cord was cut is the most elemental identity tag because it represents our first separation from the realm of molecular process. The realm of the unconscious, for both Irigaray and Deleuze and Guattari, includes the realm of embodiment, of the material, of contact and participation in the material realm prior to any cut, prior to any separation from the becomings among which we find ourselves. To act in the world, one must first achieve some sense of one's separateness from the world and the forces with which one participates and among which one finds oneself. If Irigaray suggests that it is the cutting of the umbilical cord that represents the first cut that makes social identification possible, it is because it is that cut which starts us on our journey to subjectivity. It is in establishing our position vis-à-vis our parents in the very material sense of establishing our body boundaries with respect to embodied others that we come to establish some sense of the limits of our social identities. Whether or not we can name different zones of intensity with all the names of history, it is through our embodied relationships with concrete others that we are able to consolidate the diffusion of names upon one specific social identity and so cohere as a social self. The kind of significance we attach to our initial beginnings in the body of another will have implications for how we continue to define ourselves vis-à-vis the happenings of the world and other human beings. Insofar as we degrade and denigrate our origins in another, insofar as we cannot bear the thought of ever having confused our body boundaries with those of another, we will continue to act out that denial and denigration upon the "feminine" others around us. Thus, to suggest that it is important to think about how we represent our origins in the body of another who is always feminine is to ask us to consider how we represent to ourselves our relationship to our material surroundings as well as to human others.

In "Divine Women" Irigaray comments that she wrote *Marine Lover,* *Elementary Passions,* and *L'Oubli de l'air* in the context of doing a study of our relations to the elements of water, earth, fire, and air. The elements represent for Irigaray "those natural matters that constitute the origin of our bodies, of our life, of our environment, the flesh of our passions" (S&G 57). They thus provide a vocabulary for the elements of which we are made up. This experiment with exploring affects, passions, and aspirations through a language of the elements can be seen as an attempt analogous to that of Deleuze and Guattari for rendering the happenings of our lives in language that thwarts or goes beyond the language of bodies and substances which all three feel is inadequate to the dynamic processes of actual living. What can be represented, in other words, is not all that there is. And futhermore, what can be represented often diverts us from the living movement of imperceptible becomings that occur at a more elemental level. That is, because of the organizing hierarchies of our conscious experience, we miss the singularities that continually transgress the categories we set up and confuse the representations that we would give. Whereas Deleuze and Guattari find the more "scientific" language drawn from other disciplines ("intensities," "fluxes," etc.) more attractive, Irigaray uses the more personable language of elements and corporeal feeling. She could be seen as appealing directly to the more "feminine," "intuitive" language associated with nature and magic, witchcraft and myth. By deliberately returning to a "crude" and more "primitive" language, one long since debunked by science in favor of more sophisticated descriptions, Irigaray also returns us to our own intuitive sense of a divine that we cannot see and yet feel all around us. Deleuze and Guattari deliberately avoid reference to the divine; Irigaray makes use of myth and religious language in order to evoke a sense of experience that is always reaching toward something not yet perceived.

Unlike Deleuze and Guattari, Irigaray prioritizes touch as a sense that can hint at the sensible transcendental and this divine beyond. This emphasis brings us back to our own bodies in a very personal way. While Deleuze and Guattari's lines of flight, with all the intensities and flows they entail, evoke a vivid intensification of experience, there is still room for distancing oneself from such experience. If one is nomadic and in flight, one can still leave whatever grabs on too tightly behind one. Touching upon the world brings into awareness not just the world's proximity but the world's proximity to us. It leaves us no room for situating ourselves at one step removed, and it confronts us with a form of participation in which we are no longer clearly the agent of what transpires.

Irigaray's evocation of angels of passage sounds very much like Deleuze's notion of becoming-imperceptible. Both insist on the immanent nature of vital becomings that are completely material and yet imperceptible owing to the structures of consciousness. Both delineate ways in which we might access this realm of the imperceptible, and both suggest that such access would lead to revitalizing contact with our world and with others. Both are also interested in creating ways of representing this contact that would not reduce it to the realm of the fixed, but would continually encourage fresh influx of nonrepresentable material. This means fostering another way of thinking and being — one that would be able to flow with imperceptible encounters and attune itself to the messages of angels, one that would avoid the calcification of the man of *ressentiment* and the self-centered narcissism of a masculine subject who would deny subjectivity to the feminine other. In the next two sections I elaborate further on the resonance between their two projects and argue that bringing their two vocabularies together allows a "personalized" approach to destratification, with important ethical and political implications.

Critique of Representation and the Masculine Subject

Both Irigaray and Deleuze are critical not only of conceptions of self, subject, and subjectivity which normatively promote the "neuter" (masculine), disembodied, unified subject exemplified in the Western tradition, but also of representational notions of thinking which are such a subject's counterpart. The repetition of a self-identical subject requires the repetition of self-identical objects of thought and perception. Coherent, unified subjects represent the coherent, unified objects of the world through a process which presumes that one can recognize and repeat what one has already thought or experienced. Irigaray's notion of a feminine subject and Deleuze's, and Deleuze and Guattari's, notion of a nomadic subject entail a different image of living, thinking, and speaking. I have focused on Irigaray's notion of the sensible transcendental and Deleuze's, and Deleuze and Guattari's, notion of becoming-imperceptible in characterizing their alternative conceptions of subjectivity. In the next subsection I elaborate on the similarities of their alternatives, and in the one that follows I explore the ethical and political implications of their respective conceptions of shattering mirrors and mapping lines of flight.

Feminine and Nomadic Subjectivity

Irigaray's feminine subject emerges from a social field in which masculine subjects displace corporeal labor on feminine others. The feminine subject, however, rejects the castration foisted on her by the masculine subject and instead allows her feminine desire (which knows no lack) and her feminine sexuality (which engenders difference through contact with corporeal limits) to motivate symbolic forms of thinking and living that problematize old dichotomies. I have called particular attention to how this subject is able to own her own corporeality and is thus able to engage in an integrative practice of harmonizing corporeal and conceptual logics. Deleuze's nomadic subject emerges from a social field in which traditional subjects tend to be stratified into impoverished forms of organization. The rejection of oedipalization in favor of the construction of planes of consistency (in the creation of bodies without organs and abstract machines) which put the heterogeneous singularities of life processes into continuous variation motivates novel, more intense formations in thinking and living. I have called particular attention to how the nomadic subject, by putting into continuous variation singularities traditionally bifurcated between discursive (conceptual) practices and nondiscursive (corporeal) practices, is also able to engage in a practice that amounts to integrating the corporeal and conceptual logics of subjectivity.

Irigaray insists on symbolizing an "impossible" subject. Such symbolization entails bringing the "outside" of the scenes of representations onto the scene itself and thereby brings the whole scenography of representation into crisis. This crisis can be resolved only by introducing a new way of thinking and living with an open-ended approach to the "outside" which would allow its ongoing symbolization. Constructing bodies without organs and abstract machines also entails continually bringing into thought the "outside" of all that is already conceivable and perceivable and so also precipitates a way of thinking that actively acknowledges this open-ended process rather than trying to conceal it.

Symbolizing feminine subjectivity involves insisting on starting from a map of the contemporary social field which pinpoints gender dualisms as points of creative becoming. Spiritualizing the flesh is a kind of practice that we could say brings the heterogeneous logics of the corporeal and the conceptual (in a culture that bifurcates these aspects of being human according to a sexually differentiated division of labor) into a plane of continuous variation. The feminine subject, by refusing both castration and the displacement onto her of the corporeal labor of an active masculine subject, enables both subjects to integrate corporeal and conceptual logics. This integration, since it touches both logics onto the "outside" of indeterminate forms, brings about unprecedented subjects who continually transform in concert with others. The feminine subject refers her becomings to the horizon of a feminine divine. This means that she unfolds her desire according to an immanent principle of contiguity; she opens up her flesh to the pleasure of mutually engendering, sensuous contact with others and the world. The feminine divine is an ideal of immersion in a sensuous world, rather than the untouchable ideal of an eternal form removed from the ceaselessly changing forms of life as process. Although the feminine subject has rejected castration in deference to an immanent principle of feminine desire, she still maintains a personal identity. Her morphology and psychic self are concretely determined through limit-forming interactions with others and the world in which boundaries are continually formed and reformed. Her personal identity is the identity of a self with a specific narrative and history. She initially forms boundaries in relation to a specific woman who is her mother. She continues to reshape these boundaries in the context of concrete experiences that precipitate her out of the world.

We can see how Deleuze and Guattari's notion of 'milieu' can be helpful in understanding Irigaray's feminine subject. Although a story of origins is helpful for orienting the feminine subject to a horizon that allows her to become without being rendered invisible through appropriation into the stories of other subjects, this story is clearly a creation formed in concert with others in order to delineate a personal self and body. Since Irigaray's notion of negativity problematizes dualisms such as active/passive, masculine/feminine, beginning/end, thinking of this self as emerging from a milieu makes sense. Such a self is a point of origin for agency, responsibility, and the history of a life only in the sense that one can choose this perspective on subjectivity. Living one's life toward the horizon of a feminine divine, for example, allows one to take such a perspective on the narrative of one's life. A sense of coherent agency is precipitated from a milieu in which patterns form and take on stability through a repetition of what can never be the same. Although molar aggregates may adhere to recognizable patterns, they could always be otherwise, and they shift in imperceptible ways as they repeat themselves. Personal identity entails abstracting a multiplicity or determinate set of forces from surrounding processes and giving it a narrative by relating it to an origin in the past and to a future form. Such identities and the narratives that go with their transformation over time are always somewhat arbitrary in the sense that the way we construe those identities and their narratives could always be different. Personal identity, then, may be more akin to art than philosophy since it entails linking up virtual possibilities with actualized forms. The embodied subject must approach the virtual from the finite perspective of lived experience. She must engage in sensory as well as conceptual becomings from a specific location in space and time. While chaos is a realm of incompossible events, a life lived by a personalized subject must ultimately be rendered with some degree of coherence. Disjuncts must be chosen in which incompossibles are ruled out. Like Kierkegaard's aesthete who would leave all possibility open, the nomadic subject must choose one disjunct of an either/or if she is to personalize herself in the context of a community. Because Irigaray's feminine subject lives toward a horizon of a personal becoming, she can follow an immanent principle of desire which vastly increases creative sites of resistance to existing forms of socialization at the same time that she maintains something like a personal self.

Deleuze promotes a conception of life as a nonpersonal process. Nomadic subjects deliberately defy the coherence of a subjectivity lived in keeping with compossible possibilities. They deliberately evoke the schizophrenia of someone who does not have to circumscribe the virtual through convergence upon a composite assemblage.[2] But notions of agency, responsibility, and a life-narrative assume such convergence. Although subjects can be dissolved into their virtual components, if we want to "rethink" rather than dismiss such notions, we need to create a model of subjectivity that allows such convergence at the same time that it refuses reduction of the subject to a set of already determined options. Referring the subject to an origin abstracted out of the world on the basis of matricide entails a structuring process which must always be blind to constitutive others. Referring the subject to an origin precipitated from a differentiating process could suggest a more nuanced conception of origin that could secure personal identity without fixing it or obliterating the processes out of which it emerges. Reading Irigaray and Deleuze together suggests a model of subjectivity that is sensitive to the constitutive other as well as to the pre-personal singularities of dynamic becoming.

Deleuze and Guattari's notion of becoming-other entails a reciprocity quite similar to that of Irigaray. The molecular elements of molar configurations and strata adhere because they "resonate." They could not resonate without some feedback mechanism to bring them into a specific configuration. In becoming-other, a multiplicity does not simply abandon its current form but metamorphizes into another form through the introduction of an "alien" configuration of organization. Just as Irigaray's conception of the mutual engenderment of two embodied subjects entails the transformation of both, so does the cross-circuiting of two multiplicities entail the transformation of both multiplicities. Deleuze's notion of the 'between' is thus quite similar to Irigaray's notion of mutual engenderment. The fecundity of the caress occurs between two, neither one of whom is left the same, just as Deleuze's becoming-other occurs between two who both become-other. In fact, we could supplement Irigaray's vocabulary with that of Deleuze in order to specify the nature of such mutual engenderment. An organism and subject of signification and experience organized in a particular way becomes deeply implicated in the organism and subject of signification and experience of another. Allowing "contaminating" particles of another to produce multiple effects on myself means relinquishing the self-identical repetition of a masculine form of subjectivity in order to allow new boundaries to form between self and other. Deleuze and Guattari's notions of strata and destratification, and the specific strata they delineate for human living, allow a more detailed mapping of such mutual engenderment.

Although Deleuze and Guattari's notion of becoming-other does not insist on the ethical need for recognition, they do provide a useful vocabulary for such becomings. Like Irigaray's vocabulary, their vocabulary allows for ambiguating active/passive, self/other dichotomies in a way that renders the interaction between two more like a passage of becoming than the effects of a subject acting on a passive other. So, although the failure to insist on recognition of mutually constitutive effects in any interaction between two multiplicities could allow the appropriation of another's constitutive power, Deleuze's model also allows for such constitutive power. In a social field in which marginal others were not exploited for psychic as well as economic gain, Deleuze's model could provide a way of thinking about the connections among personal subjects, as well as other kinds of multiplicities, that allows for mutual engenderment without insisting on binary oppositions in which one opposition inevitably must predominate over the other.

The Sensible Transcendental and Becoming-Imperceptible

Irigaray believes that we can intervene in social meaning systems in the interests of symbolizing "feminine" activity in human living. This "feminine" activity involves touching the corporeal and conceptual logics of the perceivable and the conceivable onto an "outside" which both nourishes and threatens stable formations of human life. Irigaray refers to this "outside" as the divine or the sensible transcendental, and rather than putting it in a realm removed from material existence, she insists on its immanence. It is thus misleading to call it an outside at all since it is external to the realm of conscious experience only in the sense of lying beyond what we can say about our experience. This "outside" is in some sense of the word extralinguistic. Like the notion of the unconscious, however, this "outside" recedes from us the moment we perceive or conceive of it: to be aware of it is to render it "inside" to corporeal and conceptual logics. Symbolizing feminine subjectivity involves spiritualizing the flesh and symbolizing an awareness of this process. Since the feminine other, on Irigaray's reading, has carried most of the burden for harmonizing corporeal and conceptual logics, symbolizing this process will entail changing the contemporary scene of representation and subjectivity by symbolizing the activity by which embodied subjects maintain their corporeal and conceptual forms of organization.

Constructing bodies without organs and abstract machines also entails symbolizing a process of integrating corporeal and conceptual logics by touching upon an "outside" that destabilizes any determinate form of organization. I have chosen to emphasize Deleuze's reading of Foucault in my reading of Deleuze's work in order to highlight the way the division between discursive and nondiscursive practices could be read into his notion of becoming-imperceptible. Although Deleuze, and Deleuze and Guattari, clearly mark places at which the distinction between what I have been calling corporeal and conceptual logics might occur (in their distinction between the double articulation of human existence into machinic assemblages and collective assemblages of enunciation, for example), their insistence on proliferating binaries deliberately problematizes the theoretical rendering of any one binary. Constructing bodies without organs and abstract machines, however, on a social field that is mapped in terms of mind/body dualisms foregrounds the cross-circuiting of such dualisms as important points of destabilization or creative resistance to contemporary forms of human life. Just as symbolizing feminine subjectivity touches us upon the sensible transcendental, so does constructing bodies without organs and abstract machines, or other forms of destratification or becoming-imperceptible, touch us upon virtual reality. Irigaray's notion of the spiritualization of the flesh involves a kind of perceptual training; one starts from the body and self one lives and engages in embodied practices which make possible attunement to something that is always at the fringes of current awareness. Such perceptual training entails a feminine kind of attunement to oneself, to others, and to one's world that is akin to Deleuze and Guattari's notion of becoming-other. The vocabulary of particles and of entering into zones of proximity with the molecular elements of another's becoming provides interesting ways to detail Irigaray's notion of percptual training. It is through the opening of stable, molar forms of organization to the molecular fluxes that are always "between" myself and my world that something new can happen. Perceptual training, then, could amount to a form of becoming-imperceptible.

The benefit of bringing these two vocabularies together is that whereas there is a tendency in Deleuze and Guattari's work to structure becoming-imperceptible as something that occurs in writing, or in doing science or philosophy, or in creating art, Irigaray's emphasis on one's personal becoming toward a divine horizon insists on perceptual training in the context of a life lived from a personal past and into a personal future. Whereas Deleuze and Guattari's nomadic subject can invent new possibilities for living in its pursuit of lines of flight, it is Irigaray's notion of the sensible transcendental that provides an image for grounding such lines of flight in an immanent notion of coherence. The wholeness of an embodied subject is not the wholeness of a subject who totalizes herself through appeal to an ideal she can never fulfill, but the wholeness of a subject who brings herself into continuous variation. That is, she constructs a body without organs which brings her molecular elements into full resonance. Nomadic subjects risk destabilization of stable forms of organization (just as feminine subjects do). They reterritorialize onto new formations through attunement to the molecular flows of the becomings around them (through becoming-other). But if, as I argued in Chapter 7, the man-standard is a kind of reference point for such nomadic journeys, then attunement to human others, in particular, will be oriented toward a molar identity which disables symbolization of processes of becoming. Deleuze and Guattari do not advocate becoming a schizophrenic; becoming-imperceptible can be carried out through one's work. The relationship of such work to one's living is not always clear. Doing philosophy, doing science, doing art allow a subject with a biography to engage in becoming-imperceptible in a specific context. The creations that emerge from such becomings — the concepts of philosophy or the affects and percepts of art — can then be used to survey forms of life and introduce new possibilities. But further characterization of how the process of living these possibilities might play out is also important. It seems to me that this is the strength of Irigaray's work. Her notion of a feminine divine allows for a personal horizon that gives us an image of thinking about how the possibilities opened up by explorations in becoming-imperceptible could be brought to bear on the living possibilities of an embodied individual.

Whereas Irigaray appeals to angelic messages and cosmic rhythms, Deleuze conjures up imperceptible encounters and the nonpersonal forces of life. Irigaray points us to a divine toward which we can become, and Deleuze delineates various approaches to a virtual chaos. Irigaray speaks of a feminine desire and feminine sexuality that could lead to singularity in love, and Deleuze speaks of "a million little sexes" which evoke the transsexual nature of us all and the infinite variability that plays out in the specific statistical formations of the individuals who actualize molar identities. If we read Irigaray and Deleuze as in some sense replicating a sexual difference in their work (with Irigaray taking on the "feminine" work of corporeality and Deleuze the "masculine" work of the conceptual), then putting their vocabularies into continuous variation could engender creative possibilities beyond both.

Shattering Mirrors and Mapping Lines of Flight

Irigaray appeals to Hegel's notion of negativity in order to develop a notion of recognition and reciprocity that goes beyond the dead end of a master-slave dialectic. She is adamant about the need for feedback loops and sounding boards; stabilization of human subjectivity requires some sort of resonating chamber. Deleuze and Guattari acknowledge this as well in their notion that becoming-other entails a reciprocal cross-circuiting and that strata are formed from resonating patterns. Whereas Deleuze and Guattari do not seem to worry about how molecular flows will stabilize and instead seem to assume that stabilization, since it is inevitable, is less important than destabilization, Irigaray is very concerned with the forms feedback mechanisms take. In particular, she is concerned that feminine others be released from a position of subservient invisibility and enabled to symbolize their own histories through reciprocal recognition. Her notion of Hegelian negativity vividly conjures up a corporeal as well as a conceptual aspect to this reciprocity: one comes to know one's own limits only by coming into contact with the limits of others. One can come to develop a corporeal logic or morphology only through contact with a world that resists and eludes one, and one can come to develop a conceptual logic only through differentiating symbolic elements on the basis of an initial corporeal differentiation.

Irigaray's depiction of the Hegelian family suggests that she would agree with Deleuze and Guattari's critique of family totalization; reducing oneself to a family function (for example, that of mother or lover) can only result in attempting to create binding relationships among human beings on the basis of universals that cannot capture them in their singularity. Like Deleuze and Guattari, she advocates another form of love, another form of relationship, one that would open up to the singularity of molecular flows and allow for a differentiating process of creating connections in the "between" of molar identities. Whereas she might call such attunement among subjects a kind of fidelity to present sensibility which follows the movement of growth (ILTY 38–39; cf. Chapter 4), Deleuze and Guattari would describe such attunement as the construction of a plane of consistency that could bring heterogeneous elements into continuous variation.

Again, it is interesting to note how Irigaray's vocabulary returns us to an explicit attention to ourselves in our embodiment, while Deleuze and Guattari's descriptions are as applicable to the conceptual personae, impartial observers, or aesthetic figures of philosophy, science, and art — perhaps even more so — as they are for living individuals. Nomadic subjects must attempt to leave their coherence behind if they are to bring about new perspectives on living. To be too wedded to one's morphology or psychic self can only thwart such a creative project. One can be schizophrenic as one writes, even if one does not want to actualize schizophrenia as an embodied subject.

What I propose is to create a plane of consistency of the work of Irigaray, Deleuze, and Deleuze and Guattari. This means putting the vocabularies of each into continuous variation in the context of attending to the fluxes and flows of my own corporeal and conceptual logics as I do so. By confronting the gaps among these vocabularies as well as the gaps between my corporeal and conceptual response to these vocabularies and the gaps in their imaging of various aspects of individual and social life, I hope, myself, to touch upon a sensible transcendental or a virtual chaos from which unprecedented morphologies and concepts can emerge. The process of reading Irigaray, Deleuze, and Deleuze and Guattari together has been exciting, stimulating, and productive (whether or not my readers agree is for them to decide!). If it has not led to the complete dissolution of either my corporeal or my conceptual boundaries as what I hope is a relatively recognizable social subject, it is probably because I have been cautious in my experimentation with their texts. At the same time that I share Deleuze and Guattari's impatience with the molar identities that block molecular flow, I also share Irigaray's concern for the other whose differences I may efface as well as for the appropriation of my own productive creativity that fluidity can entail. In a way I have to agree with Deleuze's, and Deleuze and Guattari's, restraint in nomadic subjectivity: a writing that is a becoming-imperceptible allows one to experiment in ways that one may not be ready or brave enough to risk in the actual living of one's life. And yet, Irigaray's concern for my substantive existence as a personal subject struggling to give coherent shape to herself and her life gives me reassurance and hope that such experiments could actually have transformative effects in my "personal" life as well.

Deleuze states in one of the interviews reprinted in *Negotiations* that he never wanted to "become invisible" but rather to "become imperceptible," which means, of course, that the latter is different from the former. But visibility on the social field according to the contemporary formations of perceivables and sayables is variable from subject to subject. Gayatri Spivak's notion of the subaltern gives some indication of my concern: pursuing lines of flight from a subaltern identity is a risky business if one does not have some way of warding off appropriation into mainstream modes of stabilizing subjectivity (see Spivak 1988). Irigaray gives a detailed map of how the feminine other is obliterated by an "active" (masculine) subject. We can extend her map to indicate how "active" subjects of various sorts can obliterate the constitutive effects of marginalized others in a number of ways. As a feminist, I am inclined toward promoting Irigaray's mapping of the social field, but as an anti-racist, anti-heterosexist, and post-Marxist, I would embrace other mappings of the social field as well.

Applying Deleuze and Guattari's vocabulary to Irigaray's project allows us to see how embodied subjects could also engage in nomadic living without leaving personal identity behind. Although dissolution of the self is an integral part of nomadic lines of flight, self-transformation is contingent on interaction with the responsive world and human others which gives one new form and shape. Like the fetus in the womb, no human being can escape the incredibly responsive range of forces in which we are continuously immersed. Since Irigaray does not equate opening up to such forces with regressive fusion but rather images it as creative engenderment, personal identity could entail a kind of continual transformation in a corporeal dance with others in which we acknowledged and celebrated the interdependent activity of self-making. That is, personal identity could be refigured as a continual shaping and reshaping of self in concert with others, or the continual becoming of a self with a past, present, and future, whose story was inextricably implicated with the stories of others. Given a perceptual training in which these subjects incorporated a practice of integrating corporeal and conceptual logics into their self-making, such stories would always be opened onto the sensible transcendental or the virtual. A personal story, then, could be like a diagram or a personal map with points of destabilization and creative resistance always pointing toward an open future.

Such personal maps when put into the context of larger diagrams of the social field could indicate directions for constructive social change. Irigaray has supplied a kind of map of gender relations, and Deleuze and Guattari have supplied various maps of human processes in their implication with broader life processes. Since these maps intensify points of destabilization rather than suggest a program and a new set of "preferable" molar formations, they suggest approaches toward destabilizing contemporary formations of the social field in keeping with the delineation of effects one wants to avoid. Multiple mappings of the social field can suggest multiple approaches to transforming the discursive and nondiscursive practices of contemporary society in what we could construe to be a "liberating" way. I would call those lines of flight liberating (rather than destructive) which promote active subjectivity without obliterating either the constitutive effects of interdependent others nor the latter's possibilities for getting the kind of nurturing feedback they need to stabilize an active subjectivity of their own.

Diagrams of the social field not only indicate the lines of flight that would destabilize determinate organizations of molecular flows; they also indicate immanent causes of that field's various configurations. The construction of an immanent cause (or abstract machine) allows for a galvanizing image of something to be resisted. Because an immanent cause produces effects that spread throughout the social field, what is to be resisted cannot be construed as an object or a thing, but rather must be construed as a related series of effects which produce points of creative becoming as well as stability. Active resistance then becomes the further destabilization of already unstable points rather than an attack on a specific object or thing. As we have already seen, "femininity" is one label for the unstable point of Irigaray's map of sexual difference and de-oedipalization is one way of characterizing the unstable point of Deleuze and Guattari's diagram. Various diagrams could reveal the convergence of points of resistance common to more than one abstract machine. For example, resisting the effects of Irigaray's diagram of sexual difference by further destabilizing gender fault lines could converge at certain points with resisting the effects of a diagram of racial difference. And resisting the effects of oedipalization could converge with resisting the effects of sexual difference. Diagrams, then, could help us not only to find lines of flight but also to choose particularly strategic ones with respect to the social field. Such lines of flight could still be lived out nomadically through immanent principles of desire, but they could be selected from a larger range of possibilities.

Creating a plane of consistency from the work of Irigaray, Deleuze, and Deleuze and Guattari suggests a model of subjectivity that emphasizes the subject's participation in a world of both human and nonhuman processes as well as nonhierarchical possibilities for self-transformation in concert with others. Although I have only begun to draw out some of the possibilities of their work, it is my hope that such models could open up new answers to questions about how to engage in politics across differences at the individual level as well as at the level of collective action.

Notes

INTRODUCTION

1. Various feminist accounts of body comportment and the sexed body influenced by phenomenology, poststructuralism, and/or Lacanian psychoanalysis have provided exciting new ways to look at embodiment. See references in the Bibliography to the work of Bartky, Bordo, Braidotti, Butler, Dallery, Diprose, Gatens, Grosz, Jaggar, and Young for some indication of the range of these accounts.

2. I am thinking here, for example, of the emphasis of Saussurean linguistics on the formal structure of *langue* at the expense of the pragmatic situation of embodied speakers engaged in *parole*, a reading of Lacanian psychoanalysis that privileges the symbolic dimension of subjectivity at the expense of the imaginary and the real (Kristeva's notion of the semiotic could be seen as a kind of corrective to such a reading in addition to challenging and extending the Lacanian account of embodied subjectivity), and a reading of Derrida's work that emphasizes the play of signifiers at the expense of the extralinguistic effects of the situatedness of speech acts.

3. Elizabeth Grosz has addressed the body in many articles and books. Her work, along with that of Rosi Braidotti, Judith Butler, Julia Kristeva, Margaret Whitford on Irigaray, and Irigaray herself, provided the initial inspiration for my own approach to questions about embodiment and subjectivity.

4. See Ann Ferguson's characterization of a sexual division of labor in a somewhat different context in terms of 'sex/affective production' in her classic essay "On Conceiving Motherhood and Sexuality: A Feminist-Materialist Approach" (1984).

5. See Descombes 1980 and Matthews 1996 for helpful historical overviews of French philosophy.

6. See Schrift 1995.

7. See Graybeal 1990 for a similar reading of Heidegger with reference to Kristeva's notion of the semiotic.

8. See Nagatomo 1992, 62–63, for an intriguing characterization of the approach of the Japanese philosopher Yuasa toward mind/body dualisms, which is in keeping with the kind of approach I advocate here.

9. Kristeva's work also evokes mind/body dualisms and integrative practices that can bridge them, for example, through her notions of the semiotic and symbolic. Her accounts of the semiotic and the participation and motivation of the somatic in the symbolic aspects of subjectivity are an important influence on my approach to embodied subjectivity. See Oliver 1993 and Reineke 1997 for examples of intriguing readings of Kristeva's work along these lines.

10. Obviously philosophers in other traditions as well have come to a similar conclusion.

1. Hirsh and Olson 1995; hereafter cited as JLI.

2. The people who have most influenced my own reading of Irigaray are Rosi Braidotti, Judith Butler, Elizabeth Grosz, and Margaret Whitford. I am grateful for their exciting and insightful interpretations of Irigaray's project. For excellent orientations to Irigaray's project which take into account the French philosophical tradition out of which Irigaray emerges see Burke 1994a, Grosz 1989 (chaps. 1, 4, and 5), and Whitford 1991a. The collection *Engaging with Irigaray* (Burke, Schor, and Whitford 1994) gives a good idea of the new wave of interest in Irigaray's work in keeping with Whitford's groundbreaking study *Luce Irigaray: Philosophy in the Feminine* (Whitford 1991a).

3. Also see Deutscher 1994, 92, for a similar point. Elizabeth Hirsh makes an analogous point from the perspective of the "practicable" of the psychoanalytic situation (between analysand and analyst) and the theory of psychoanalysis (1994, 302, 307). The category of the feminine in the determinate forms it takes in specific contexts turns out to open onto what Judith Butler calls the "excessive" feminine — that which must be excluded for the binaries of representation to operate (Butler 1993, 39). Irigaray's reception in this country was initially somewhat hostile; there has been much debate over whether or not her work presupposes some kind of biological essentialism. Tina Chanter's excellent book *Ethics of Eros*, which carefully situates Irigaray's work in the philosophical tradition from which it comes, should lay this view to rest (1995, chap. 1). Also see Schor's essay "This Essentialism Which Is Not One" (in Burke, Schor, and Whitford 1994, 57–78), Whitford 1989, and Weed 1994 for useful orientations to this question.

4. This view comes out of Lacan's linguistic rereading of Freud: if the norm for subjectivity is masculine, and the feminine is defined as a specific kind of deviation from that norm (as Irigaray eloquently argues in *Speculum*), then insofar as a woman approaches that norm, she is speaking as a masculine, rather than feminine, subject. For a helpful introduction to Lacan from a feminist perspective, see Grosz 1990b.

5. For other renderings of this critique, see Grosz 1989, 104–26; Oliver 1995, 10–16; and Whitford 1989 and 1991a, chaps. 2 and 3.

6. Cynthia Willett gives an intriguing account of the tactile dance that occurs between infant and primary caretakers as a crucial prefiguration of autonomous selfhood and sociality drawn from Irigaray and from Daniel Stern's account of attunement in early childhood development (see, e.g., 1995). Also see Kelly Oliver's characterization of a bodily logic that prefigures linguistic logic in relation to Julia Kirsteva's work in her introduction to *The Portable Kristeva* (Oliver 1997).

7. "Is it necessary to add, or repeat, that woman's 'improper' access to representation, her entry into a specular and speculative economy that affords her instincts no signs, no symbols or emblems, or methods of writing that could figure her instincts, make it impossible for her to work out or transpose specific representatives of her instinctual object-goals? The latter are in fact subjected to a particularly peremptory repression and will only be translated into a *script of body language*. Silent and cryptic. Replacing the fantasies she cannot have — or can have only

when her amputated desires turn back on her masochistically, or when she is obliged to lend a hand with 'penis-envy' " (S 124).

8. "Among women, the relationship to sameness and to the mother is not mastered by the *fort-da*. The mother always remains too familiar and too close. In a way, the daughter has her mother under her skin, secreted in the deep, damp intimacy of the body, in the mystery of her relationship to gestation, to birth, and to her sexual identity. Furthermore, the sexual movement characteristic of the female is whirling round rather than throwing and pulling objects back as little Ernst does. The girl tries to reproduce around and within her an energetic circular movement that protects her from abandonment, attack, depression, loss of self. Spinning round is also, but in my opinion secondarily, a way of attracting. The girl describes a circle while soliciting and refusing access to her territory. She is making a game of this territory she has described with her body. There is no object here, in the strict meaning of the word, no other that has had to be introjected or incorporated. On the contrary, girls and women often set up a defensive territory that can then become creative, especially in analysis" (S&G 98).

9. That daughters are not able to objectify their mothers in the same way as sons is for Irigaray also a dangerous situation — one that she believes needs to be rectified through the project of creating symbolic support for feminine subjectivity and relationships among women. For the dangers, see Irigaray 1981a.

10. An important essay in any consideration of Irigaray's refiguration of sexuality is "The Fecundity of the Caress: A Reading of Levinas, *Totality and Infinity*, Phenomenology of Eros," included in *An Ethics of Sexual Difference* (1993a). I have more directly addressed this essay elsewhere (Lorraine 1994). The title points to Irigaray's affinity for the work of Emmanuel Levinas, who was an important influence on Irigaray's notions of the irreducible difference of the other and an ethics of alterity. Also see Irigaray 1991b. For a good introduction to this influence in Irigaray's work as well as her critique of Levinas, see chap. 5 of Chanter 1995. Also see Ince 1996; Grosz 1989, 153–58; and Whitford 1991a, 165–68.

11. See Chanter 1995, 146–59, 164; Berry 1992; and chap. 7 of Grosz 1995 for more on Irigaray's conception of time.

12. I discuss Irigaray's notion of the sensible transcendental later in this chapter and in Chapter 3.

13. Tina Chanter examines the methodological similarity between Heidegger's approach to the question of the meaning of Being and Irigaray's approach to the question of sexual difference in chap. 4 of *Ethics of Eros* (1995).

14. This interview is published in *This Sex Which Is Not One* under the title "The Power of Discourse and the Subordination of the Feminine" (TS 68–85).

CHAPTER 2. IRIGARAY'S NIETZSCHE

1. Quoted in Oppel 1993, 88.
2. "C'est un appel et un refus. Je ne crois pas qu'il faille parler là de haine" (Irigaray 1981b, 48).

3. Jacques Derrida makes this point in *Spurs*. Also see Krell 1986, Schrift 1994, and Shapiro 1991. See Oliver 1995 for a critique of these approaches from a feminist perspective.

4. Kelly Oliver draws from Irigaray's work, among others, in arguing that "although Nietzsche proposes a way of reading and writing that opens onto its other, a reading and writing from the body, this body is always a masculine body" (1995, 25). She presents an extended development of this argument in her book *Womanizing Nietzsche*; see chap. 4 (83–125) for her reading of *Marine Lover*. In my reading, I am more concerned with Irigaray's reading of Nietzsche in the context of developing an understanding of her work in light of my own project than with either validating or contesting it in terms of Nietzsche's texts.

5. The resonance to Derrida's motif of the eardrum is striking here. Indeed, Oliver reads *Marine Lover* as implicitly addressed to Derrida as well as Nietzsche (1995, 85). See Chanter 1995, chap. 6, for more on Irigaray's relationship to Derrida.

6. Teresa Brennan (1992) provides a fascinating account of energetic interchange in relationship to femininity and masculinity drawn from psychoanalytic theory which elaborates a scenario similar to this one.

7. The law of castration, she implies, involves the universalization of "the interdict-impossibility of Dionysiac sensuality" and the "virtual renunciation of Apollo's enchantment unless it be to privilege identification's value as mask" (ML 93).

8. As Oliver puts it: "Following Nietzsche, and yet going beyond him, Irigaray argues that Christians have forgotten the most important part of Christ's message: incarnation. They have forgotten that Christ is a bodily incarnation of god. Like Dionysus he is god-man; like Dionysus he represents the unity of the human and the divine. But whereas with Dionysus, Eros is too violent and rips up the body, with Christ, Eros disappears altogether" (1995, 124, citing ML 176–77).

9. Oliver in discussing Irgaray's reading of Nietzsche comments: "Nietzsche's gods — Dionysus, Apollo, and Christ — all appropriate the power of their mothers, sisters, or lovers without acknowledging their debt. They invent ways to give birth to themselves in order to forget that they were born of their mothers. Nietzsche's doctrine of the eternal return of the same is another way of telling a story in which man gives birth to himself without woman" (1995, 125).

10. I discuss Deleuze's notion of the eternal return in more detail in Chapter 6.

11. See Shapiro 1989, 91–92, for a similar reading.

12. Oliver is speaking of the notion of the eternal return here; she agrees with Irigaray that Nietzsche's texts enact a form of matricide: "While, against Irigaray, I believe that Nietzsche does move us out of a metaphysics that annihilates the value of the body, at the same time he cannot admit the value of the feminine pregnant maternal body" (1995, 113). My own view is that Irigaray is actually more sympathetic toward Nietzsche than Oliver suggests. It is because Nietzsche is able to go so far in bringing the body back into philosophy that Irigaray can make the move to bring the sensuous body into play.

13. Thus, despite the obvious difference between Irigaray's reading of the eter-

nal return and that of Deleuze, the practice taken from Nietzsche by each may be more closely aligned than the content of their differing conceptions of the eternal return would indicate.

14. Irigaray, in mocking Nietzsche for depicting the feminine other in terms of veils and sails, wings and flight, is also mocking Derrida's reading of Nietzsche in *Spurs*.

15. See the section titled "The Umbilical Cord to a Space of Wholeness," in the next chapter.

16. Derrida tends to play with oppositions in order to open up the subordinate category and then move onto an undecidable. If the feminine is no more than an oppositional category, then he too has failed to recognize truly what is foreign about it and so has lost an opportunity by "forgetting" it.

CHAPTER 3. IRIGARAY'S SENSIBLE TRANSCENDENTAL

1. For an intriguing account of this fiery becoming, see Berry 1994.

2. In a reading of a passage on mirrors from Plato's *Timaeus* (46a–c), Irigaray mocks the relay of mirrors that so carefully creates an "economy of light" but "without risk of combustion and death": "The Words of the Father depend for their effect upon a measured and harmonious reflection of each part within the whole, untroubled by searchlights by night or eclipses by day. This rigorous distribution of each speck of brightness, of which only the information is retained, is set up by relays of mirrors — as well as filters, lenses, paraphragms, camerae obscurae, projection and reproduction screens — which divide up 'Being' as a whole into fragments suitable to each 'being' " (S 148–49).

3. "They indicate that Matter is sterile, not female to full effect, female in receptivity only, not in pregnancy: this they accomplish by exhibiting Matter as approached by what is neither female nor effectively male but castrated of that impregnating power which belongs only to the unchangeably masculine" (S 179).

4. "But now, by a stroke of almost incredible boldness, it is the singular subject who is charged with giving birth to the universe all over again, after he has brought himself back into the world in a way that avoids the precariousness of existence as it is usually understood" (S 182).

5. Compare this claim to Irigaray's critique of Nietzsche's Dionysus; the ecstatic dismemberment of a Dionysian frenzy can only constitute, from Irigaray's view, alienating detachment from one's body rather than the embrace of one's corporeality.

6. For more on this kind of wholeness, see the characterization of intrauterine life described in the next section. Also note the resonance of this description with the image of the feminine sea depicted in *Marine Lover* (cf. the discussion of this image in Chapter 2).

7. Deutscher argues that the feminine ideal entails participation in the divine in an open-ended process of becoming rather than an ideal from which a woman is severed (1994, 102).

8. Whitford relates this process to the death drive and the violence of unsymbolized affects associated with the body; symbolizing unconscious drives so that they can be integrated into conscious self-representation could mediate some of the violence of contemporary self-other relations in more productive ways (1991a, 145).

9. Also see the discussion of corporeal and conceptual logics in the Introduction.

10. We might compare this description of perceptual disharmony to Nietzsche's characterization of the man of ressentiment. The man of ressentiment withdraws from the infinite changeability of life; he opts for transcendent images of heaven rather than remaining "true to the earth." According to Nietzsche's valuation, this indicates that his mind and spirit are "sick." To be "healthy" would entail embracing life (Nietzsche 1966). Whereas Irigaray emphasizes a kind of balance that can be struck between conceptual and perceptual economies within the context of openness to another, Nietzsche emphasizes the light-hearted dance of a warrior intent on a self-sufficient form of nobility. For Deleuze's account of Nietzsche's man of ressentiment, see Chapter 6.

11. Also see JTN 37–44. See Oliver 1995, 187–93, for a compelling account, drawn from Irigaray and Kristeva, of the placenta as a medium of exchange providing a model for ethical relationship.

12. For Freud to analyze the reel game of the small boy, then, as gaining mastery over the coming and going of the mother is at two steps removed on Irigaray's analysis. The string of the reel the little boy throws out and pulls back in is meant not to connect him to his mother but to represent an umbilical cord. That is, Freud reads the cord as pulling in the mother, but Irigaray is suggesting that in giving such a reading, Freud is covering over a nostalgia for the womb, which is precisely not the mother but an environment within the mother specific to fetal development (S&G 35).

13. For a fascinating account of Irigaray's reading of the veil, see Schwab 1994.

14. Since it is the positions of active (masculine) subject and supportive (feminine) other that are at issue in the transformation of the cultural symbolic and imaginary, homosexual couples are not excluded from this transformative possibility. In fact, an important part of Irigaray's project entails contesting the cultural reduction of women to a maternal function. See Grosz 1994b for more on this topic.

15. See Chapter 1, for a discussion of this type of cultivation in the context of sexuality.

16. See Chanter 1995, 163–64; Grosz 1989, 168–72; and Whitford 1991a, 55–56, 60–62, for more on Irigaray's use of language evoking the elements.

CHAPTER 4. SHATTERING MIRRORS

1. Some of Irigaray's disappointment emerges, for example, at the beginning of *I Love to You.*

2. See Chapter 1 for a discussion of Irigaray's articulation of a specifically feminine alternative to masculine sexuality.

3. As in my reading of Irigaray's Nietzsche, I am more concerned with developing Irigaray's project here than in supporting or contesting Irigaray's reading of Hegel. For a good introduction to Irigaray's use of Hegel in the context of Antigone's story, see chap. 3 of Chanter 1995.

4. "Happiness must be built by us here and now on earth, where we live, a happiness comprising a carnal, sensible and spiritual dimension in the love between women and men, woman and man, which cannot be subordinated to reproduction, to the acquisition or accumulation of property, to a hypothetical human or divine authority. The realization of happiness in us and between us is our primary cultural obligation" (ILTY 15).

5. Irigaray, unlike Deleuze, affirms rather than contests Hegelianism. Although I do not address the differences between Irigaray's and Deleuze's readings here, such a comparison would be fruitful for demonstrating how one could develop a notion of differentiating recognition along the line of thought discussed here, one that could move beyond the binary oppositions of traditional self-other comparisons.

6. Irigaray says nothing about hermaphroditism, transsexualism, transvestism, or other forms of gender "transgressions." But since these certainly exist and Irigaray is certainly aware of this fact, we must take her argument here as pertaining to the impossibility of avoiding gender designations entirely.

7. Irigaray sums up her research into the differences between language use by women and men as follows: "Women seek communication, especially dialogue, but they particularly address themselves to *lui/il* (him/he) whose interest is not intersubjective exchange and who is more oriented towards the past than towards the present or the future; . . . Men are interested in the concrete object if it is theirs (my car, my watch, my pipe, etc.), or in the abstract object insofar as it is proper to a man or sanctioned by the already existing community of men, their psychological states, or their genealogical and familial problems; they rarely seek dialogue and remain within a collectivity that is poorly defined but marked by the masculine gender" (ILTY 95).

8. "Intentionality thus artificially remains turned in a privileged direction: toward *he/they*, and with no return to the female self nor between female selves. The *he/they* becomes a pseudo-transcendence to which *she* is oriented, losing her subjectivity on the way, and thus the possibility of real communication.

Communication, exchange between people, intersubjectivity — the privileged loci of the least alienated female identity — are thus held back from appropriation by the female gender and from reciprocity between the sexes. With no return to the self, woman/women cannot truly engage in dialogue. They concern themselves with men — especially fathers and sons — situate themselves in familiar surroundings, hope for the future and continually try to communicate, particularly in the form of a question that might actually be a hope of being returned to themselves through the response they receive. And so in various ways they ask: Do you love me? The question really means: What am I for you? Or, Who am I? or, How can I return to myself?" (ILTY 98)

9. Irigaray contrasts her notion of listening to the 'Thou' of philosophers such

as Buber by saying that their notion of 'Thou' involves trapping the mystery of the other in irreducibility. She claims that doing so amounts to reducing the difference of the other to sameness and similarity by referring the other to an ecstatic model "outside the judgment of consciousness" (ILTY 118).

10. "Interdependency between subjects is no longer reduced to questions of possessing, of exchanging or sharing objects, cash, or an already existing meaning. It is, rather, regulated by the constitution of subjectivity. The subject does not vest its own value in any form of property whatsoever. No longer is it objecthood, having or the cost of having that governs the becoming of a subject or subjects and the relation among them. They are engaged in a relationship from which they emerge altered, the objective being the accomplishment of their subjectivity while remaining faithful to their nature" (ILTY 127).

CHAPTER 5. DELEUZE'S PROJECT

1. Elizabeth Grosz has characterized two kinds of approaches to theorizing the body in "twentieth-century radical thought" in terms of an "inscriptive" approach which conceives the body as a surface on which social institutions inscribe themselves and an approach that emphasizes the "lived body" or the body as it is experienced (1995, 33). She lists Nietzsche, Foucault, and Deleuze as theorists who take the first approach, and although she does not explicitly align Irigaray with the latter approach, there are more phenomenological overtones to Irigaray's work than to Deleuze's. As Grosz points out, it is not clear that these two approaches are not ultimately incompatible. My reading of Deleuze mitigates the gap between the two approaches by emphasizing the processes of writing and thinking as processes that engage the reader, writer, or thinker in a form of schizoanalysis or destratification which opens up the lived experience of the reader, writer, or thinker to the unthinkable thoughts and unperceivable sensations of the "outside."

2. I am using Constantin Boundas's wording here. See his excellent article on this topic, "Foreclosure of the Other: From Sartre to Deleuze" (1993, 35).

3. Deleuze and Guattari present no systematic critique of the masculinist bias of psychoanalytic theory as such, and yet their critique of the normative subject of Lacanian psychoanalysis, as we will see, entails a critique of oedipal masculinity with important points of convergence with that of Irigaray.

4. Cf. May 1991, 32–33.

5. Translator's note, Lacan 1978, 280. Also see Lacan's characterization: "The real is distinguished . . . by its separation from the field of the pleasure principle, by its desexualization, by the fact that its economy, later, admits something new, which is precisely the impossible" (167).

6. The difference between the molar and the molecular is a matter not of size but of type of organization. The term 'molecular' comes from biochemistry. Philip Goodchild, in a discussion of the application of these terms to social processes, describes molar organization as that of groups which are subjugated to an external authority and molecular organization as that of groups whose product influences

their own process (1996a, 159). It is the latter quality that gives a more fluid, changeable character to molecular processes.

7. The notion of the body without organs is one of Deleuze and Guattari's stranger notions and, like their other concepts, tends to mutate in different contexts. The connection between this notion and Freud's notion of the death instinct should become apparent. See Goodchild 1996a, 77–80 and 83, and Massumi 1992, 70–71, for useful discussions of this notion.

8. Richard Boothby at one point in his fascinating book *Death and Desire* defines Freud's notion of the death drive as presenting "the struggle against the repressive strictures of the ego waged by that portion of organismic energies that have remained excluded by it" (1991, 96). On Deleuze and Guattari's rereading of the death instinct, the resistance is produced not by a determinate set of energies but rather by the conflict immanent in any determinate organization between stabilized form and its unactualized alternatives.

9. For an account of the oedipalization of desire in connection with Deleuze's reading of Nietzsche, see Schrift 1995, 77–78. Also see Goodchild 1996a, 100–104, for a discussion of de-oedipalization more explicitly related to the social production of capitalism.

10. Compare this description to the description given by Irigaray (cited in Chapter 1) of the feminine reader/writer who "puts a torch" to all codes.

11. Deleuze and Guattari distinguish three types of "social machines." The capitalist machine is the machine of our own society. Two earlier machines are the "savage territorial machine" and the "barbarian despotic machine." "Each type of social machine produces a particular kind of *representation* whose elements are organized at the surface of the socius: the system of connotation-connection in the savage territorial machine, corresponding to the coding of the flows; the system of subordination-disjunction in the barbarian despotic machine, corresponding to over-coding; the system of co-ordination-conjunction in the civilized captialist machine, corresponding to the decoding of the flows" (A-O 262). See Goodchild 1996a, 90–100, for a more extended discussion of these three social machines.

12. Deleuze thus counters the notions of the real and the possible with that of the virtual and the actual. For helpful commentary on Deleuze's notion of the virtual, see Boundas 1996a, Clark 1997, Goodchild 1996a and b, Olkowski 1996, Patton 1996c, Piercey 1996, and Smith 1995.

13. Paul Patton gives a very lucid and useful characterization of this project in terms of Deleuze's conception of the Platonic image of thought and the conception of thought with which Deleuze counters this tradition (1994, 144–45).

14. I am quoting from Daniel Smith's highly helpful account of this aspect of Deleuze's thought (1996, 30).

15. Deleuze himself does not characterize this mode of being as "feminine," unless one takes Deleuze and Guattari's comments on becoming-woman (which I discuss in Chapter 7) as indicating such a characterization. I am using this adjective here in the context of evoking a resonance with Irigaray's work.

16. I find such a model to be both personally empowering and potentially politically effective as an alternative to the model for self-presentation assumed in

identity politics. Developing a vocabulary for mapping imperceptible becomings could make possible an alternative approach to characterizing the singular conditions of local terrains without sacrificing the power of self-presentation. Writing as a becoming-imperceptible is thus, on the reading I give here, not about relinquishing the desire for visibility and political empowerment, but is rather about an alternative model for achieving visibility.

17. The same, of course, could be said for many philosophers. Deleuze's explicit project of changing the image of thought from that of a model of recognition to one premised on a logics of difference and multiplicity makes the integrative nature of his project more obvious.

18. Patton describes concepts as "autopoetic entities" (1996c, 4). Also see his essay "Concept and Event" (1996a, 322).

19. See Chapter 8 for another example.

20. Goodchild comments that "Deleuze inverts values by replacing the transcendental model of thought with the body" (1996b, 39). Although Deleuze does not give a phenomenology of the body, he "seeks the unthinkable body, the body which acts upon thought and escapes thought" (39–40).

21. That is, our perception abstracts phenomena from the becomings that condition them. This entails separating the forces of dynamic becoming from what they can do. We will see in the next chapter that the separation of force from what it can do is Deleuze's definition of Nietzsche's notion of reactive force.

CHAPTER 6. DELEUZE'S NIETZSCHE

1. For more on the nature of this experiment in the context of the post-Heideggerian French reception of Nietzsche, see Alan Schrift's highly useful account in his book *Nietzsche's French Legacy* (1995, chap. 3). Also see Schrift 1990 for a contrast between the Heideggerian and French readings of Nietzsche.

2. Schrift gives an interesting account of Deleuze's link between desire and the will to power and states that the desiring-machine of *Anti-Oedipus* is "a machinic, functionalist translation of Nietzschean will to power." This translation enables Deleuze to avoid situating desire in a "substantive will, ego, unconscious, or self" (1995, 68). Schrift goes on to argue that this makes possible a conception of the subject as "a process of multiple becoming in which anything can be connected to anything else" (71).

3. Deleuze cites some passages from *Interpretation of Dreams*, "The Unconscious," and *Beyond the Pleasure Principle* to lay out Freud's "topical hypothesis." Despite Freud's reservations about this hypothesis, Deleuze finds it interesting that "we find all the elements" of it in Nietzsche's work (NP 112). Cf. Freud 1965, 574–83.

4. See Bogue 1989, 31, for a helpful characterization of this ethical doctrine.

5. See Salanskis 1996, 69, and Conway 1997 for interesting readings of the throw.

6. Michael Hardt gives the example of the worker who attacks work; it is by at-

tacking her own "essence" — the values that define her as a worker — that the worker in effect destroys herself and then is able to create (1993, 44).

7. "Only the extreme forms return — those which, large or small, are deployed within the limit and extend to the limit of their power, transforming themselves and changing one into another. Only the extreme, the excessive, returns; that which passes into something else and becomes identical. That is why the eternal return is said only of the theatrical world of the metamorphoses and masks of the Will to power, of the pure intensities of that Will which are like mobile individuating factors unwilling to allow themselves to be contained within the factitious limits of this or that individual, this or that Self. Eternal return or returning expresses the common being of all these metamorphoses, the measure and the common being of all that is extreme, of all the realised degrees of power. It is the being-equal of all that is unequal and has been able to fully realise its inequality" (D&R 41).

8. Goodchild's discussion of the eternal return as the solution to the practical problem of the passage of time is the inspiration for this correlation (cf. Goodchild 1996b, 50–57). I am simplifying Deleuze's account of the three syntheses presented in chap. 2 of *Difference and Repetition* (70–128).

9. In *Difference and Repetition*, Deleuze more explicitly draws the first synthesis from Hume's conception of habit as the contraction of successive instants in a living present. The resonance with Bergson's notion of habit should be clear. The notion of the sensory-motor schema is an important theme in *Cinema 1* and *Cinema 2* (Deleuze 1986 and 1989).

10. There is, of course, much more that could be said about this form of time. *Cinema 2: The Time-Image* presents an extensive discussion of it in the context of a philosophical perusal of the concepts to which cinema (and especially modern cinema in the case of the time-image) gives rise.

11. I want to emphasize that it is the images that suggest safeguarding one's individuality and not Deleuze himself. Deleuze nowhere advocates anything like being "yourself" or preserving one's individuality.

CHAPTER 7. DELEUZE'S BECOMING-IMPERCEPTIBLE

1. Deleuze's admiration for Nietzsche should be qualified with Deleuze's caution that Nietzsche's grandiose and dangerous task entailed "a new way of exploring the depth. . . . He could not stand to stay on the fragile surface, which he had nevertheless plotted through men and gods. Returning to a bottomless abyss that he renewed and dug out afresh, that is where Nietzsche perished in his own manner" (LS 108). Deleuze prefers the surface to either the heights or the depths. (Cf. Deleuze's discussion of the surface throughout *The Logic of Sense* and his characterization of philosophy in relation to height, depth, and surfaces in the eighteenth series of *The Logic of Sense* [127–33] and the genesis of the subject in relationship to height, depth, and surfaces in the twenty-seventh through twenty-ninth series [186–209].)

2. In the next chapter I discuss the notion of an abstract machine more fully in the context of Foucauldian cartography.

3. Deleuze and Guattari avoid using terms such as 'human being' or 'person' in their descriptions; such terms suggest a clear-cut demarcation between a human being and the rest of the world. As I pointed out in Chapter 5, Deleuze and Guattari's conception of the individual insists upon her ongoing and all-encompassing immersion in a world. Stratification and destratification involve individuals who are always implicated in assemblages and strata that defy traditional conceptions of where human beings end and the world "out there" begins.

4. Brian Massumi, the translator of *A Thousand Plateaus*, chose to "import" 'signifiance/interpretance' into English without modification and notes that they are borrowed from Benveniste and are typically translated as "signifying capacity" and "interpretive capacity" in the English translations of Benveniste's work (ATP xviii). I use the term 'significance' to cover both aspects of an individual's relation to social systems of meaning. Goodchild discusses the three strata in more detail than I do here in chap. 6 of *Deleuze and Guattari* (1996a).

5. Deleuze and Guattari's examples of becoming-other in *A Thousand Plateaus* provide other examples of this kind of process. I address some of these examples later in this section.

6. See ATP 21 for an extended definition of the rhizome.

7. As Massumi puts it: "The body without organs is a region of the Milky Way marked by a constellation but including an infinity of background stars visible at varying degrees of intensity. . . . The behavior patterns that begin to develop are the constellation as perceived from a civilization center. The glare of city lights begin [sic] to obscure all but the brightest stars in its region of the sky: in the end, only the 'meaningful' ones outlining the constellation's symbolic shape remain" (1992, 71).

8. Grosz says that "the empty BwO empties itself too quickly, disarrays itself too much, so that it closes in on itself, unable to transmit its intensities differently, stuck in repetition. It does not deny becoming; rather, it establishes a line of flight that is unable to free the circulation of intensities, making other, further connections with other BwOs impossible" (1994c, 171).

9. Of course, although Deleuze and Guattari do not say so, if the masochist does not succeed in producing new assemblages with new flows of desire which affect the surrounding social field, the BwO she has constructed is an empty one.

10. The images are first found on page 10 of *The Castle*: "As K was going out, he noticed a dark portrait in a dim frame on the wall . . . the bust portrait of a man about fifty. His head was sunk so low upon his breast that his eyes were scarcely visible, and the weight of the high, heavy forehead and the strong hooked nose seemed to have borne the head down" (Kafka 1992).

11. Although I think there are interesting comparisons to make between memory as a block of becoming and the active memory of the future discussed in Chapter 6, there are important enough dissimilarities that I will not pursue such a comparison here.

12. Cf. "Investigations of a Dog" and "The Metamorphosis," both in *Franz Kafka: The Complete Stories* (Kafka 1971).

13. Cf. Deleuze and Guattari's example of the wasp and orchid as rhizome (ATP 10).

14. Rosi Braidotti makes a similar point (1996, 308–14). Also see Braidotti 1991, 1993, and 1994a, b, c, and d; Grosz 1994c, 174–80, and 1994c; and Olkowski 1994.

15. I realize of course that Deleuze and Guattari's 'war machines' are not to be equated with war. A full account of this term would involve an account of their conception of the State, which is beyond the scope of this book. Still, if confronted with a choice between Irigaray's vocabulary drawn from the elements (earth, sea, sky, fire, air, etc.) and Deleuze and Guattari's military vocabulary, I have to admit to preferring the former.

CHAPTER 8. MAPPING LINES OF FLIGHT

1. Foucault characterizes what he distinguishes in terms of the nondiscursive and discursive realms in *The Archaeology of Knowledge* as the visible and the articulable in *Birth of the Clinic* and *Discipline and Punish*, and Deleuze follows him in this. Deleuze claims that visibilities are multisensorial complexes: "Visibilities are not defined by sight but are complexes of actions and passions, actions and reactions, multisensorial complexes, which emerge into the light of day" (F 59). I am interpreting the nondiscursive realm as the perceivable realm of material reality. This would align it with what I have been calling the corporeal.

2. Cf. Chapter 7.

3. See Chapter 7 for a discussion of strata.

4. Moira Gatens presents a fascinating account of Deleuze's reading of Spinoza as a "social cartography" by which to map individuals and an ethology or an "ethics of the molecular" (1996b). Deleuze's reading of Spinoza is crucial to his project (cf. Deleuze 1992). For more on this connection, see Armstrong 1997, Bogue 1989, Diprose 1994, Goodchild 1996b, Grosz 1994c, and Hardt 1993.

5. I am not doing justice to Deleuze's notion of the fold here. Deleuze devotes his book on Leibniz, *The Fold*, to this notion. See Goodchild (1996b, 135–38) for an interesting discussion of Deleuze's reading of Foucault on this point in relation to the notion as it emerges in the *Cinema* books.

6. This concept of chaos should be connected with the concept of the virtual discussed in Chapter 5.

7. Deleuze and Guattari's characterization of science not only provides an interesting contrast to their characterizations of philosophy and art but suggests as well that science is also a process of destratification. I confine myself here to a discussion of philosophy and art since these activities are more directly relevant to the concerns of my own project.

8. The Kantian *cogito* introduces the component of time into the Cartesian *cogito* and consists of four components: "I think, and as such I am active; I have an existence; this existence is only determinable in time as a passive self; I am therefore determined as a passive self that necessarily represents its own thinking activ-

ity to itself as an Other that affects it" (WP 31–32). For another rendering of the example of the Cartesian cogito, see Patton 1996a, 318–19, in which Patton presents a highly lucid account of the interrelationship of concepts, events, and the virtual.

9. This is not to say that the creation of concepts does not inevitably affect the embodied philosopher — even if these effects do not become immediately manifest at the level of representational consciousness.

10. The translations are courtesy of Daniel W. Smith.

CHAPTER 9. CORPOREAL CARTOGRAPHIES

1. Deleuze and Irigaray have a complex relationship with metaphors and their use which I have not addressed here. Since metaphors are premised on the kind of representational thinking they both subvert, metaphors — as well as models — are suspect. Constantin Boundas argues that Deleuzian theorizing rejects "preformed" models in favor of projects that are virtual "and yet real — real in a future anterior mode; The virtual cannot be imitated; it can only be constructed" (1996b, 337). In suggesting that Irigaray's metaphor of intrauterine experience could be read as the construction of a BwO, I am thinking in terms of this kind of project. My use of the term 'models of subjectivity' also refers to a model that is "real in a future anterior mode" rather than pre-formed; the kind of models I am working with here must always be thought of in terms of an open-ended project.

2. Daniel Smith gives this helpful gloss on the nomadic subject and its relationship to an actual individual: "Rather than being closed upon the compossible and convergent world they express from within (the monadic subject), beings are now torn open and kept open through the divergent series and incompossible ensembles that continually pull them outside themselves (the nomadic subject). . . . An individual is a multiplicity, the actualization of a set of virtual singularities that function together, that enter into symbiosis, that attain a certain consistency. But there is a great difference between the singularities that define the virtual plane of immanence and the individuals that actualize them and transform them into something transcendent. . . . What he [Deleuze] calls 'schizophrenization' is a limit-process in which the identity of the individual is dissolved and passes entirely into the virtual chaosmos of included disjunctions" (Smith 1997, xxviii–xxix).

Bibliography

Ansell-Pearson, Keith. 1993. "Nietzsche, Woman, and Political Theory." In *Nietzsche, Feminism, and Political Theory*, edited by P. Patton, 27–48. New York: Routledge.

———. 1994. *An Introduction to Nietzsche as Political Thinker: The Perfect Nihilist.* New York: Cambridge University Press.

———, ed. 1997a. *Deleuze and Philosophy: The Difference Engineer.* New York: Routledge.

———. 1997b. "Deleuze Outside/Outside Deleuze: On the Difference Engineer." In *Deleuze and Philosophy: The Difference Engineer*, edited by K. Ansell-Pearson, 1–22. New York: Routledge.

———. 1997c. "Viroid Life: On Machines, Technics, and Evolution." In *Deleuze and Philosophy: The Difference Engineer*, edited by K. Ansell-Pearson, 180–210. New York: Routledge.

Armstrong, Aurelia. 1997. "Some Reflections on Deleuze's Spinoza: Composition and Agency." In *Deleuze and Philosophy: The Difference Engineer*, edited by K. Ansell-Pearson, 44–57. New York: Routledge.

Bartky, Sandra. 1990. *Femininity and Domination: Studies in the Phenomenology of Oppression.* New York: Routledge.

Baugh, Bruce. 1993. "Deleuze and Empiricism." *Journal of the British Society for Phenomenology*, 24:1, 15–31.

Beddoes, Diane. 1997. "Deleuze, Kant, and Indifference." In *Deleuze and Philosophy: The Difference Engineer*, edited by K. Ansell-Pearson, 25–43. New York: Routledge.

Bergson, Henri. 1991. *Matter and Memory.* Translated by N. M. Paul and W. S. Palmer. New York: Zone Books. Originally published as *Matière et mémoire* (Paris: Presses Universitaires de France, 1908).

Berry, Philippa. 1992. "Woman and Space According to Kristeva and Irigaray." In *Shadow of Spirit: Postmodernism and Religion*, edited by P. Berry and A. Wernick, 250–64. New York: Routledge.

———. 1994. "The Burning Glass: Paradoxes of Feminist Revelation in *Speculum*." In *Engaging with Irigaray: Feminist Philosophy and Modern European Thought*, edited by C. Burke, N. Schor, and M. Whitford, 229–246. New York: Columbia University Press.

Bogue, Ronald. 1989. *Deleuze and Guattari.* New York: Routledge.

———. 1991. "Rhizomusicosmology." *Substance*, 66, 85–101.

———. 1996a. "Deleuze's Style." *Man and World*, 29:3, 251–68.

———. 1996b. "Gilles Deleuze: The Aesthetics of Force." In *Deleuze: A Critical Reader*, edited by P. Patton, 257–69. Cambridge: Blackwell.

Boothby, Richard. 1991. *Death and Desire: Psychoanalytic Theory in Lacan's Return to Freud.* New York: Routledge.

Bordo, Susan. 1993. *Unbearable Weight: Feminism, Western Culture, and the Body.* Berkeley: University of California Press.

Boundas, Constantin V. 1993. "Foreclosure of the Other: From Sartre to De-leuze." *Journal of the British Society for Phenomenology*, 24:1, 32–43.
——. 1994. "Deleuze: Serialization and Subject-Formation." In *Gilles Deleuze and the Theater of Philosophy*, edited by C. V. Boundas and D. Olkowski, 99–116. New York: Routledge.
——. 1996a. "Deleuze-Bergson: An Otology of the Virtual." In *Deleuze: A Critical Reader*, edited by P. Patton, 81–106. Cambridge: Blackwell.
——. 1996b. "Transgressive Theorizing: A Report to Deleuze." *Man and World*, 29:3, 327–41.
Boundas, Constantin V., and Dorothea Olkowski, eds. 1994. *Gilles Deleuze and the Theater of Philosophy*. New York: Routledge.
Braidotti, Rosi. 1989. "The Politics of Ontological Difference." In *Between Feminism and Psychoanalysis*, edited by T. Brennan, 89–105. New York: Routledge.
——. 1991. *Patterns of Dissonance: A Study of Women in Contemporary Philosophy*. New York: Routledge.
——. 1993. "Discontinuing Becomings: Deleuze on the Becoming-Woman of Philosophy." *Journal of the British Society for Phenomenology*, 24:1, 44–55.
——. 1994a. "Feminism By Any Other Name." *differences*, 6:2 and 3, 27–61.
——. 1994b. *Nomadic Subjects: Embodiment and Sexual Difference in Contemporary Feminist Theory*. New York: Columbia University Press.
——. 1994c. "Of Bugs and Women: Irigaray and Deleuze on the Becoming-Woman." In *Engaging with Irigaray: Feminist Philosophy and Modern European Thought*, edited by C. Burke, N. Schor, and M. Whitford, 111–37. New York: Columbia University Press.
——. 1994d. "Toward a New Nomadism: Feminist Deleuzian Tracks; or, Meta-physics and Metabolism." In *Gilles Deleuze and the Theater of Philosophy*, edited by C. V. Boundas and D. Olkowski, 159–86. New York: Routledge.
——. 1996. "Nomadism with a Difference: Deleuze's Legacy in a Feminist Per-spective." *Man and World*, 29:3, 305–14.
Brennan, Teresa, ed. 1989. *Between Feminism and Psychoanalysis*. New York: Routledge.
——. 1992. *The Interpretation of the Flesh: Freud and Femininity*. New York: Routledge.
Burgard, Peter J., ed. 1994. *Nietzsche and the Feminine*. Charlottesville: University Press of Virginia.
Burke, Carolyn. 1994a. "Irigaray Through the Looking Glass." In *Engaging with Irigaray: Feminist Philosophy and Modern European Thought*, edited by C. Burke, N. Schor, and M. Whitford, 37–56. New York: Columbia University Press.
——. 1994b. "Translation Modified: Irigaray in English." In *Engaging with Irigaray: Feminist Philosophy and Modern European Thought*, edited by C. Burke, N. Schor, and M. Whitford, 249–61. New York: Columbia University Press.
Burke, Carolyn, Naomi Schor, and Margaret Whitford, eds. 1994. *Engaging with Irigaray: Feminist Philosophy and Modern European Thought*. New York: Columbia University Press.
Butler, Judith. 1987. *Subjects of Desire: Hegelian Reflections in Twentieth-Century France*. New York: Columbia University Press.
——. 1990. *Gender Trouble: Feminism and the Subversion of Identity*. New York: Routledge.
——. 1992. "Contingent Foundations: Feminism and the Question of 'Postmod-

ernism.'" In *Feminists Theorize the Political*, edited by J. Butler and J. W. Scott. New York: Routledge.

——. 1993. *Bodies That Matter: On the Discursive Limits of "Sex."* New York: Routledge.

——. 1994. "Against Proper Objects." *differences*, 6:2 and 3, 1–26.

Butler, Judith, and Joan W. Scott, eds. 1992. *Feminists Theorize the Political.* New York: Routledge.

Chanter, Tina. 1995. *Ethics of Eros: Irigaray's Rewriting of the Philosophers.* New York: Routledge.

Chisholm, Dianne. 1994. "Irigaray's Hysteria." In *Engaging with Irigaray: Feminist Philosophy and Modern European Thought*, edited by C. Burke, N. Schor, and M. Whitford, 263–84. New York: Columbia University Press.

Clark, Tim. 1997. "Deleuze and Structuralism: Towards a Geometry of Sufficient Reason." In *Deleuze and Philosophy: The Difference Engineer*, edited by K. Ansell-Pearson, 58–72. New York: Routledge.

Colombat, André P. 1991. "A Thousand Trails to Work with Deleuze." *Substance*, 66, 10–23.

——. 1996. "November 4, 1995: Deleuze's Death as an Event." *Man and World*, 29:3, 235–49.

Conway, Daniel W. 1993. *"Das Weib an sich*: The Slave Revolt in Epistemology." In *Nietzsche, Feminism, and Political Theory*, edited by P. Patton, 110–29. New York: Routledge.

——. 1997. "Tumbling Dice: Gilles Deleuze and the Economy of *Répétition*." In *Deleuze and Philosophy: The Difference Engineer*, edited by K. Ansell-Pearson, 73–90. New York: Routledge.

Dallery, Arlene B. 1990. "Sexual Embodiment: Beauvoir and French Feminism *écriture féminine*." In *Hypatia Reborn*, edited by A. Y. Al-Hibri and M. A. Simons, 270–79. Bloomington: Indiana University Press.

Deleuze, Gilles. 1964. *Proust et les signes.* Paris: Presses Universitaires de France.

——. 1977a. "Active and Reactive." In *The New Nietzsche: Contemporary Styles of Interpretation*, edited by D. B. Allison, 80–106. Cambridge: MIT Press.

——. 1977b. "Nomad Thought." In *The New Nietzsche: Contemporary Styles of Interpretation*, edited by D. B. Allison, 142–49. Cambridge: MIT Press.

——. 1981. *Francis Bacon: Logique de la sensation.* Paris: éditions de la Différence.

——. 1983. *Nietzsche and Philosophy.* Translated by Hugh Tomlinson. New York: Columbia University Press. Originally published as *Nietzsche et la philosophie* (Paris: Presses Universitaires de France, 1962).

——. 1984. *Kant's Critical Philosophy: The Doctrine of the Faculties.* Translated by Hugh Tomlinson and Barbara Habberjam. Minneapolis: University of Minnesota Press. Originally published as *La Philosophie critique de Kant* (Paris: Presses Universitaires de France, 1963).

——. 1986. *Cinema 1: The Movement-Image.* Translated by Hugh Tomlinson and Barbara Habberjam. Minneapolis: University of Minnesota Press. Originally published as *Cinéma 1, L'Image-mouvement* (Paris: Minuit, 1983).

——. 1988a. *Foucault.* Translated by Seán Hand. Minneapolis: University of Minnesota Press. Originally published as *Foucault* (Paris: Minuit, 1986).

——. 1988b. *Spinoza: Practical Philosophy.* Translated by Robert Hurley. San Francisco: City Lights Books. Originally published as *Spinoza: philosophie pratique* (Paris, Minuit, 1981, rev. ed. of 1970 ed.).

———. 1989. *Cinema 2: The Time-Image*. Translated by Hugh Tomlinson and Robert Galeta. Minneapolis: University of Minnesota Press. Originally published as *Cinéma 2, L'Image-temps* (Paris: Minuit, 1985).

———. 1990. *The Logic of Sense*. Translated by Mark Lester. New York: Columbia University Press. Originally published as *Logique du sens* (Paris: Minuit, 1969).

———. 1991. *Bergsonism*. Translated by Hugh Tomlinson and Barbara Habberjam. New York: Zone Books. Originally published as *Le Bergsonisme* (Paris: Presses Universitaires de France, 1966).

———. 1992. *Expressionism in Philosophy: Spinoza*. Translated by Martin Joughin. New York: Zone Books. Originally published as *Spinoza et le problème de l'expression* (Paris: Minuit, 1968).

———. 1993. *The Fold: Leibniz and The Baroque*. Translated by T. Conley. Minneapolis: University of Minnesota Press. Originally published as *Le pli: Leibniz et le baroque* (Paris: Minuit, 1988).

———. 1994a. *Difference and Repetition*. Translated by P. Patton. New York: Columbia University Press. Originally published as *Différence et répétition* (Paris: Presses Universitaires de France, 1968).

———. 1994b. "He Stuttered." In *Gilles Deleuze and the Theater of Philosophy*, edited by C. V. Boundas and D. Olkowski, 23–29. New York: Routledge.

———. 1995. *Negotiations: 1972–1990*. Translated by Martin Joughin. New York: Columbia University Press. Originally published as *Pourparlers* (Paris: Minuit, 1990).

———. 1997. *Essays Critical and Clinical*. Translated by Daniel W. Smith and Michael A. Greco. Minneapolis: University of Minnesota Press. Originally published as *Critique et clinique* (Paris: Minuit, 1993).

Deleuze, Gilles, and Félix Guattari. 1983. *Anti-Oedipus: Capitalism and Schizophrenia*. Translated by Robert Hurley, Mark Seem, and Helen R. Lane. Minneapolis: University of Minnesota Press. Originally published as *L'Anti-Oedipe: capitalisme et schizophrénie I* (Paris: Minuit, 1972).

———. 1986. *Kafka: Toward a Minor Literature*. Translated by Dana Polan. Minneapolis: University of Minnesota Press. Originally published as *Kafka: pour une littérature mineure* (Paris: Minuit, 1975).

———. 1987. *A Thousand Plateaus: Capitalism and Schizophrenia*. Translated by Brian Massumi. Minneapolis: University of Minnesota Press. Originally published as *Mille plateaux: capitalisme et schizophrénie II* (Paris: Minuit, 1980).

———. 1994. *What Is Philosophy?* Translated by Hugh Tomlinson and Graham Burchell. New York: Columbia University Press. Originally published as *Qu'est-ce que la philosophie?* (Paris: Minuit, 1991).

Deleuze, Gilles, and Claire Parnet. 1987. *Dialogues*. Translated by Hugh Tomlinson and Barbara Habberjam. New York: Columbia University Press. Originally published as *Dialogues* (Paris: Flammarion, 1977).

Derrida, Jacques. 1978. *Writing and Difference*. Translated by Alan Bass. Chicago: University of Chicago Press.

———. 1979. *Spurs; Nietzsche's Spurs*. Translated by Barbara Harlow. Chicago: University of Chicago Press.

———. 1985. *The Ear of the Other: Otobiography, Transference, Translation*. Translated by Peggy Kamuf. Lincoln: University of Nebraska Press.

Descombes, Vincent. 1980. *Modern French Philosophy* Translated by L. Scott-Fox and J. M. Harding. Cambridge: Cambridge University Press.

Deutscher, Penelope. 1994. " 'The Only Diabolical Thing about Women . . . ': Luce Irigaray on Divinity." *Hypatia*, 9:4, 88–111.

Diprose, Rose. 1993. "Nietzsche and the Pathos of Distance." In *Nietzsche, Feminism, and Political Theory*, edited by P. Patton, 1–26. New York: Routledge.

———. 1994. *The Bodies of Women: Ethics, Embodiment and Sexual Difference*. New York: Routledge.

Ferguson, Ann. 1984. "On Conceiving Motherhood and Sexuality: A Feminist-Materialist Approach." In *Mothering: Essays in Feminist Theory*, edited by J. Trebilcot. Totowa, N.J.: Rowman and Allanheld. Reprinted in Ann Ferguson, *Sexual Democracy: Women, Oppression, and Revolution* 66–95. Boulder: Westview Press, 1991.

Foucault, Michel. 1965. *Madness and Civilization: A History of Insanity in the Age of Reason*. Translated by Richard Howard. New York: Vintage.

———. 1970. *The Order of Things: An Archaeology of the Human Sciences*. New York: Vintage.

———. 1972. *The Archaeology of Knowledge and The Discourse on Language*. Translated by A. M. Sheridan Smith. New York: Pantheon Books.

———. 1973. *The Birth of the Clinic: An Archaeology of Medical Perception*. Translated by A. M. Sheridan Smith. New York: Vintage Books.

———. 1977. *Language, Counter-Memory, Practice: Selected Essays and Interviews*. Translated by Donald Bouchard. Ithaca: Cornell University Press.

———. 1978. *The History of Sexuality*. Vol. 1. *An Introduction*. Translated by Robert Hurley. New York: Vintage Books.

———. 1979. *Discipline and Punish: The Birth of the Prison*. Translated by Alan Sheridan. New York: Vintage Books.

———. 1985. *The History of Sexuality*. Vol. 2. *The Use of Pleasure*. Translated by Robert Hurley. New York: Vintage.

———. 1986. *The History of Sexuality*. Vol. 3. *The Care of the Self*. Translated by Robert Hurley. New York: Vintage.

Freud, Sigmund. 1961. *Beyond the Pleasure Principle*. Translated by James Strachey. New York: W. W. Norton.

———. 1965. *The Interpretation of Dreams*. Translated by James Strachey. New York: Avon Books.

Gatens, Moira. 1992. "Power, Bodies, and Difference." In *Destabilizing Theory: Contemporary Feminist Debates*, edited by M. Barrett and A. Phillips, 120–37. Stanford: Stanford University Press.

———. 1996a. *Imaginary Bodies: Ethics, Power, and Corporeality*. New York: Routledge.

———. 1996b. "Through a Spinozist Lens: Ethology, Difference, Power." In *Deleuze: A Critical Reader*, edited by P. Patton, 162–87. Cambridge: Blackwell.

Goodchild, Philip. 1996a. *Deleuze and Guattari: An Introduction to the Politics of Desire*. London: Sage.

———. 1996b. *Gilles Deleuze and the Question of Philosophy*. Cranbury, N.J.: Associated University Presses.

Graybeal, Jean. 1990. *Language and "The Feminine" in Neitzsche and Heidegger*. Bloomington: Indiana University Press.

Grisham, Therese. 1991. "Linguistics as an Indiscipline: Deleuze and Guattari's Pragmatics." *Substance*, 66, 36–54.

Grosz, Elizabeth. 1989. *Sexual Subversions: Three French Feminists*. Sydney: Allen & Unwin.

———. 1990a. "Contemporary Theories of Power and Subjectivity." In *Feminist Knowledge: Critique and Construct*, edited by S. Gunew, 59–120. New York: Routledge.

———. 1990b. *Jacques Lacan: A Feminist Introduction*. New York: Routledge.

———. 1993. "Bodies and Knowledges: Feminism and the Crisis of Reason." In *Feminist Epistemologies*, edited by L. Alcoff and E. Potter, 187–215. New York: Routledge.

———. 1994a. "A Thousand Tiny Sexes: Feminism and Rhizomatics." In *Gilles Deleuze and the Theater of Philosophy*, edited by C. V. Boundas and D. Olkowski, 187–210. New York: Routledge.

———. 1994b. "The Hetero and the Homo: The Sexual Ethics of Luce Irigaray." In *Engaging with Irigaray: Feminist Philosophy and Modern European Thought*, edited by C. Burke, N. Schor, and M. Whitford, 335–50. New York: Columbia University Press.

———. 1994c. *Volatile Bodies: Toward a Corporeal Feminism*. Bloomington: Indiana University Press.

———. 1995. *Space, Time, and Perversion: Essays on the Politics of Bodies*. New York: Routledge.

Hardt, Michael. 1993. *Gilles Deleuze: An Apprenticeship in Philosophy*. Minneapolis: University of Minnesota Press.

Heaton, John M. 1993. "Language Games, Expression, and Desire in the Work of Deleuze." *Journal of the British Society for Phenomenology*, 24:1, 77–87.

Heidegger, Martin. 1962. *Being and Time*. Translated by John Macquarrie and Edward Robinson. New York: Harper and Row.

———. 1977. "Who Is Nietzsche's Zarathustra?" In *The New Nietzsche: Contemporary Styles of Interpretation*, edited by D. B. Allison, 64–79. Cambridge: MIT Press.

Hirsh, Elizabeth. 1994. "Back in Analysis: How to Do Things with Irigaray." In *Engaging with Irigaray: Feminist Philosophy and Modern European Thought*, edited by C. Burke, N. Schor, and M. Whitford, 285–316. New York: Columbia University Press.

Hirsh, Elizabeth, and Gary A. Olson. 1995. "Je — Luce Irigaray": A Meeting with Luce Irigaray." *Hypatia*, 10:2, 93–114.

Hodge, Joanna. 1994. "Irigaray Reading Heidegger." In *Engaging with Irigaray: Feminist Philosophy and Modern European Thought*, edited by C. Burke, N. Schor, and M. Whitford, 191–210. New York: Columbia University Press.

Holland, Eugene W. 1991. Deterritorializing "Deterritorialization" — From the *Anti-Oedipus* to *A Thousand Plateaus*. *Substance*, 66, 55–65.

Hollywood, Amy M. 1994. "Beauvoir, Irigaray, and the Mystical." *Hypatia*, 9:4, 158–85.

Ince, Kate. 1996. "Questions to Luce Irigaray." *Hypatia*, 11:2, 122–40.

Irigaray, Luce. 1981a. "And the One Doesn't Stir without the Other." *Signs*, 7:1, 60–67.

———. 1981b. *Le Corps-à-corps avec la mère*. Paris: éditions de la Pleine Lune.

———. 1983a. *La Croyance même*. Paris: éditions Galilée.

———. 1983b. *L'Oubli de l'air: chez Martin Heidegger*. Paris: Minuit.

———. 1985a. *Parler n'est jamais neutre*. Paris: Minuit.

———. 1985b. *Speculum of the Other Woman*. Translated by Gillian Gill. Ithaca: Cornell University Press. Originally published as *Speculum de l'autre femme* (Paris: Minuit, 1974).

———. 1985c. *This Sex Which Is Not One*. Translated by Catherine Porter and Carolyn Burke. Ithaca: Cornell University Press. Originally published as *Ce Sexe qui n'en est pas un* (Paris: Minuit, 1977).

———. 1986. "The Fecundity of the Caress." In *Face-to-Face with Levinas*, edited by R. A. Cohen. New York: State University of New York Press.

———. 1989. "Equal to Whom?" *Differences*, 1:2, 59–76.

———. 1991a. *Marine Lover of Friedrich Nietzsche*. Translated by Gillian C. Gill. New York: Columbia University Press. Originally published as *Amante marine* (Paris: Minuit, 1980).

———. 1991b. "Questions to Emmanuel Levinas: On the Divinity of Love." In *Re-Reading Levinas*, edited by R. Bernasconi and S. Critchley. Bloomington: Indiana University Press.

———. 1992. *Elemental Passions*. Translated by Joanne Collie and Judith Still. New York: Routledge. Originally published as *Passions élémentaires* (Paris: Minuit, 1982).

———. 1993a. *An Ethics of Sexual Difference*. Translated by Carolyn Burke and Gilian C. Gill. Ithaca: Cornell University Press. Originally published as *éthique de la différence sexuelle* (Paris: Minuit, 1984).

———. 1993b. *Je, Tu, Nous: Toward a Culture of Difference*. Translated by Alison Martin. New York: Routledge. Originally published as *Je, tu, nous* (Paris: Grasset, 1990).

———. 1993c. *Sexes and Genealogies*. Translated by Gillian C. Gill. New York: Columbia University Press. Originally published as *Sexes et parentés* (Paris: Minuit, 1987).

———. 1994a. "Ecce Mulier? Fragments." In *Nietzsche and the Feminine*, edited by P. J. Burgard, 316–31. Charlottesville: University Press of Virginia.

———. 1994b. *Thinking the Difference: For a Peaceful Revolution*. Translated by Karin Montin. New York: Routledge. Originally published as *Le Temps de la différence: pour une révolution pacifique* (Paris: Livre de Poche, 1989).

———. 1996. *I Love to You: Sketch for a Felicity within History*. Translated by Alison Martin. New York: Routledge. Originally published as *J'aime à toi: esquisse d'une félicté dan l'histoire* (Paris: Grasset, 1992).

Jaggar, Alison M., and Susan Bordo, eds. 1989. *Gender/Body/Knowledge: Feminist Reconstructions of Being and Knowing*. New Brunswick: Rutgers University Press.

Kafka, Franz. 1971. *Franz Kafka: The Complete Stories*, edited by Nahum N. Glatzer. New York: Schocken Books.

———. 1992. *The Castle*. Translated by Willa and Edwin Muir. New York: Schocken Books.

Klein, Anne C. 1994. "Presence with a Difference: Buddhists and Feminists on Subjectivity." *Hypatia*, 9:4, 112–30.

Klossowski, Pierre. 1997. *Nietzsche and the Vicious Circle*. Translated by Daniel W. Smith. Chicago: University of Chicago Press.

Koelb, Clayton. 1994. "Castration Envy: Nietzsche and the Figure of Woman." In *Nietzsche and the Feminine*, edited by P. J. Burgard, 71–81. Charlottesville: University Press of Virginia.

Kozel, S. 1996. "The Diabolical Strategy of Mimesis: Luce Irigaray's Reading of Maurice Merleau-Ponty." *Hypatia*, 11:3, 114–29.

Krell, David F. 1986. *Postponements: Woman, Sensuality, and Death in Nietzsche*. Bloomington: Indiana University Press.

———. 1994. "To the Orange Grove at the Edge of the Sea: Remarks on Luce Irigaray's *Amante marine.*" In *Nietzsche and the Feminine,* edited by P. J. Burgard, 185–209. Charlottesville: University Press of Virginia.

———. 1996. *Infectious Nietzsche.* Bloomington: Indiana University Press.

Kristeva, Julia. 1980. *Desire in Language: A Semiotic Approach to Literature and Art.* New York: Columbia University Press.

———. 1991. *Strangers to Ourselves.* Translated by Leon S. Roudiez. New York: Columbia University Press.

Lacan, Jacques. 1977. *Écrits: A Selection.* Translated by Alan Sheridan. New York: W. W. Norton.

———. 1978. *The Four Fundamental Concepts of Psycho-Analysis.* Translated by Alan Sheridan. New York: W. W. Norton.

Land, Nick. 1993. "Making It with Death: Remarks on Thanatos and Desiring-Production." *Journal of the British Society for Phenomenology,* 24:1, 66–76.

Levin, David M. 1985. *The Body's Recollection of Being: Phenomenological Psychology and the Deconstruction of Nihilism.* Boston: Routledge & Kegan Paul.

———. 1987. "Mudra as Thinking: Developing Our Wisdom-of-Being in Gesture and Movement." In *Heidegger and Asian Thought,* edited by G. Parkes. Honolulu: University of Hawaii Press.

Levinas, Emmanuel. 1969. *Totality and Infinity: An Essay on Exteriority.* Translated by Alphonso Lingis. Pittsburgh: Duquesne University Press.

Lingis, Alphonso. 1994. "The Society of Dismembered Body Parts." In *Gilles Deleuze and the Theater of Philosophy,* edited by C. V. Boundas and D. Olkowski, 289–303. New York: Routledge.

Lorraine, Tamsin. 1994. "Irigaray and Confusing Body Boundaries: Chaotic Folly or Unanticipated Bliss?" In *Transitions in Continental Philosophy,* edited by A. B. Dallery and S. H. Watson with E. M. Bower. Albany: State University of New York Press.

Lungstrum, Janet. 1994. "Nietzsche Writing Woman/Woman Writing Nietzsche: The Sexual Dialectic of Palingenesis." In *Nietzsche and the Feminine,* edited by P. J. Burgard, 135–57. Charlottesville: University Press of Virginia.

Macherey, Pierre. 1996. "The Encounter with Spinoza." In *Deleuze: A Critical Reader,* edited by P. Patton, 139–61. Cambridge: Blackwell.

Mackay, Robin. 1997. "*Capitalism and Schizophrenia*: Wildstyle in Full Effect." In *Deleuze and Philosophy: The Difference Engineer,* edited by K. Ansell-Pearson, 247–69. New York: Routledge.

Martin, Jean-Clet. 1994. "Cartography of the Year 1000: Variations on *A Thousand Plateaus.*" In *Gilles Deleuze and the Theater of Philosophy,* edited by C. V. Boundas and D. Olkowski, 265–88. New York: Routledge.

———. 1996. "The Eye of the Outside." In *Deleuze: A Critical Reader,* edited by P. Patton, 18–28. Cambridge: Blackwell.

Massumi, Brian. 1992. *A User's Guide to Capitalism and Schizophrenia: Deviations from Deleuze and Guattari.* Cambridge: MIT Press.

———. 1996. "The Autonomy of Affect." In *Deleuze: A Critical Reader,* edited by P. Patton, 217–39. Cambridge: Blackwell.

Matthews, Eric. 1996. *Twentieth-Century French Philosophy.* New York: Oxford University Press.

May, Todd. 1991. "The Politics of Life in the Thought of Gilles Deleuze." *Substance,* 66, 24–35.

———. 1993. "The System and its Fractures: Gilles Deleuze on Otherness." *Journal of the British Society for Phenomenology*, 24:1, 3–14.
———. 1994. "Difference and Unity in Gilles Deleuze." In *Gilles Deleuze and the Theater of Philosophy*, edited by C. V. Boundas and D. Olkowski, 33–50. New York: Routledge.
———. 1996. "Gilles Deleuze and the Politics of Time." *Man and World*, 29:3, 293–304.
Mortensen, Ellen. 1994. "Woman's Untruth and *le féminin*: Reading Luce Irigaray with Nietzsche and Heidegger." In *Engaging with Irigaray: Feminist Philosophy and Modern European Thought*, edited by C. Burke, N. Schor, and M. Whitford, 211–28. New York: Columbia University Press.
Muraro, Luisa. 1994. "Female Genealogies." In *Engaging with Irigaray: Feminist Philosophy and Modern European Thought*, edited by C. Burke, N. Schor, and M. Whitford, 317–34. New York: Columbia University Press.
Nagatomo, Shigenori. 1992. "An Eastern Concept of the Body: Yuasa's Body-Scheme." In *Giving the Body Its Due*, edited by M. Sheets-Johnstone, 48–68. Albany: State University of New York Press.
Nancy, Jean-Luc. 1996. "The Deleuzian Fold of Thought." In *Deleuze: A Critical Reader*, edited by P. Patton, 107–113. Cambridge: Blackwell Publishers.
Nietzsche, Friedrich. 1966. *Thus Spoke Zarathustra: A Book for All and None*. Translated by Walter Kaufmann. New York: Penguin.
Oliver, Kelly. 1993. *Reading Kristeva: Unraveling the Double-Bind*. Bloomington: University of Indiana Press.
———. 1995. *Womanizing Nietzsche: Philosophy's Relation to the "Feminine."* New York: Routledge.
———, ed. 1997. *The Portable Kristeva*. New York: Columbia University Press.
Olkowsi, Dorothea. 1996. "Beside Us, In Memory." *Man and World*, 29:3, 283–92.
———. 1994. "Nietzsche's Dice Throw: Tragedy, Nihilism, and the Body without Organs." In *Gilles Deleuze and the Theater of Philosophy*, edited by C. V. Boundas and D. Olkowski, 119–40. New York: Routledge.
Oppel, Frances. 1993. " 'Speaking of Immemorial Waters': Irigaray with Nietzsche." In *Nietzsche, Feminism, and Political Theory*, edited by P. Patton, 88–109. New York: Routledge.
Patton, Paul, ed. 1993. *Nietzsche, Feminism, and Political Theory*. New York: Routledge.
———. 1994. "Anti-Platonism and Art." In *Gilles Deleuze and the Theater of Philosophy*, edited by C. V. Boundas and D. Olkowski, 141–56. New York: Routledge.
———. 1996a. "Concept and Event." *Man and World*, 29:3, 315–26.
———, ed. 1996b. *Deleuze: A Critical Reader*. Cambridge: Blackwell.
———. 1996c. "Introduction." In *Deleuze: A Critical Reader*, edited by P. Patton, 1–17. Cambridge: Blackwell.
Piercey, Robert. 1996. "The Spinoza-intoxicated Man: Deleuze on Expression." *Man and World*, 29:3, 269–81.
Plant, Sadie. 1993. "Nomads and Revolutionaries." *Journal of the British Society for Phenomenology*, 24:1, 88–101.
Plotnitsky, Arkady. 1994. "The Medusa's Ears: The Question of Nietzsche, the Question of Gender, and Transformations of Theory." In *Nietzsche and the Feminine*, edited by P. J. Burgard, 230–53. Charlottesville: University Press of Virginia.

Polan, Dana. 1994. "Francis Bacon: The Logic of Sensation." In *Gilles Deleuze and the Theater of Philosophy*, edited by C. V. Boundas and D. Olkowski, 229–54. New York: Routledge.

Reineke, Martha. 1997. *Sacrificed Lives: Kristeva on Women and Violence*. Bloomington: Indiana University Press.

Rich, Adrienne. 1986. *Of Woman Born: Motherhood as Experience and Institution.* Tenth Anniversary Edition. New York: W. W. Norton.

Rosenberg, M. E. 1993. "Dynamic and Thermodynamic Tropes of the Subject in Freud and in Deleuze and Guattari." *Postmodern Culture*, 4:1, 1–43.

Rowley, Hazel, and Elizabeth Grosz. 1990. "Psychoanalysis and Feminism." In *Feminist Knowledge: Critique and Construct*, edited by S. Gunew. New York: Routledge.

Sadler, T. 1993. "The Postmodern Politicization of Nietzsche." In *Nietzsche, Feminism, and Political Theory*, edited by P. Patton, 225–43. New York: Routledge.

Salanskis, Jean-Michel. 1996. "Idea and Destination." In *Deleuze: A Critical Reader*, edited by P. Patton, 57–80. Cambridge: Blackwell.

Schor, Naomi. 1994a. "Previous Engagements: The Receptions of Irigaray." In *Engaging with Irigaray: Feminist Philosophy and Modern European Thought*, edited by C. Burke, N. Schor, and M. Whitford, 3–14. New York: Columbia University Press.

——. 1994b. "This Essentialism Which Is Not One: Coming to Grips with Irigaray." In *Engaging with Irigaray: Feminist Philosophy and Modern European Thought*, edited by C. Burke, N. Schor, and M. Whitford, 57–78. New York: Columbia University Press.

Schrift, Alan D. 1990. *Nietzsche and the Question of Interpretation: Between Hermeneutics and Deconstruction*. New York: Routledge.

——. 1994. "On the Gynecology of Morals: Nietzsche and Cixous on the Logic of the Gift." In *Nietzsche and the Feminine*, edited by P. J. Burgard, 210–29. Charlottesville: University Press of Virginia.

——. 1995. *Nietzsche's French Legacy: A Genealogy of Poststructuralism*. New York: Routledge.

Schwab, Gail M. 1994. "Mother's Body, Father's Tongue: Mediation and the Symbolic Order." In *Engaging with Irigaray: Feminist Philosophy and Modern European Thought*, edited by C. Burke, N. Schor, and M. Whitford, 351–78. New York: Columbia University Press.

Shapiro, Gary. 1989. *Nietzschean Narratives*. Bloomington: Indiana University Press.

——. 1991. *Alcyone: Nietzsche on Gifts, Noise, and Women*. Albany: State University of New York Press.

Smith, Daniel W. 1995. "Deleuze's Concept of the Virtual and the Critique of the Possible." Paper given at the International Association for Philosophy and Literature Conference at Villanova University.

——. 1996. "Deleuze's Theory of Sensation: Overcoming the Kantian Duality." In *Deleuze: A Critical Reader*, edited by P. Patton, 29–56. Cambridge: Blackwell.

——. 1997. "Introduction: 'A Life of Pure Immanence': Deleuze's 'Critique and Clinique' Project." In *Essays: Critical and Clinical* by Gilles Deleuze, translated by Daniel W. Smith and Michael A. Greco, ix–lvi. Minneapolis: University of Minnesota Press.

Spivak, Gayatri C. 1988. "Can the Subaltern Speak?" In *Marxism and the Interpre-*

tation of Culture, edited by C. Nelson and L. Grossberg, 271–313. Urbana: University of Illinois Press.

Stern, Daniel. 1985. *The Interpersonal World of the Infant: A View from Psychoanalysis and Developmental Psychology*. New York: Basic Books.

Stivale, Charles. 1991. "Introduction: Actuality and Concepts." *Substance*, 66, 3–9.

Surin, Kenneth. 1991. "The Undecidable and the Fugitive: *Mille Plateaux* and the State-Form." *Substance*, 66, 102–13.

Tapper, Marion. 1993. "*Ressentiment* and Power: Some Reflections on Feminist Practices." In *Nietzsche, Feminism and Political Theory*, edited by P. Patton, 130–43. New York: Routledge.

Theisen, Bianca. 1994. "Rhythms of Oblivion." In *Nietzsche and the Feminine*, edited by P. J. Burgard, 82–103. Charlottesville: University Press of Virginia.

Tirrell, Lynne. 1994. "Sexual Dualism and Women's Self-Creation: On the Advantages and Disadvantages of Reading Nietzsche for Feminists." In *Nietzsche and the Feminine*, edited by P. J. Burgard, 158–82. Charlottesville: University Press of Virginia.

Weed, Elizabeth. 1994. "The Question of Style." In *Engaging with Irigaray: Feminist Philosophy and Modern European Thought*, edited by C. Burke, N. Schor, and M. Whitford, 79–110. New York: Columbia University Press.

Welchman, Alistair. 1997. "Machinic Thinking." In *Deleuze and Philosophy: The Difference Engineer*, edited by K. Ansell-Pearson, 211–27. New York: Routledge.

Whitford, Margaret. 1989. "Rereading Irigaray." In *Between Feminism and Psychoanalysis*, edited by T. Brennan, 106–26. New York: Routledge.

——. 1991a. *Luce Irigaray: Philosophy in the Feminine*. New York: Routledge.

——, ed. 1991b. *The Irigaray Reader: Luce Irigaray*. Cambridge: Blackwell.

——. 1994a. "Irigaray, Utopia, and the Death Drive." In *Engaging with Irigaray: Feminist Philosophy and Modern European Thought*, edited by C. Burke, N. Schor, and M. Whitford, 379–400. New York: Columbia University Press.

——. 1994b. "Reading Irigaray in the Nineties." In *Engaging with Irigaray: Feminist Philosophy and Modern European Thought*, edited by C. Burke, N. Schor, and M. Whitford, 15–33. New York: Columbia University Press.

Willett, Cynthia. 1995. *Maternal Ethics and Other Slave Moralities*. New York: Routledge.

Young, Iris M. 1990. *Throwing Like a Girl and Other Essays in Feminist Philosophy and Social Theory*. Bloomington: Indiana University Press.

Zourabichvili, François. 1996. "Six Notes on the Percept on the Relation between the Critical and the Clinical." In *Deleuze: A Critical Reader*, edited by P. Patton, 188–216. Cambridge: Blackwell.

Index

Deleuze's reading of, 18, 136–65
Irigaray's reading of, 48–66
Nietzschean subject, 69–72, 143–46,
    161, 175
Nietzsche and Philosophy (Deleuze),
    140–45, 165
nihilism, 150–55, 161
nomadic, the, 220–21, 227–39
    subject, 5, 11, 14, 114, 125–26,
    134–37, 154, 188–91

oedipalization, 116–28, 135–41, 171,
    187–88, 208, 221–29, 238
deterritorializing, 176–83
and Nietzsche, 143–45, 161, 163–66
Oliver, Kelly, 63–64, 74, 76, 80
opinion, 207, 210, 214
origin, 25–30, 47, 83–86, 91, 128–29,
    221–27, 230–31
L'Oubli de l'air (Irigaray), 226
outside, the, 181, 190–93, 196–204,
    209–10, 214, 229, 232–33, 239
and immanence, 19, 76, 168–70
and patriarchy, 45, 66
overman, 145, 150–51, 161–62

Parnet, Claire, 128
Parsifal (Wagner), 148
perception
    art of, 66, 79, 88–92, 216
    training in, 160, 233–37
percepts, 203, 210–12, 234
plane, 193, 200, 203
    of composition, 203, 210, 213–14
    of consistency, 5, 166–72, 180,
        189–93, 203–5, 229, 236–38
    of immanence, 203–5, 208–9
    of organization, 166–67, 170, 173,
        182, 189–90, 193
Plato, 68, 72, 75, 207
Plotinus, 68, 72, 75
possible, the, 126–27, 206
poststructuralism, 9, 13, 19
psychoanalysis, 19–29, 42, 48, 81, 86, 91,
    186, 202

and corporeal logic, 78, 83
moving beyond, 17, 113, 116, 163–76,
    183, 221–25
Lacanian, 8, 12, 17, 117, 122

real, the, 117, 126–27, 138, 190, 206
receptivity, 33, 40, 73–77, 105–6, 174,
    188–89, 198
reciprocity, 21, 86, 100, 136, 231, 235
recognition, 93, 101, 110, 114, 134, 136,
    146, 162
    Hegelian, 97–98, 101–2
    model of, 111, 129–33
repetition, 25–26, 35, 79–82, 86,
    111–12, 154, 162, 201
    of identity, 51–52, 225–32
    and the eternal return, 18, 146,
        157–58
representation, 19, 50, 77–79, 129–30,
    175, 199, 211–15, 239
    and the feminine, 26–30, 37–46, 224
    and memory, 157–59, 179
    of origins, 220–28
    scene of, 25, 86–90, 138, 229
    Western system of, 65–68, 111–14
resistance, 191, 200–203, 209, 231–33,
    237–38
ressentiment, 139, 150–54, 158, 175,
    228
reterritorialization, 123, 137, 207, 234
    and molar identity, 163, 183–84
    and Kafka, 174–80
rhizome, 170, 177, 183, 185, 190
rights, 93, 95, 103

same, the, 111, 116, 130, 140, 146,
    148–49, 152, 157, 162–63
    logic of, 161
Saussure, Ferdinand de, and linguistics, 8
Scherer, René, 181
schizo, 116, 122–23, 171
schizoanalysis, 17–18, 114, 137–45, 172,
    183, 187, 194, 202
    and destratification, 123–25, 165–68
    and psychoanalysis, 166, 168, 172

LaVergne, TN USA
04 April 2011
222869LV00001B/89/P

9 780801 485862